Hobey

Hobey Goodale

Cover: Hobey in 1927

TABLE OF CONTENTS

DEDICATION

This book is dedicated to the memory of my loving wife of sixty years, Nancy. She was also the mother of our four children who are important people in this book—the story of my life. Nancy was the one who started by encouraging me to get going with the writing, and, when I would slack off, she would nag me kindly to get the job done. Unfortunately, she will never see the final product, but she could probably quote it word for word because of the many times she read the manuscript looking for errors. Nancy was a good critic—suggesting changes, mostly for the better, and encouraging me to finish the job.

PREFACE

I have lived for eight-plus decades and seen one century pass into another. I have also seen the end of one millennium and am enjoying the new one. In my short span on this earth, I have seen many changes here on Kaua'i and throughout the world.

When I first was brought to Kaua'i, it was on a boat, and it wasn't before ten years had gone by that I had my first airplane ride. Now, the only way to travel between the islands is by air. The propeller has given way to the jet engine. The first automobiles in my family had standard transmissions, and, now, the automatic is the standard transmission.

Our island economy has gone from agriculture to tourism. No more pineapple except for local use, and no sugar plantations either, where in the thirties there were twenty-eight. Cattle ranching has changed. Very few cattle are slaughtered locally anymore, most of the calves are shipped to the mainland for fattening. The railroad replaced the oxen trains, and now trucks have replaced the rail. What sugar is produced, only on the island of Maui, is shipped in bulk instead of in burlap sacks. Some fruit and vegetables are still grown commercially. Taro was replaced by rice, but now rice has been replaced by taro.

On the national scene, there was a great depression and recovery in the nineteen thirties. America and its allies were in a world war with a victory in the nineteen forties. The first use of nuclear fission ended that war. There was a war in Korea and one in Viet Nam with no definite outcomes and two wars in Iraq—one of which we are still fighting.

I can remember when we got our first radios, and, then, in the fifties, TV sets came along. Then came computers—large commercial ones first and then smaller ones for the general public. Now, a family with children might have one for the parents and one for each child. Communication by telephone is standard, but email is running a close second.

The cellular telephone is taking over everything. You can now call almost anywhere on earth and talk to people. You can also take a picture and even record video with your cell phone. Plus, seeing someone with a phone glued to his or her ear while driving down the road at sixty to eighty miles an hour is almost normal.

Icarus with his waxed wings fell to his death because he flew too close to the sun. Then came the airplane and then the jet and then the rocket, and man was put into earth's orbit. Almost a half century ago, man landed on the moon and returned to earth. Now, we are sending rockets to check on the climate of Mars and other planets. We have telescopes in space that send us pictures of other celestial bodies, and, recently, we sent a rocket to successfully intercept a comet. Jules Verne and the Nautilus have been superseded by nuclear submarines that can circle the earth without surfacing. What will man do next? All this in one lifetime is hard to visualize, but it has happened. What is to come in the next eighty years?

In my lifetime, the introduction of exotic plants has just about ruined the native forests. And most of them do no good whatsoever. Good agricultural land is being developed faster and faster, traffic is too heavy for our roads, and even having the assurance of fresh drinking water is becoming a problem. Local fishing, which used to sustain a population of between 300,000 and 500,000, is now being sorely taxed, and restrictions are being put in place to protect certain species at their breeding times.

I have done a great deal of traveling in my life and have not found any other place I would rather live. Kaua'i is home!

At the urging of my children and grandchildren, I am putting into words the story of my life.

CHAPTER ONE

Forefathers

In 1818 or early 1819, at the urging of a group of young Hawaiian men who had come to New England to learn to read and write, the American Board of Foreign Missions started assembling a group of young couples who were willing to brave a strange new world and bring the Word of God and the written word to the Hawaiian people. So, on October 23, 1819, seven couples and three young Hawaiian men sailed from Boston, Massachusetts, on the brig *Thaddeus*. The voyage took 164 days before they made landfall at Kailua on the island of Hawai'i. After a couple of days waiting for permission to land, they were allowed on shore. The *Thaddeus* then sailed for Honolulu where everyone disembarked, and, here, each couple was assigned to a different island.

The Reverend Samuel Whitney and his wife Mercy Partridge were assigned to the island of Kaua'i and landed at Waimea. Here they lived and worked with the native people for what would become the rest of their lives. In the early 1840s, Samuel Whitney was afflicted with breathing difficulties and started seeking for a place where he could receive medical attention. In December of 1845, he arrived at Lahaina, Maui, and, within two days, he was dead. He was buried in Lahaina. Mercy Whitney remained in the couple's original home at Waimea on Kaua'i and was beloved by the Hawaiian people with whom she worked until she herself died on December 26, 1872. She is buried in the Waimea Foreign Church Cemetery, and the inscription on her gravestone is in English on one side and Hawaiian on the other. Up until the early 2000s, someone put flowers on her grave every Memorial Day.

The Whitney's had four children. Their third child was a son, Henry Martyn Whitney, who was sent back to New England for schooling at the age of seven in the care of a ship's captain. Henry studied to be a printer. He then returned to Hawai'i after seventeen years and settled in Honolulu. When he finally returned to Kaua'i to see his mother, he landed at Kōloa. When the Hawaiian residents found out who he was, they set up a relay to bring the news to Mrs. Whitney in Waimea, in advance of his arrival, so that she knew of his coming well before he got to Waimea. There was much celebrating the return of her son by the local people because Mrs. Whitney had been so loved by them. This is one story. Another, from Mercy's journal, is that the ship Henry arrived on anchored in Waimea Bay, and he walked to the house and surprised her. He only stayed for a day or so.

Henry Martyn Whitney, because of his occupation as a printer, is credited for starting the *Honolulu Commercial Advertiser*, which has now become the *Honolulu Star-Advertiser*. The Crown appointed him Postmaster General of the Kingdom of Hawai'i in 1847. He designed and had printed the first postage stamps for the kingdom. They were for two cents, five cents, and thirteen cents. The two-cent stamp is known as the "Missionary Blue," and, in 1995, one sold for 1.2 million dollars at auction. There are only twenty-eight used stamps known to exist. I collect stamps but do not have any.

Henry's daughter Emma married William Whitmore Goodale, who was a sugar plantation manager. His last plantation was in Waialua on O'ahu. Their son, Holbrook March Goodale, my father, graduated from the Naval Academy in 1921. After serving in the Navy for the required years, he resigned his commission and went into commercial flying in Honolulu. In 1921, right after his graduation, Holbrook married Juliet Rice, and they had two sons. They were divorced some time in 1925, and, then, Holbrook was killed in an airplane crash in 1927.

The ninth company of missionaries left Boston on November 14, 1840 and arrived in Hawai'i in May 22, 1841, after a voyage of 188 days, which included stops at Rio de Janeiro, Brazil, and Santiago, Chile. There were only four couples in this company, and one of them was William Harrison Rice, my great-great grandfather, and his wife Mary Sophia Rice Hyde, my great-great grandmother. They were actually bound for the Whitman Mission in Walla Walla in the Oregon Territory. However, when the mission in Honolulu found out that they were teachers, they were asked to stay. They refused, saying that they had promised to go to Oregon and that they would fulfill their commitment.

After a few days of re-provisioning the ship, called the *Gloucester*, they sailed for the Pacific Coast. After three or four days at sea, the ship was caught in a severe storm, and the travelers had to return to Honolulu to repair damage to the masts and sails. This time, William Rice agreed to stay in the islands because, he said, God had showed him where he wanted him to do his work. If, indeed, he had continued on to Washington and the Whitman Mission, he and his wife would have been massacred along with the rest of those at Mission. The Lord was looking after them.

After being accepted by the Honolulu Mission, the Rices were sent to

Hāna on Maui. When Mrs. Rice was about ready to have their first baby, she chose to go to Wailuku where the only doctor lived and practiced. The couple left Hāna by outrigger canoe, and, by the time they got to Ke'anae Peninsula, the ocean was so rough that they had to go ashore. Mrs. Rice had to have help on the steep slope up the path out of Ke'anae. Once on top, she was able to walk all the rest of the way to Wailuku. She arrived safely, and, in due time, her baby was born strong and healthy. The Rices served in Hāna for two years and, then, returned to Honolulu to teach at Punahou.

While at Punahou, Mr. Rice taught school while Mrs. Rice saw that the children were cared for. She did all the housework and was housemother to all the mission children who were boarders.

My grandfather, Charles Atwood Rice, tells of his father having to watch where the chickens made their nests so that he could collect the eggs for the table. My grandfather said that he had done the same when he went to Punahou, along with milking the cows. Both Rices were fluent in the Hawaiian language and used the old form of inflections. I was never taught to speak Hawaiian, and I regret it to this day.

In 1854, the American Board of Foreign Missions stopped any further support for the Hawaiian Mission, so the missionaries had to find other means of employment. Some stayed in the islands, and the rest went back to New England. William Harrison Rice's brother-in-law, Paul Isenberg, asked him to move to Kaua'i and become the manager of the Lihue Plantation for him. He agreed and moved his entire family to Kaua'i. In the course of his employment in Līhue, Mr. Rice had an irrigation system built, and this system of ditches is still in use today.

My grandfather was the second son of William Hyde and Mary Waterhouse Rice. He was born on Kaua'i and was educated at Punahou and Heald College in California. He managed the family farm at Kīpū until April of 1942 when the last of the sugarcane was harvested. The old cane fields became a cattle ranch and are still a cattle ranch today.

After his father, William Hyde Rice, died, the farm was willed to his eight children in equal shares. Later, Charles Rice started to buy the shares from his siblings, and, by 1941, he had purchased the shares of all his brothers and sisters with the exception of one-fifth of one-eighth of one of the brother's shares along with the full one-eighth share of Harold Rice. Harold later sold his shares to Jack Waterhouse. I had wanted to buy those shares but was not allowed to.

My grandfather served in the Territorial House of Representatives for several years and then the Territorial Senate until the middle thirties. In the middle thirties, he switched from the Republican Party to the Democratic

3

Party because he didn't agree with the way the Territory was being run by the plantations and the Republican Party. He later was elected to the Constitutional Convention and helped formulate the document that is in force today.

My grandfather married Grace King, and they had two daughters, Edith Kapiolani and Juliet Atwood. Edith married John Christopher Plews, and Juliet, my mother, first married Holbrook March Goodale and then Fredrick Warren Wichman. Mother had two sons with Holbrook Goodale and one son with Fred Wichman. After divorcing Fred Wichman in 1943, she became active in the Red Cross in San Francisco during World War II. She also volunteered at the Allied Arts Guild in Menlo Park, California, until 1945 when she returned to Kaua'i to live. Mother was able to buy some shares in the Haena Hui and built her home there. She lived in this home until 1962 when she, then, built a home on Mokoi Street in Līhue. She was the moving force in the formation of the Kauai Museum. She died in her home at Hā'ena in 1987. Her ashes were scattered in the garden behind her Hā'ena home.

My paternal great-great grandparents Samuel Whitney and Mercy Partridge Whitney in 1819. Portraits by Samuel B. Morse.

My maternal great-great grandparents William Harrison Rice and Mary Sophia Hyde Rice, 1841.

My great grandfather Henry Martyn Whitney, the Whitney's son, who was sent to America at eight years of age for an education. He had hearing problems so became a printer and returned to Hawaii eighteen years later.

William Whitmore Goodale, my paternal grandfather.

Aunt Catherine Carter, my father's sister.

Ens. Holbrook March Goodale, my father, at the time of his graduation from the Naval Academy at Annapolis, Maryland.

The Rice Family: Daisy Wilcox Rice, Philip Rice. Second Row: Charles Rice, Mary Waterhouse Rice, Emily Rice Sexton, William Hyde Rice, Mary Rice Scott. Back Row: William Henry Rice and wife Mary Agnes Rice, Harold Rice. Inset: Arthur Rice, circa 1890.

William Hyde Rice holding his first great-grandson, while his wife Mary Waterhouse Rice who is blind, looks on. In the background are the grandparents Charles and Grace King Rice. This picture was taken at his baptism on December 25, 1923.

CHAPTER TWO

The Early Years 1923–1936

After resigning his commission from the Navy, my father moved back to Honolulu and became a barnstorming pilot. He and Mother had a home on Wiley Street in the Nu'uanu section of Honolulu. So, when I was born, Mother naturally went to the best children's hospital available in Honolulu—the Kauikeolani Children's Hospital now known as Kapiolani Medical Center for Women and Children. I was born on October 8, 1923. My birth certificate number is 94077, and it is located in volume 150 and registration number 3587. I was named Holbrook March Goodale, Jr. after my father. In December of the same year, Mother brought me to Kaua'i to present me to my grandparents and great-grandparents.

In those days, there was not a pier or a jetty in Nāwiliwili Harbor. The interisland ships had to anchor just outside the main surfing area and transfer all the passengers and freight ashore by lighter. Mother always told, with great glee in later years, how I was handed from one large brown hand to another large brown hand, bouncing up and down in the lighter while they were trying to get a good hold on me. Mother recalled being terrified at the time. But, as you can see, the transfer was made successfully, as I am still here.

My grandparents, Charles and Grace Rice, lived on Kalapaki Beach, the property having been a wedding present from grandfather's parents. While we were on Kaua'i, the family decided to have me baptized. It was Christmas day of 1923. The ceremony was conducted by an Episcopal clergyman by the name of Carver, who just happened to be on the island at the time. There would be no Episcopal churches on Kaua'i until 1925, when All Saints Church was built in Kapa'a. My baptism took place at the Līhue home of my great-grandparents.

My great-grandfather, William Hyde Rice, was the last governor of Kaua'i under the Hawaiian monarchy. Queen Lili'uokalani appointed him to the post of governor of Kaua'i, but he was promptly kicked out after the overthrow in 1893 because of his loyalty to the queen. I was the only great-grandchild who he ever saw before he died in early 1924. He was buried with his parents in the Lihue Cemetery.

My great-grandmother, Mary Waterhouse Rice, was born in Honolulu and moved to Kaua'i after she was married. She and my great-grandfather had eight children, five boys and three girls. By the time I came along, she was blind from glaucoma. She was a self-sufficient person. You couldn't fool her by trying to disguise your footsteps; as soon as she heard your step she knew who it was.

A funny story about William Hyde Rice and Mary Waterhouse Rice is that, after they were married in Honolulu at her parents' home, she was given a hogshead each of brandy, rum, and port wine as part of her dowry. Mary Waterhouse was the daughter of John T. Waterhouse, a merchant in Honolulu who was originally from Tasmania. The Waterhouse home was known as the house of the groaning board because of the large amounts of food that was served at every meal. There were almost always two different kinds of meat, one at each end of the table, at the main meal of the day. Upon their arrival on Kaua'i, the new Mrs. Waterhouse's mother-in-law, Mary Sofia Rice, said that the brandy was medicinal but that rum and port were from the devil. She, then, had the rum and port hogsheads stove in, and all the liquor was lost in the sand. The first missionaries to the island were strict Calvinists, and intoxicating liquor was not to be tolerated. It is said that nearby Hawaiians scooped up the wet sand and tried to salvage what liquor they could.

Mother divorced my father in 1925 and moved to Kaua'i where, on August 11, my brother Charles was born in Līhue. My father later remarried, and I understand that I have a sister somewhere but no one in the family has ever talked about her. On October 16, 1927, my father was flying a commercial photographer over the Mormon Temple at Lā'ie on O'ahu when the plane stalled and crashed into a nearby cane field. All four people in the plane were killed. I was only four years old at the time, so I don't remember my father at all. About fifty years later, my Aunt Edith Plews gave me a copy of *The Honolulu Advertiser* that described the entire event.

In 1926, Mother married Frederick Wichman, and we moved back to Honolulu and lived on Old Pali Road in Nu'uanu. My stepfather was a partner in Dusenberg and Wichman with a seat on the Honolulu stock exchange. Their offices were on Bishop Street in downtown Honolulu. Mother said that, when she would go there for the mail, she would toot the horn at the front of the building and a young Chinese man would run out with her mail. The young man was Chin Ho who later became one of the wealthiest and influential men in Hawai'i.

My brothers and I were reared under the premise that little children were to be seen and not heard. Manners of every kind were drilled into us at an early age, and any infraction or lapse was dealt with immediately and often severely. My grandfather was a very kind and caring person and never disciplined us severely. Our uncle, Jack Plews, was a proper Englishman who never raised his hand to us, although we got his message immediately. Our stepfather, Fred Wichman, was another matter. His Teutonic blood was on the surface at all times. Punishment was both quick and severe. Many are the times I couldn't sit comfortably after a spanking from him.

When we lived on Old Pali Road, I was a handful. I had to be watched all the time, which was an impossibility. So my parents had a cage built outside for me and my brother Charles. It had no covering at the top, so I soon learned to climb out. The first time, I didn't let my brother out and he started crying. I was busted. I learned my lesson, but so did my parents. In response, they had a chicken wire top put on. That only kept me in for a while. One day, while trying to dig my way out from under the shelter with my hands, I uncovered an ancient Hawaiian stone adze, which I used to break one wire from the covering. From there, I unwound the wire until I had a hole big enough for me to get through. This time, I didn't forget to let Charlie out. I can't remember what we did after that time, but I know that was the last time we got loose. I still have that adze in my collection. Another thing that I did, for which I got a good paddling, involved the circular planter in the driveway planted to blue agapanthus lilies. One day, when the lilies had just started to send up buds, I went into the circle and broke off all the young buds. Boy, did my bottom burn. In June of 1928, my brother Bruce was born, so that made three boys.

In April of 1929, my stepfather said that the stock market was no good, something was amiss. So he sold out to his partner and bought a small ranch on Kaua'i in the Wailua Homestead area. He and Mother built a beautiful house on the ranch, and we moved in about the time of the crash in October of 1929. We later learned that his partner had lost everything and committed suicide.

Right after we moved into the new house, I came down with a disease the doctors could not diagnose. My fever would rise to 103 degrees and stay there for several days at a time. One of the top doctors in Honolulu came to Kaua'i to see me and said, "This boy will never live." Well, I fooled him in the long run. However, I was kept in bed for almost six months. Dr. Jay Kuhns, our family doctor (and also doctor for Lihue Plantation, Grove Farm, and Kīpū), never gave up on me. He and I became fast friends. One day, a Hawaiian woman came up to see Mother, and, on walking up to the front door, she noticed some red tī leaves growing beside it. She told Mother that having red tī there was very bad luck and that she should get rid of them immediately. The reasons for this, she said, was that red tīplants were reserved for royalty and one was supposed to plant the red tī leaf in the back of the house. This Mother did, and, soon after that, I started to get better.

Like any family, we all got the childhood diseases. One time, all three of us got the measles at the same time. What a circus that was! Another time, one Christmas Eve, I came down with the mumps and couldn't go to my grandparents' home for Christmas Eve dinner. I had been out all day with the local ranchers working their cattle. When I got home, I told my mother that I had a sore throat. She took one look at me and said, "You have the mumps." She put me right to bed, and I had to stay home that night.

After I recovered from my mysterious illness, I started school. I was sent to Olohena School in the Homesteads. It was a three-room schoolhouse with grades kindergarten through eight. I was the only Caucasian child in school and got kicked around a lot. This treatment lasted for about a year and a half. By then, my brother Charles was ready for school, so we transferred to the Lihue Grammar School. From the Homesteads, we had to go through Kapaʻa to get to Līhue. I guess we had to go to Līhue because it was a Grammar School that had regular classrooms and annex units. The annex units were for those of us who were the most proficient in the English language. We had a more accelerated course of studies.

At about this time, my stepfather and grandfather decided that I, as the eldest and one who was more deft with my hands, should learn how to carve all varieties of meat and fowl. I found carving came quite easily to me. My grandfather was not a very skilled carver, but he always gave you a good, thick slice of roast beef when he carved. My uncle Jack Plews, being English, had learned the art of carving paper-thin slices, especially when it came to ham. One time, when I was twenty, my grandfather told me to invite the Plews for dinner on his birthday. I was also instructed to ask him what kind of meat he would like. His answer was duck, and, then, he added, "That's because it is the hardest bird in the world to do a good carving job on." He quickly relented and said he would like a good steak.

In those days, a steak was a T-bone and was about an inch thick. Each person in our family would receive an entire steak. There is a saying in our family, "It's very good cold." These words meant that anything you couldn't eat at that sitting you could take home for another meal. Fred Wichman was a good carver, but he did not cut slices as thin as those of Uncle Jack. Some of the happiest times growing up were Sunday nights in Wailua when we had to cook our own dinners. Fred Wichman was a good cook, especially with Chinese dishes. On those nights, the whole family worked in the kitchen helping in any way we could while he did the cooking. Sometimes we thought that we were punished unduly hard for infractions of table manners. In retrospect, since then I have never been uncomfortable about table manners no matter where I am.

In the fall of 1930, Kaua'i's only Ford dealer, a man known as King Baggot, ran for election to the Territorial House of Representatives and won. On the night of the election, after the votes were counted and he knew that he had been elected, he went home to bed. Baggot never woke up; he died of a massive heart attack that very night. His stock in the Ford dealership was put up at auction, and my grandfather was the winning bidder. My grandfather then persuaded his two sons-in-law to run the dealership. Jack Plews became the manager and Fred Wichman the sales manager. Now, since my stepfather would be coming to Līhue every day, it would be no problem getting us to school.

My brothers and I got along fairly well, but there were definitely a number of incidents when we did not. However, once I tried to cut my brother Charlie's finger off with a lawn mower. I cut his finger pretty badly but not off. He got back at me later at the dinner table once when I was persistently teasing him. His response was to reach across the table and jam a fork into my left forearm. The fork was left just hanging there. Another time, my youngest brother, Bruce, chased me with a machete. I ran into the license plate of a parked car and took a gouge out of my forearm. When Mother took me to the doctor's office, the nurse (who was male) looked at the incision and said that it would have to be soaked so the flap of skin could be softened. Only then, could the doctor could pull it together to sew up. The nurse gave us some solution and said to come back in approximately three hours. Then, the doctor would give me stitches. Mother and I went to the Tip Top Cafe and had a sandwich for lunch. Then, we went to the movies. After the show was over, we went back to the doctor's office, and I had my arm sewed up. I still have a horseshoe scar on my left forearm as a memento. My brothers were furious at me when they heard that we had been to the movies.

From 1930 to 1936, I was pretty much a loner around the house, as I would get into a lot of trouble by teasing my youngest brother Bruce. He was the apple of his father's eye, and I would usually get a spanking for making him cry. I learned early on to get away from the house and trouble. It was at these times that I started to go out with the cowboys and do cattle work. All the cowboys were Hawaiian and all commands were in Hawaiian. I had to know what they were saying, or I'd be left going west when everybody else was going east. Even though I never learned Hawaiian, I got pretty good at the simple directions and didn't get lost too often.

I had my own horse and a rawhide lasso, so I was well equipped. On weekends, I would go into the homesteaders' pastures and help them with their cattle work. One time while riding, when I was eight years old, I roped a full-grown cow. My hands were too small to hold all the rope, so some of the loops fell and wrapped around my right ankle. I had tied the rope onto the pommel of my saddle with a slipknot, so I just pulled the end of the rope and the knot came undone. But, as the rope threaded out, it burned the skin on my ankle. To this day, I still have a scar. I was very lucky that this incident turned out in such a way, for I could easily have lost my foot.

One Sunday, I went out with John Vilela, a rancher who also worked as a yardman for Mother, and I helped him with the branding of his calves. When the work was all done, his mother called us all for lunch. She spoke almost no English, only Portuguese, and she sure could cook. This was the first time I had ever eaten rabbit. I also ate bread cooked in an outdoor oven, and I even had a drink of some homemade wine. The branding was fun, but the food was divine.

I also loved to go swimming in the North Fork of the Wailua River, which was right below our house. There were goldfish in the river, and I would swim and chase them until they tired and tried to hide under rocks. That's when I would dive down and catch them. I always went out fishing by myself and went swimming in the river even when there was a lot of water rushing downstream. The most fun was when the river was in about half flood. I would jump over a seven- or eight-foot falls into the pool below. Nobody told me not to do this, but, today, I know how foolish I was to go swimming alone.

When I was young, there wasn't a rock high enough to scare me from jumping off it. I loved diving from high places. I would often bring the goldfish from the river home in a bucket and put them in one of the three little lily ponds that Mother had built in the yard. It took me quite a long time to figure out why the goldfish kept disappearing. We had three cats, and they were all as good of fishermen as I was.

Another form of sport was to go after frogs. I would bait a hook with a red rag and try to get them to latch on, or, if that failed, I would just jump in after them when they dived into the water. I got quite proficient at both methods. Then, one time, a young Japanese girl, whose father was a rice farmer in the lower Wailua River Valley, was working for us. She took me out one night with a kerosene lantern, and she showed me how to catch frogs by blinding their eyes and grabbing them. After about an hour, we caught almost three-dozen frogs before calling it quits. The next day, it was my job to clean the frogs. I thought that the work would never end.

In those days, there were no large- or small-mouthed bass in the Wailua

River, so there were still a lot of large 'o'opu in the river. Every September, there would be heavy rains, and the river would flood. Then, down would come the 'o'opu to spawn. During August, the men on the East Kauai Water Company would build a ramp-like weir onto which the floodwaters would push the 'o'opu and strand them. The 'o'opu were then easy picking—a little muddy-tasting but still good eating. The roe was the best eating of all. Some of the 'o'opu were at least fifteen inches in length and would weigh about two pounds. 'O'opu are fish that go down to the river mouth to spawn; then, after the eggs hatch, the young spend about a month in the ocean. The young fish, at this point called hinana, make their way back to the river and up toward the headwaters to grow until it is time for themselves to spawn. The Hawaiian names for the two predominate species of 'o'opu are nākea and nōpili. The nōpili has a suction-cup-like fin beneath its gills that it actually uses to climb up some pretty serious waterfalls. However, since the introduction of both the large-mouth and the small-mouth bass, the 'o'opu is scarce. The only places where they remain somewhat plentiful are the Wainiha and Kalalau Streams.

We three boys learned to swim at Kalapaki, and we took to the water like ducks. After we were pretty proficient, my grandfather bought three surfboards for us. No one in Nāwiliwili had the slightest clue about how to use them, and it's a wonder that none of us ever got hurt. One summer, when I was about nine years old, Doris Duke Cromwell, the wealthy tobacco heiress came to Kaua'i on her yacht. With her was Sam Kahanamoku, Duke Kahanamoku's younger brother. When he saw us fumbling around with our surfboards, he came out into the water and taught us how to really use a surfboard. With me, it didn't take long. But, my two brothers never did become avid surfers. I guess I was rather precocious, for soon I was looking for the biggest waves I could find. It wasn't long after that when some of the local boys–Goro Sadaoka, John Makanani, and John Ah You–got into the swing of surfing and then we always had company.

In 1935, my grandfather had a surfboard made for me in Honolulu. I have a letter from Duke Kahanamoku explaining what a wonderful sport surfing was and that this board was coming to me. When it came, I was king of the hill. I surfed on it from 1935 to 1945, until I joined the Army.

In the late thirties, Bill Paia married a Nāwiliwili girl and had brought his own board from Honolulu with him. Richard Sakoda was the first to get a hollow board. Those boards were about fifteen feet long and four inches thick and made out of plywood. They were good to paddle because they were buoyant, but they were hard to handle in big surf. Our boards in those days had no leashes, like today. So, if we lost our board, we had to swim for

CITY AND COUNTY OF HONOLULU
OFFICE OF THE SHERIFF
HONOLULU HALE

HONOLULU, HAWAII   March 28, 1935.

Mr. Hobey Wichman,
Lihue, Kauai.

My dear Hobey:

Your grandpa, the Honorable Chas. A. Rice, has
informed me that you are very much interested in surfing
and that you are encouraging the boys around your place to
take up this sport. I will tell you this: Surfing is a
sport equal to none in this world. It is in a class by
itself and if one starts as young as you have, it will make
you a healthy and clean young man and the exercise you
get out of it will come in handy in your later life. I
owe my swimming strength to surfing and from what your
grandpa tells me, you are quite expert. I invite you, whenever you are in Honolulu, to come up with me to the big
surf at Waikiki and I am sure you will have a thrilling
time.

Peter Makia, one of the beach boys, is making you
a very nice board and we are all helping him and I am sure
that when you get it, you will be very proud of it.

Again, I wish you luck as an expert surfboard operator,
remaining, always your friend,

Very truly yours,

Duke P. Kahanamoku

Sheriff, City and County of Honolulu.

Letter from Duke Kahanamoku to Hobey in 1935 announcing his new surfboard.

it. We would only surf in Kalapaki Bay because, before World War II, we were too young to drive a car, and, during the war, there wasn't enough gas to go looking for waves as the kids do today.

At Kalapaki, the main break was over by the seawall. The kids still surf there today, but they don't have one of the most formidable hazards that we had back then. In good surf, if you sat at the takeoff point and looked down into the water, you could see a large anchor fluke looking back at you. In the seventies, a coastguardsman by the name of Ivey removed the anchor from the reef and brought it to shore. Luckily, the anchor hurt no one. The anchor was put into the reef as a mooring for ships to tie up to before there was any breakwater or jetty in Nāwiliwili.

The way we surfed back then, we always tried to be ready for the second wave in a set because it was the steepest and gave you the best ride. With the wooden boards of those days, the object was to get the longest ride you could. The finless boards were not as maneuverable as the fiberglass ones the kids use today. Sometimes, when there was a south swell with big surf running, we would go out to the lighthouse below the sixteenth hole of the Kiele Golf Course and catch a wave and ride it almost all the way to the beach.

One time, when we were surfing in very small waves, I was on a wave standing up and went right over a five-foot long barracuda. When the barracuda realized that something big had gone over him, he disappeared in a hurry. Another time, in early 1945, three of us were out on a Monday afternoon sitting on our boards waiting for a wave when a four- or five-foot shark swam right between John Makanani and myself. I can't remember who the third person was, but he was Hawaiian. After spotting a shark that close to us, the two Hawaiian boys lay down on their boards and paddled to shore as fast as they could. They carried their boards down the beach to the beach house at Kalapaki. I waited until a good wave came along, caught it, and rode it as far as I could. Then, I paddled over to the beach right in front of the beach house where we stored the boards. The two Hawaiian boys told their mother what had happened that afternoon. Later, I heard that she told them that the shark was my ʻaumakua or guardian spirit. They were also told never to try and harm me in the water as the shark would come and protect me. I since learned from Robert Keuma, Sr. that his grandfather kept a shark and fed it from the big rock in the middle of the beach at Kalapaki. When the old man knew that he was going to die, he called the shark one last time, fed him, and released him from his duties of caring for him. A good story, and I've heard other tales of these guardian angels. I never told the boys or anyone else for a long time that Mondays were the days we slaughtered cattle, and I must have had the smell of blood on me to have interested the shark.

Unfortunately, my board from Duke was lost in the tsunami of April 1, 1946. After the war was over, and I got married and had children, I got on a surfboard one more time—in 1953 when our son David was four years old. Nobody much was surfing then, so I went on to other sports.

On my tenth birthday, Uncle Philip Rice, who was also my godfather, gave me a single-shot, twenty-two rifle as a present. My grandfather had already taught me how to use a rifle, so I had a pretty free rein on using the rifle. I learned how to sight and aim by shooting myna birds and got to be a pretty good shot. Down at Kalapaki, the lily pond was almost one acre in size and was just crawling with frogs. The banks of the pond were planted with taro, which we used for the tender young leaves. But, there was no way to get the frogs with lantern or flashlight. I started to shoot them and would keep my grandfather well supplied with frog legs. There was one problem. I would run out of ammunition. A good friend of my grandmother's, a Mrs. Swan, whose husband worked in the Grove Farm office, loved frog's legs. For a dozen pairs of frog legs, she would get me a box of five hundred rounds of ammunition. All I had to do was keep her supplied with frog legs, and I would never want for ammunition. One time when I was at Kalapaki, I had caught five or six frogs but didn't have a burlap bag to keep them in. So, I put them in the bathtub for the night. Needless to say, the next morning, they were not in the bathtub but all around the bathroom. My grandmother wasn't too happy with me.

When we started to go to school in Līhue, we would have to get up early in the morning, have breakfast, and be ready to roll by six-thirty in the morning. We lived above the hill called Puʻu Pilo in the Wailua Homesteads and would drive into Kapaʻa town and then onto Līhue. The house that my stepfather and Mother built is now part of the Hindu temple. After school, we would go over to Garden Island Motors and wait for my stepfather (who by now was "dad" to me) to finish work and then drive all the way back through Kapaʻa and up into the Homesteads. The present Poliahu Road was originally undertaken in 1935 because Dr. Jay Kuhns had purchased a place in the Homesteads, and he needed a faster route to get to the hospital in Līhue.

Some days after school, we would go to the movies. One year, the daughter of the manager of the Lihue Theater had the hots for my brother Charlie and he got to go to the movies for free every day. Boy, were the rest of us jealous.

Dad worked as sales manager of Garden Island Motors until the repeal of Prohibition. That's when he opened a liquor store called Kauai Factors in Nāwiliwili. He first sold Hau Blossom gin and a sweet drink that the Filipinos called "anisado," along with three kinds of sweet wine—port, muscatel, and tokay. These wines came in large barrels and had to be put in gallon bottles to be retailed. Some afternoons, while we were waiting to go home with our dad, I would get a paper cup and fill it with wine, a different one every day, and drink it. I would go to sleep in the car on the way home. Our dad could never get any of the good brands of bourbon and scotch because the plantation store had the all the good brands to themselves and wouldn't let him buy any to sell.

One day, someone told Dad about a man in San Francisco who ran a "fire sale" business. So, our dad went to the city and tried to get an appointment to see him. After a two-day wait, he finally got into the inner office.

The man behind the desk said, "What do you want to sell me?"

Dad said, "I don't want to sell you anything. I want to buy something."

Then, after Dad told him of the situation in Hawai'i, they began a friendly relationship. Now, Kauai Factors, as the store was known, began to sell the best brands available. Some of the liquor and wines were even better than those the plantation storeowner could get. After getting the liquor business in good shape and profitable, our dad branched out into selling house paint and picked up the well-known General Paint line. He kept active in the liquor and paint businesses until he left for Oregon and Hay Creek Ranch in 1936.

In 1933, just before I was ten, my grandfather took me with him to visit his brother Harold, who had a ranch on the slopes of Haleakalā. We sailed from Kaua'i on the interisland steamer *Waialeale* to Honolulu and on the SS *Haleakala* to Maui. The old home where we stayed was in Kula and looked down over to the West Maui Mountains. While there, Uncle Harold gave me a two-iron golf club and some balls and sent me out into the yard to fool around. As I was hitting the balls, a young Japanese boy ran across the yard just as I hit a shot. I hit him in the head; then, he fell down but got right up and went screaming back to his house. We found out later that he wasn't hurt, but it has sure made me wary from that point on of anyone within range. Uncle Harold used to tease me about the incident and said that, when the boy grew up, he was a genius at figures and that I must have pounded some sense into him.

While on Maui, we went horseback riding across my great uncle's ranch, One day, we drove newborn calves and their mothers into a corral where the calves were earmarked and vaccinated for blackleg and then turned them into another pasture. I never forgot this procedure, and, later, when managing Kīpū Ranch, I instituted the same practice on our cows and calves. Another day, we rode up into the West Maui Mountains and looked down into Lahaina. The next day, my grandfather and I drove into to Lahaina. There we met Caleb Burns, the manager of the Pioneer Mill Company, a sugar plantation on Maui's west side. Burns had just been named by American Factors as the new manager of the Lihue Plantation Company.

After our stay on Maui was over, we flew back to Oʻahu in an eight-seat amphibian plane. We sat right behind the pilot and copilot and talked to them the whole way back to Oʻahu. The copilot showed me the altimeter and said that we were 8,000 feet above sea level. I was amazed that we were so high. In Honolulu, we stayed for a couple of nights at the Alexander Young Hotel and then took the steamer *Waialeale* back to Kauaʻi.

In 1934, I again went to Honolulu with my grandfather to see an Army Review in honor of President Roosevelt's visit to Hawaiʻi. We drove out to the Schofield Barracks and spent the entire afternoon watching tanks and trucks pulling field artillery pieces by the reviewing stand. We were able to get a good look at the president as he sat at the place of honor. It was quite a sight for an eleven-year-old boy to see. It is amazing in retrospect that, only seven years later, most of the equipment I saw that day would become obsolete. That evening, I had dinner in our room at the Young Hotel while my grandfather went to a reception for the president. I was too young to go.

The next evening, we returned to Kauaʻi by boat. I loved going to Honolulu with my grandfather because one of the stops was always the Kewalo Inn. I would always have a lobster stuffed with fried rice while my grandfather would have a steak. This meal was always one of the highlights of a trip to Honolulu, and, later, while at ʻIolani, my grandfather would take me out to dinner when he came to Honolulu.

Every summer, our family would spend two to three weeks at Kīpū Kai. Kīpū Kai is a valley on the south side of Kauaʻi accessible through a gap in the Hoary Head Range on the east side of Mount Hāʻupu. The trail follows an old Hawaiian pathway up the side of the mountain to the pass and then down the other side. Most of the trail was paved with good-sized rocks, so it was not muddy. An ancient Hawaiian legend told of the chief going over the trail in really wet weather when the trail was very slippery. It is said that he slipped and fell to the ground and got all muddy. Then and there, he decreed that the trail be paved with rocks. We would go over the trail and not give the steepness a second thought, but others felt differently. On the Kīpū Kai side of the trail, there was one place that, for about fifty feet, it went down at almost a forty-five degree angle. But, again, we never thought about how steep it was.

One time, Jeanette McDonald, the star of the operetta *Indian Love Call*, and her husband Gene Raymond came over as guests of the Philip Rices and never took a deep breath at the trail. Another time, the Philip Rices had Bill Boyd, "Hopalong Cassidy," as their guest, and, when he saw the steep trail, he got off his horse and walked to the bottom. After that episode, Hopalong Cassidy was a nobody on Kaua'i. He had ruined his image as a daring cowboy forever. Many other distinguished guests visited Kīpū Kai during the twenties and thirties. I have photocopies of the old guest book, which is fascinating to read.

My brothers and I would spend our time swimming, looking for shells on the beaches, and fishing with a pole and baited hook. We caught all kinds of fish. We usually let them all go, unless the maid who watched us when we were small wanted to keep one or two for herself to eat. Our grandfather and the other adults only wanted moi and āholehole, both delicious, white-fleshed fish, that were caught by Hina, the resident caretaker.

Hina had several sons and two daughters. His wife Chise and their daughters would do all the housework while the men would take care of the chickens and turkeys along with all the ranching chores including growing sweet corn and other vegetables. One son, Shigeru, was my age and we hit it off right from the start. Shige had a throw net, and his father taught me how to use it. Shige and I would always want to go fishing, but Hina wouldn't let us go until certain chores were done. After the two weeks were over and it was time to return to Līhue, I would beg to stay longer. Hina would tell my mother that it was okay for me to stay with them and that he would see that I worked right along with his sons.

One day, we had worked for most of the day cleaning out the chicken coops and didn't have time to go fishing. Hina said that, if Shige and I would hoe weeds in the cornfield the following day and make a pile of weeds big enough to fill the dumpcart, we could go fishing. We jumped at the chance of getting off work early because most of the weeds were of a variety that were pretty big and we thought we could fill the dumpcart pretty early in the day. Well, we went to work with a vengeance. Hina didn't come out with the dumpcart until after lunch. What we didn't realize was that the sun had wilted the weeds so that we had only about three quarters of a load. Hina initially told us that we had to hoe some more to fill the cart, but he soon relented and let us go fishing. Two ten-year olds learned a hard lesson of the real world. Hina joked about this incident for many years afterwards.

In the late thirties, Hina quit his job at Kīpū and went to work for Walter

Dillingham on his ranch at Mokulēʻia on Oʻahu. I only saw Hina twice after he left—once after I had been drafted and was at Schofield Barracks on my way to California and once when I was in Honolulu for the Statewide 4-H Beef Roundup. I happened to be there because some of the steers KīpūRanch had sold to children of Kauaʻi were in Honolulu for the state finals.

Shige went on to become a pretty successful building contractor in Honolulu and also was a staunch backer of Junior Golf. One lesson I learned while staying with Hina was how to use chopsticks. During his family's meals, they had sweet Japanese onion pickles that I loved. To keep me from eating too many at one time he said, "If you want to eat those pickles, you have to pick them out of the jar without sticking the chopstick into them, and you have use your chopsticks to pick them up one at a time." Have you ever tried to pick up a small, round onion with chopsticks? If you want something bad enough, you learn how to get the job done.

After Kīpū Kai, the family went to Kokeʻe for the rest of the summer. My grandmother loved it up there. She loved roses and other temperate flowers, along with apples, peaches, and plums. We would travel up the mountain with at least two cars and a staff of three or four servants. One car would go down to Waimea once a week to get ice for the iceboxes, for there was no electricity up there. On Saturday noon, a car with servants would go to Līhue so they could be with their families for Sunday. They would return on Monday with all the supplies needed for the next week, along with the mail. I developed my love for gardening up at Kokeʻe by working with the roses and other flowers. There would always be at least four horses brought up for the summer. There was a pasture for the horses, and, every morning, they were rounded up and given a bucket of rolled barley. This was so we could catch them easier. While my grandmother was still active, we used to go riding every afternoon all over the mountains. There were no blackberries, banana poka, or strawberry guava in those days. However, it was a joy just to go out for a ride.

The apples that were grown at Kokeʻe were mostly seedlings from apples that we bought at the stores. The apples were quite tart and made for good pies. Our cook, Iwamoto, would peel and core the apples and then slice them with a mandolin. The slices would be about one-thirty-second of an inch thick. After he had the crust in the pie pan, he filled it with the sliced apples and plenty of washed brown sugar and cinnamon. The pies were always one-and-one-quarter inch thick in depth and were served hot with cream from the dairy in Līhue.

Our dairy was stocked with Ayrshire cows that produce a very high butterfat content milk. The surplus milk was run through a cream separator.

The skim milk went one way and the cream another. After about twenty-four hours in the icebox, the cream would solidify and wouldn't pour, so it had to be spooned out of the bottle. We used the cream in lieu of butter on apple pie, pancakes, and waffles. We also made butter out of any extra cream. Later, after World War II began, and butter was rationed, we made around twelve pounds a week. What butter my grandfather's family didn't need we gave to friends and other family members. The milk wasn't pasteurized, so during the War we couldn't sell any milk to the military. After the War, we sold the cows to Hilo Dairy, run by the Nishida brothers, in the Wailua Homesteads. A particular disadvantage for our family was that our cows were all milked by hand and milkers were hard to find.

The dairy barn was located right around where the parking lot for Hamura Saimin Stand is today. That whole block was pasture area for the cows, including where the Salvation Army Thrift Shop is all the way down to Kalena Street. The pasture had over twenty large kiawe trees on it, and the cows loved to eat the kiawe beans that had ripened and fallen to the ground. In the thirties, my grandfather subdivided the area. The big building on Kress Street was built by S. H. Kress, of the five-and-dime fame, and was our first and only five-and-dime store for many years. On the lower eastern side of the street is Barbeque Inn run by the Sasaki family. The Sasakis are the only family of the original owners left on the whole block. The Hamura block was developed in the fifties after the dairy was sold.

In 1935, the Civilian Conservation Corps (CCC) Camp was started at Koke'e. They opened existing trails and developed others so that, every summer, there were some new places to explore. One afternoon during that year, my grandmother, grandfather, Chiyuki Hada, who was one of our servants, and I went on a horseback ride along a trail that we hadn't been on yet that year. A bee stung my grandmother's horse, and my grandmother was thrown and broke her arm. My grandfather and I stayed with her while Chiyuki went back for a car to take her home. He came back, and the two of them helped my grandmother into the car left for home. I had to lead the other two horses back to the camp. By the time I returned, my grandmother had gone to see a doctor. She never got on a horse again.

One year, my grandfather got a big tent for us boys, and we spent the summer sleeping out in it. Our carpenters built a form around the outer boundary of the ground, and we filled it with about two feet of the hay-like grasses from the yard. This became our mattress, and it was quite comfortable. That summer, my brother Charles and some other kids started a gossip sheet and circulated it among all the people summering at Koke'e. It was quite well received by almost everyone.

One sport that I enjoyed throughout my childhood was trout fishing. In the twenties, the Department of Fish and Game imported some rainbow trout from Southern California. The waters of Koke'e were cool enough so that they could spawn. I fished in the Koke'e Stream from our camp to where the tunnel took the water underground to the Pukalua Reservoir. The biggest fish that I ever caught was fourteen inches long. He was a cagey old rascal, though, as he would not take a fly or a worm. Previously, I had read in a sports magazine that if you could tickle a fish's belly you could slowly work your hand up to his gill and just lift him out of the water. I tried this method, and it was easier than one would expect. The fish wasn't very good-tasting though; like the 'o'opu, he tasted rather muddy. Later, "Dolly Varden" trout were introduced. They grew to be pretty big but could not reproduce because the water was not quite cold enough for them. This was lucky for the rainbow population because Dolly Varden loved to eat baby rainbows.

I can remember where the first blackberry plants were planted. They were brought in by Dr. Nils P. Larsen and planted next to his house just down the road from my grandfather's camp. When we knew that Dr. Larsen wasn't around, we would sneak over and try to find some ripe berries to eat. By 1938, the blackberry bushes had started to spread. My grandfather hired an old Japanese man to dig up any plants he could find. This same man would work on the blackberries from June to September every summer for four years until 1941. Once World War II started, all bets were off, as we couldn't get out to Koke'e any more because of gasoline rationing. By the time the War was over, it was too late—the blackberry bushes had taken over. The same holds true for the banana poka and the strawberry guava. Black Wattle, a species of Acacia, was imported from Australia in 1934 when the CCC started their reforestation of Koke'e. Now, though, these trees have become pests in the area. Another potential pest is the Pyrocantha, a shrub that has pretty orange and red berries that birds like to eat. It seems to be spreading around the park area, and someone has been digging out the existing plants. The Myrica faya tree, which is from the Portuguese controlled Madeira Islands in the Atlantic Ocean, was brought to Hawai'i in the late 1800s by Portuguese immigrants. This tree has nitrogen-fixing capabilities enabling it to dominate native species of trees and spread. In addition, in Portugal the cattle eat the leaves, but, here in Hawai'i, our cattle have better things to eat. So, this tree grows profusely. The flowering plant lantana, a pretty ornamental, has been a pest for so many years it is almost considered by some to be native. I have many scars on my arms from plowing through lantana while chasing cattle. Unfortunately, our native plants evolved in an atmosphere most benevolent and have no natural defenses for the exotic invaders.

When school was not in session, to keep from getting into too much mischief, I would spend a lot of time in Kalapaki where my grandparents lived. While growing up in Kalapaki, most of my daylight hours were spent in trees and in the water. I could climb coconut trees like a monkey, and we ate coconuts all the time. Mangos were a treat as was tamarind and any other fruit we could get our hands on. One sport we liked to play was tag up in the trees. If your feet touched the ground, you were automatically it. One of our favorite trees was the big banyan that is now part of the Menehune Gardens. After we had determined who would be "it," the rest of us would climb as high up in the tree as possible and wait for the "it." When he got close to us, we would jump off the branch we were on and into the branches below us and wait again. We would repeat this until we got close to the ground and, then, scamper up a different branch to the top again. This game was kind of dangerous, but none of us ever fell out of a tree. I better mention that banyan branches are very strong and supple, and they never snap like some other trees' branches. The tamarind is even stronger that the banyan.

Another fun place to play tag was where Hale Kauai is today. This was the Wilcox family's beach home. The waves used to lap at the shore at the bottom of the Hale Kauai driveway before the breakwater and jetty were built in 1930. There was a grove of coconut trees, fifteen feet tall at the time, that had been planted with each tree about fifteen to twenty feet apart. Their fronds overlapped each other so it was easy for us to hold on to two fronds from separate trees and sit in thin air. When "it" came up one tree, we would let go the frond from that tree, move around to the other side, and grab a frond from another neighboring tree. Again, we were lucky no one ever got hurt.

However, there was one time I got into a tree accident. The first Tarzan movie had just come to Kaua'i, and I guess I was trying to emulate Tarzan when the branch I was hanging from broke and I fell to the ground. My feet were only about three feet from the ground when this happened, but it caused me to limp. After a few minutes, I finally went in and told my grandmother what had happened. She got my grandfather to take me to the hospital for an x-ray. The image showed a greenstick fracture of my left shin. Bad news travels fast. So, by the time we got home, the word was out and a Hawaiian couple, Enoka and Beatrice Lovell, asked my grandfather if they could try a Hawaiian remedy for broken bones. My grandfather called Dr. Kuhns and asked him about this treatment, and he said we could go ahead. Dr. Kuhns was always a great advocate of the native medicines. Early the next morning, the Lovells appeared with a bowl of liquid. They slowly bathed my leg, which was stretched out in the sun, all morning. The liquid they used was made of the pounded root of the blue Hawaiian morning glory and a handful of a native pennywort that grows on exposed rock outcroppings watered by springs. I could feel something pulling the skin of my leg but nothing hurt. After they finally emptied the bowl, they said that it was enough and went home. Regardless, the next day, the doctor put my leg in a cast, and I wore that for six weeks. Two other boys broke their legs that same day, and they were the same kind of breaks as mine. I was out of my cast in six weeks, but the other two boys had to wait three more weeks before they could get out of their casts.

My grandfather had two boats at Kalapaki—one was a twelve footer powered by a ten horsepower outboard engine, and the other was a ten footer powered by oars. When I got to be about nine, we would take the rowboat out in the bay when there was no surf. About this time, we got interested in fishing, and the boat was an ideal platform to get our lines into deeper water. Our casting equipment was crude by today's standards, but the fish weren't as sophisticated either. Our main targets were pāpio and barracuda.

One day, the father of one of my best friends Goro Sadaoka asked us if we would like to go fishing in the Menehune Fishpond. He told us that his friend, Mr. Chiba, the caretaker of the fishpond, was having trouble with the barracuda eating the baby mullet they were trying to raise. We were eager to go. One Saturday morning, five of us young nine year olds set out early from Kalapaki and rowed up to the fishpond, a distance of over two miles. When we got there, Mr. Chiba told us where to fish. He also told us that we could put crab nets out in the river for Samoan crabs, but we were not to catch any crabs from the pond. This we did and drooled at the huge crabs we saw in the pond. All we caught were five crabs that were four inches or so across the back. The ones in the pond were seven and eight inches. All the while, we were casting for barracuda. At this we were pretty successful. We caught about ten; one was almost eight pounds. At around two o'clock, Mr. Chiba came out to see how we were doing and told us it was time for us to start for home. He was very pleased with our catch of barracuda and asked how many crabs we had caught. We showed him our catch. His comment was, "Not bad, all river crabs." Then, he took a long-handled scoop net and scooped up two huge crabs, tied their pinchers together so that they couldn't pinch us, and said, "You were good boys, so take these crabs to your grandmother." When we compared the river crabs with the crabs from the pond, we noticed that the river crabs were all brown from the mud while the pond crabs were a clean blue color. We talked about this for quite a while afterwards. It was a good lesson that honesty is the best policy. The row back to Kalapaki was quite strenuous, as it was against the wind and tide all the way. Nevertheless, we were happy about the day, and we traveled there several times more by oar and later, when we were older, by motorboat.

When I got to be twelve years old, I was allowed to take the motorboat out in the bay. By then, we had discovered spear fishing, and one of the better places was along the inside of the breakwater. My grandfather was not one who enjoyed going out in a small boat, and he made me promise that we would never take the boat outside the breakwater. I kept my promise. One of the hardest things for us kids was to get the boat into the water. We finally learned how to put logs under the boat and roll it in and out of the water. On the far side of the bay, we would go diving for Samoan crabs. We could find them hiding under the rocks with only their pinchers showing. We would spear them and put them right on a small grill we had set up on shore. We did this with lobsters we speared on the outside of the breakwater when it was very calm. We cooked any shellfish that we speared and ate them right away so we wouldn't get food poisoning by letting them sit and spoil.

We would also travel all the way up the river to the end of the tidewater when the mangos were ripe. There was one place where the mango trees hung over the water. So, we could tie up to the branches of the trees and climb right up into the mango trees without ever touching land. One time, three of us took the boat up the river for a camping trip. Two of my classmates, Goro Sadaoka and Takuji Fujimura, had joined the Boy Scouts and were anxious to show me their skills. We set up a tent on the riverbank and tried to make a fire. However, there wasn't any dry firewood, so we had to eat out of the cans. That wasn't too bad, but, by about nine o'clock, it started to rain and ended up raining the rest of the night. We were a sad-looking group the next morning.

One day, when another group of boys and myself had had enough surfing for a while, we caught a chicken and plucked the feathers off and got it ready for cooking. I said that we should try and kalua the bird instead of broiling it. A couple of the boys went and got some small round rocks, while the rest of us collected firewood to heat the rocks. We dug a small pit and set the fire. When the rocks came, we put them on the wood and lit the fire. In the meantime, I gathered some tī leaves. When the fire had burned down and the rocks properly heated, a bed of tī leaves was laid over the rocks and the chicken put on the tī leaf bed and covered with more tī leaves. The whole thing was covered with earth and left to cook. After about two hours, we came back from more surfing and opened the imu. The chicken looked white, but we thought that it might still be raw. One of the boys twisted off a leg, and the bone came off in his fingers. We knew the bird was done. We made short work of the chicken and agreed that we should do this again.

Another time, this same group of boys went over to Wanini, which is now called 'Anini, to go diving around the big reef. It took us three days to drive there. We speared many fish notably the uhu or parrotfish, which has a nice, white, flakey flesh. While diving the second day, I was stung by a Portuguese man-of-war right across my face on the upper lip under my nose. It stung like the dickens, and, the next day when I went back into the water, itched like the devil. The itching from the sting recurred every time I went into the ocean for about a week.

As we got older, our horizons broadened. We were now able to take the outboard motor boat across the bay from Nāwiliwili where we could hunt goats along the mountainside. The only gun that we had was the twenty-two long rifle that had been given to me. Once, when the stevedores were on strike, most of them were living in the old skating rink in Nāwiliwili and didn't have much to eat. We went goat hunting and shot four goats. We kept one for the boys and sold the other three to the strikers for a dollar-fifty apiece. If we had not field dressed the goat, we would have gotten at least double for them. Most of the strikers were Filipino and they often like the innards best.

Another time when we were hunting goats, we caught six little kids. I already had a pen built because I had used it to hold goats before. Now, I was ready for new ones. Three were nannies, and three were billies. We raised all but one of the billies to maturity. One billy died soon after capture, but the others thrived. We castrated one billy, and, when he was big enough, we ate him. The three nannies became the foundation for a herd of about sixty goats. During the War, there were times when there would be two or three Filipino men waiting for me to get home from work. They wanted to buy one of the goats from me. I made enough from selling goats to buy all the fencing I needed to pasture them. Just before I went into the Army, we put all the goats on a truck and took them to Kīpū and released them in one of the pastures. Most of them were still there when I returned three years later.

THREE SHORT STORIES ABOUT TIME
WITH MY GRANDPARENTS

THE ʻAUKUʻU

When I was about three-and-a-half years old and staying with my grandparents at Kalapaki, an amusing thing happened. My grandmother loved to play bridge. One day, while she and three other women were playing bridge, they heard a noise on the roof. One of the women asked my grandmother what the noise was. My grandmother replied, "It's probably just an ʻaukuʻu." The ʻaukuʻu is a native night heron. Another of the women said that she had never seen an ʻaukuʻu and would like to go out and try to catch a glimpse. The other women agreed. When they got outside to where they could look up on the roof, there was no ʻaukuʻu, only little Hobey. My grandmother very calmly called to me and said, "Show Nana how you got up there." Like an idiot, I ran across the roof to the lattice that followed from the roof to the ground and climbed down the way I had gotten up. As soon as my feet touched the ground, I started up the lattice again as fast as I could go. But I was not faster than my grandmother. She caught me, and that ended the escapade.

CAPTAIN JACK

Before the days when Nāwiliwili became the main port of Kauaʻi, all the East Side shipping docked at Ahukini. The sugar warehouse was there, and the bags of sugar would be brought to the pier by a conveyer from the warehouse above the pier area to be loaded on the ships. Ahukini was a small harbor, and docking a ship could be difficult at times, especially when there was big surf running and the wind was blowing, as can be the case at times.

The captain of the port was a man named Jack Bertrand. Captain Jack was a man with a large vocabulary of four letter words in several languages and would use them if anything wasn't to his liking. His sons told of the large parrot that was at their house. The parrot could hear Captain Jack down at the pier from his built-in cage on the front lanai. The parrot was beginning to accumulate an impressive vocabulary and could imitate Captain Jack quite well. In fact, the parrot swore so well that Mrs. Bertrand started complaining. Her husband solved the problem by sending two carpenters to move the parrot to the back of the house. It could be that Mrs. Bertrand could no longer hear the parrot from the back or that it lost its vocabulary when it could no longer hear Captain Jack.

My grandfather would often take me down to Ahukini to watch the ships being unloaded of their incoming freight or loaded with sugar. Most of the time Captain Jack was around, and he would come over to our car and talk with us. Very often when we were there we would hear Captain Jack cussing someone out. Needless to say, I learned some of those choice words. The story goes that, when I was about four and a half or so, I was trying to hammer a nail into a piece of wood and hit my finger with the hammer. The same way I had heard Captain Jack cut loose with a string of four letter words when something went wrong, I let loose a pretty fair string of cuss words.

My grandmother happened to be in the vicinity and heard me and said, "Hobey! Where in the world did you learn that language?!"

I promptly replied, "From Captain Jack."

I'm not sure, but I think I got my mouth washed out with soap. But, that hasn't deterred me at all.

SUGARCANE VARIETIES

My grandfather used to take me around Kīpū, and, while he checked out how the sugarcane was growing, he would teach me the names of all the varieties of cane by their color and growth characteristics. He took great pleasure in showing me off to his friends. One day, he had Jack Bottomley to show around Kīpū. Mr. Bottomley, the President of American Factors, was a rather austere man and didn't have much of a sense of humor. Grandpa was showing off my knowledge of the various sugarcanes to Mr. Bottomley, and, as we were going around the plantation, Mr. Bottomley would ask me, "What variety is this or that cane?" and I would answer him with the correct name.

Finally, we came to a field of corn, and Mr. Bottomley said, "Little boy, what is that variety of cane?"

My reply was, "You goddamned fool, that's corn." My grandfather had a hearty laugh at my response. I don't know how Mr. Bottomley took my answer, but he didn't ask me any more questions.

Grace King Rice, my grandmother.

Juliet Rice as a young woman.

Christmas card with Hobey, Jr. and dogs.

Hobey in 1927 with trike.

Hobey at twenty-three months old on horse.

Hobey at Kokeʻe, 1929.

Hobey and Charlie boy.

Hobey and Charlie playing at Kalapaki in the late 1920s.

Fred Wichman, Juliet, Hobey, Charles, and Bruce at Pihanakalani for our Christmas picture in 1935. Our last Christmas together in Hawai'i.

CHAPTER THREE

Nāwiliwili in the 1930s

Most of the rest of my story is centered on Kaua'i, so I thought this would be good place to tell you something about the port of Nāwiliwili. Nāwiliwili in the 1930s was a lazy, little town just coming awake. Two piers had just been completed. Pier one had a covered building on it, but pier two was just a concrete slab with railroad tracks and mooring bitts. The tracks were installed as a backup for Ahukini so that, when Ahukini was not able to handle sugar ships because of high surf, they could still use Nāwiliwili. The rails were connected to the web of tracks that went from Anahola on the north side to Makaweli on the south side. The bags of sugar were loaded at the mill in Līhue and then taken to Nāwiliwili to be loaded on the ship. The sugar in the bags weighed one hundred pounds. In those days, there was no limit to the weight a stevedore might be asked to move, and one hundred pounds was not thought of as excessive. A cargo net would be placed on the ground, and the bags would be placed by hand onto the cargo nets and hoisted up and into the hold of the ship where they were dropped. The stevedores would move the bags around so there was always a level to build the next layer on. This procedure went on until the hold was filled and the hatches battened down. Only the sugar from Kīlauea, Grove Farm, Kīpū, and Lihue Plantations came to Nāwiliwili for shipment. All the south shore plantations shipped their sugar out of Port Allen (until 1958 when the bulk sugar storage building was built and no one would take bagged sugar). The rivalry between the east side of the island and the west side was quite fierce, and the rivalry did not die for many years.

Canned pineapples would come from the cannery in Kapa'a, where the Pono Kai Condominiums are today, and would come to the pier by rail. There were no pallets for the sugar, but pallets were used to move the cases of pineapples. Forklifts were not used in those days, so most of the work was done by hand labor. The railroad went from the pier to two long sheds, which were located near where today's Nāwiliwili Park is today. The sheds protected the flat cars from rain until they were needed at the dock. The railroad continued over the present footbridge between JJ's and Duke's, through the area of the Marriott's Porte Cochere, and, then, up the hill to Ahukini.

In 1958, the bulk sugar plant was built, and the gantries and conveyer belts were installed. All the plantations had gone from bagging their sugar to hauling it in bulk to the storage building. Now, all sugar on Kaua'i left from Nāwiliwili, and the loading process was accelerated by at least five times.

The area where the Matson storage yard is today was a large lumberyard, and, then, next to it was a large hall built by the American Legion. The most important use of the hall was as a roller skating rink. Up to that time, all the roller-skating was on Pier Two and, as one would expect, there were several beginners who went off the pier into the bay. No one was ever hurt, but they would have to go home for a change of clothes. There were no lights or music to skate by until the hall was built.

Next to the skating rink were Don's Drug store, a pool hall, and a barbershop. Since the mid-thirties, I have had my haircut either at this shop or at its successor Kawamoto's in Līhue. Sadao Kawamoto was the last barber at the old barbershop. The Kauai Sales Building was a two-story building. The second story was a sort of salesmen's hotel, which K. C. Yamasaki rented out to the Drummers. The Drummers were sales people from Honolulu who made regular calls to the small merchants and mom-and-pop stores all over the island. The Drummers calls were sometimes the only way a small guy could get any merchandise because the plantation stores had a virtual monopoly on the island and didn't want competition. The Kauai Sales Building was opposite the Banyan Harbor Apartments of today. Further inland from all these buildings is Papalinahoa, where the Wilcox family had their beach home. In the forties, this home became the clubhouse for the Kauai Yacht Club. The former Hale Kauai building now sits on that site.

The Anchor Cove area was the base yard for the Nawiliwili Transportation Company. This company had large trucks and passenger cars to hire for the few tourists who visited the island. The drivers of these cars were colorful characters who all had wild stories to tell the visitors. The main bridge through Nāwiliwili was a divided two-lane bridge that is still in use today. The present big bridge wasn't built until the late thirties.

The Shell Service Station is now a motorcycle rental site, and the warren of small shops and homes across the road are gone having been replaced by a small shopping and eating complex. Kalapaki as a residence is no more. The April 1, 1946 tsunami wiped out my grandfather's home and other buildings. The two ten-story towers built for hotel rooms are now timeshare rental units. Chris Hemmeter had built another large ten-story building in the valley where the old Kauai Inn buildings were, for over two-hundred new hotel rooms for the Marriott chain. All the streams in the valley have been diverted through underground culverts so that they all empty into Nāwiliwili Stream.

Nāwiliwili as it looked in 1900. No breakwater or sea wall and filled in land.

Old Nāwiliwili Pier, circa 1920.

Kalapaki Bay, 1920.

Lily Pond Kalapaki Bay, 1930.

Hukilau at Kalapaki Bay, pre-breakwater.

Kalapaki Bay, post-breakwater.

CHAPTER FOUR

'Iolani & Oregon 1937–1941

In 1936, our dad got itchy feet and wanted to move somewhere else. He looked into a ranch in central Oregon and did a buy-trade deal with the owner. After Christmas of my sixth year of school, I was sent to 'Iolani Episcopal School for Boys in Honolulu as a seven-day boarder. Boy! Was it hard at first! All the students had been there since September and had made friends already. At first, I felt alone because I didn't know anyone. But, the first morning, Frank Lovell took me under his wing and into the dining hall where he sat me with all his friends. Frank was quite a bit older than I but from Nāwiliwili where his father was a deputy sheriff. His friends were all football players and had huge appetites. When the serving bowl of oatmeal was brought to the table, the fellow who sat at the head of the table took the bowl, scraped the whole dish of cereal onto his plate, and handed the bowl to the person next to him. This person went to the kitchen and had the bowl filled again, and he took all the contents for himself. This procedure continued until it was my turn. Finally, I got my chance, and, by then, everybody was done eating.

After breakfast, it was off to class. What a difference from the easy ways of Lihue Grammar School on Kaua'i. I soon got into the swing of things and everything got better. In the spring, there were no organized sports for the younger boys, but we made up touch football games and played tennis whenever the bigger boys would let us on the courts. Twice a week, in the afternoon, we would walk down to the Nu'uanu YMCA for swimming. This was a walk of about eight blocks. But there was a store where we could buy shaved ice and other goodies along the way, so we didn't mind the walk.

School hours were from eight in the morning to three in the afternoon five days a week with an hour of study hall in the evenings. There was also an hour and a half of study hall every Saturday morning. During the seven years that I boarded at 'Iolani, we had chapel (mostly morning prayer), and sometimes it was both morning prayer and vespers in the evenings before supper. On Sundays, we had to go to an early Sunday service at school and then have breakfast. After breakfast, we had to get dressed up in coat and tie and walk ten blocks to St. Andrew's Cathedral for a full service with a long sermon. This service started at eleven o'clock and lasted for at least one hour. After that, it was back to school for Sunday dinner. This schedule was the one we followed only for the first two and a half years; then, we switched to the Hawaiian service led by Father Bray, our football coach, at nine-thirty in the morning. For the first two years, I sang in the boys' choir on Sunday mornings. My uncle, Reginald Carter, who was married to my father's sister Catherine, was the organist. So, I got to join the choir. This was a wonderful set up. He paid me twenty-five cents for the Sunday service and the same for choir practice on Thursday afternoons. When fifty cents was all you got for a weekly allowance, this extra money was very welcome. When my voice started to change, the gravy train was all over. Once my voice completely changed, I was a half octave off, so I sounded flat.

At the end of the school year, in June 1937, my grandparents, my brother Charles, and I left on the *Malolo*, later the *Matsonia*, bound for California and Oregon for the summer. "Malolo" is the Hawaiian word for flying fish. The *Malolo* rolled from side to side. When they refurbished the ship and installed stabilizers, they changed the name to *Matsonia* so people would not think it was the same old ship that rolled a lot. It was a smooth trip until we got close to the California Coast; then, it got rough. I am a good sailor, so it didn't bother me. But my brother got very seasick. We landed at San Pedro, and our dad and Mother were waiting for us on the dock. We motored up to Oakland because all the San Francisco hotels were on strike. I don't remember much about Oakland. I guess that was because we went over the Oakland Bay Bridge into San Francisco almost every day. One day, our dad took us three boys to the Blum candy factory. Boy! Was the smell of chocolate enticing! Mr. Blum had a big box of chocolates on his desk, but he wouldn't let us have any until we had toured the whole factory and saw how the candy was made. By then, after seeing all that chocolate, eating a piece of chocolate didn't sound too enticing. Mr. Blum gave us the box of chocolates and said that they would be more appealing later. After Blum's, we went to Jack's Restaurant for lunch. It was the first time I had ever seen waiters in black suits. It was at this luncheon that I was introduced to the famous San Francisco sourdough hard rolls.

After about five days in the Bay Area, we left for Oregon by way of Vallejo and San Raphael on Highway 101, as the Golden Gate Bridge had not yet been completed. That first night, as we were headed north, we stopped at the Benbow Inn. We got in early and saw a large lake, so we boys went swimming. The water was colder than in Hawai'i, but we didn't care. In 1983, Nancy and I, while on our way north to Sun River in Oregon, stopped for the night at the Benbow Inn. There was no lake, and, when I asked what had happened to it, I was told that they removed the dam in the fall before the winter rains and hadn't put the dam back in yet. Big, long planks were used to dam the water to make a reservoir that created the lake.

The next day was spent driving through the redwoods. I have been through them several times since then, but I am always amazed by the size of the trees. The rest of the trip up to Hay Creek is a little hazy, but we spent one night at Grants Pass and the next day motored north to Eugene, Oregon. We travelled over the McKenzie Pass into Bend and then up to Madras on Route 97. Then, we travelled twelve miles east from Madras over an unpaved road to reach Hay Creek Ranch. When we got to Hay Creek, the shearing of the sheep had been completed, and the nine bands of sheep were well on their way up into the mountains for the summer. (Note: The sheep numbered over ten thousand, as a band of sheep is about one thousand ewe and their lambs, with one herder to watch over them.) After we got settled, it was time to move the cattle herd up into the summer range in the Ochoco Mountains. I was given a horse to ride, and, with the cowboys, we started to collect the cows and their calves. After a week of this activity, we had almost all the cattle collected and ready for the big push into the mountains. When the morning of the big push began, everything was going according to plan. Then, we got into some trees, and the cows couldn't find their calves. No matter how hard we tried, we couldn't keep them from turning back. Finally, we gave up and tried to get as many as possible back into the pasture we had started from. We spent the next week rounding up the strays. The order of the march was changed from going through the trees to going along the road to Princeville and then up the road into the mountains and Summit Prairie where there were lush summer grasses. The total distance of this drive was about one-hundred miles of dusty, unpaved county roads.

The first day's drive was out of the upper pasture down to Ranch Headquarters. This was an uneventful day. The next day, was also uneventful until we got to where we were going to spend the night. Then, the fun began just like in the movies of the old Wild West. We had to take shifts and ride herd around the cattle all night so that they would not break back and head for home. The next night, it was the same drill. The following day, we headed east from Princeville and up to a ranch where the boss there let us pasture our herd for a day of rest. After this day of rest, we started out again. By then, the cattle were pretty used to being herded along and didn't cause any more trouble. That night, we stopped at a small pasture with plenty of good water and grass for the cattle. That night was full moon, so, at one-thirty in the morning, we started to move the herd because it was a long hard climb up into the summer range. It was just about daybreak as we started up the steepest climb. Some of the youngest calves started to tire, so I was given the job of babysitting the five calves that wouldn't go with their mothers anymore. I had them all tied up to trees where they just laid down and went to sleep. I guess I did, too, for I was awakened by the sound of a truck and a lot of voices. A truckload of CCC boys were on their way to work in the forest. They stopped the truck, bailed out, came over, and asked me what the animals were. These young men were all from New York City and had never seen calves before. They asked me if they could pet the calves, and I told them to go ahead. The fellows were like little children with each with a new toy. After about half an hour, our pickup truck arrived and the petting party had to be broken up. The calves were loaded into the pickup and headed off to the mountains and their mothers.

I have forgotten to mention that one of the unpleasant things we had to look forward to was the shots. Since we were going into the mountains for the summer with sheep, we had to get inoculated against Rocky Mountain Fever. The shots themselves weren't too bad, but the ache and flulike symptoms were most uncomfortable. I guess it was a good idea that I had the shots because I spent a lot of time with the sheep. After this, the shots were automatic every summer.

We got the main herd into the pastures where they would stay until fall when the calves would be sold. After the main herd was safely in their pastures, two cowboys and I went back to where we had started three weeks previously to round up stragglers that had been missed earlier. After about a week, we had assembled forty cows and their calves. We, then, took them through the mountains on the same trail that we had tried to take the main herd. The first day, we went about twenty miles with no trouble at all. At the end of the day, we reached a small pasture that was owned by the ranch and that was used for a way stop for both cattle and sheep (both on their way into the mountains in the spring and back in the fall).

After taking care of our horses, one of the cowboys said to me, "Let's go catch some trout for dinner." There was a small creek running through the pasture. We had hooks and line with us, so we cut willow poles and rigged up our poles and line. Bait was our next concern, and we found periwinkles under the rocks in the stream and used them to bait our hooks. With three or four periwinkles each, we started to fish. In no time at all, we caught five trout of about six to seven inches in length. We used the eyeballs of the fish we had caught for additional bait, and, in a short time, we caught forty-two trout. This was enough for our supper and breakfast the next morning.

After breakfast, we saddled up the horses, rounded up the cows and calves and started out for our destination, Summit Prairie. By four that afternoon, we turned our cows and calves into the pasture with the cattle already there and went to the bunkhouse to get ready for supper. In two days, we had accomplished what had taken ten days with the main herd.

After bringing all the cattle together, we spent the summer fixing fences and doing other chores until August when we started to brand the calves. The branding took about a week. Then, there were sheep to take out of the hills to be doctored for all kinds of ailments. Another sheep-camp duty was to help move camps for the sheepherders. This happened every one to two weeks depending on the amount of grass available at a particular camp area. Certain sheepherders were good cooks, and, when we went to move their camp, a forest ranger was sure to show up for a meal of young venison or government mutton, as it was known. The rangers never cited the herders because they knew that the herders would never kill more than they could eat.

One night, while returning to our camp from a hard day's work, our driver said, "Here is a nice prairie with a stream in it. Let's take a bath." We got undressed and got in the cold water. It was about nine o'clock at night, and the water was pretty cold. But it was good to get rid of the dust. While sitting in the water looking up at a clear sky filled with millions of stars, I remembered the last verse of "Home On The Range"—"How often at night when the heavens are bright with the light of the glittering stars, have I stood there amazed and asked as I gazed, does their glory exceed that of ours?" All of a sudden, from the surrounding hills, the coyotes started their howling. It was an eerie experience and one that I'll never forget.

One of our summer jobs was to supply the sheepherders with their food needs. At the Hay Creek headquarters, there was a big commissary stocked with everything the herders would need for the summer. I helped stack all the cases of canned fruit and vegetables and hung sides of bacon out of reach of the porcupines. Porcupines loved salt and would eat right through the floorboards that had been soaked with fat from the drippings of the bacon sides. In this regard, porcupines were pests. One good thing about porcupines is that their flesh tastes just like pork. The quills are quite flammable, and, when a porcupine carcass is set on a campfire, it is ready to eat when the fire has burned out.

One day, our dad, J. Hudson White, the ranch foreman, and I drove to the north end of Summit Prairie to look at the Merritt Ranch. This was a beautiful small ranch of between five- to six- hundred acres with a nice stream running through it. Old Mr. Merritt had just died, and his children wanted to sell the property because none of them were interested in ranching. Summit Prairie was in the mountains and was snowbound in the winter. In 1938, Dad was able to buy the ranch, and it became a valuable addition to our summer range.

By the end of August, it was time to return to the islands for school. We headed back to San Francisco where we could get a ship back to the Hawai'i. San Francisco was a wonderful city for us to sightsee. We went to Fishermen's Wharf and ate crab and oysters and had a great time looking at fishing boats. One day, we drove to Stanford University because our dad had wanted us to see where he had gone to school. The trip back to Hawai'i was uneventful as was the trip back to Kaua'i. We were on Kaua'i for about a week and then back to Honolulu and 'Iolani School. This was the year 1937, when my brother Charlie joined me at 'Iolani.

Back at school, it wasn't long until I got into trouble again. One evening, I threw a hardboiled egg at a passing car and hit it. The driver came into school and saw the headmaster. The headmaster, Father Stone (or "Pohaku" as we called him), came to study hall and asked if anyone knew who had done the throwing. Right away, a boy said that he had seen me take an egg from the table after breakfast. I was busted. I was put on campus restriction until Christmas vacation and was also warned that, if anything happened to the "squealer," I would be expelled. It was a long three months of not seeing a movie or leaving the campus except to go to football games. One positive thing that came out of the experience was I got a good foundation in all my schoolwork, and that made my later years a lot easier.

When Christmas vacation arrived and I was able to get away from school and go back to Kaua'i, I was one happy kid. We stayed with our grandparents at Kalapaki. Most of the days were spent surfing and swimming in the ocean and renewing friendships with Kaua'i friends. When the ocean wasn't too rough, we would go spear fishing in the bay.

After Christmas, it was back to the old grind. Twice a week, we would go to Nu'uanu YMCA for swimming. It was then that I got interested in competitive swimming. For the years of seventh, eighth, and ninth grades, we were just getting started learning strokes and starts and turns, plus doing laps totaling one mile two or three days a week. Competitive swimming came later. When we started full training, it was one mile swimming using arms and kicking, one mile using only arms, and one mile holding a small board and kicking. Then, the coach would have us do sprints for as long as he wanted. Needless to say, we got into pretty good condition. I was always too small for football, so I started swimming for the school in my sophomore year. Before the interscholastic season started, we would swim for the Nuʻuanu YMCA team. Most of the meets were held in the evenings, and, in the spring of the year, it would get pretty cold. The worst pool was the one at the University of Hawaiʻi because the wind and rain would sweep down Mānoa Valley and you felt as though you were going to freeze when you got out of the water after a race. I was a decent swimmer but not super, but good enough to earn my letter for the two years I swam for the varsity.

While restricted to campus, I started collecting koa haole (*Leuceana leucocephala*) seeds for my grandfather. He wanted to plant some in the pastures at Kīpū. It took me about a year, but I was able to collect about one-hundred pounds of seed from the side hill in back of the campus. He paid me five dollars for the seeds and had them shipped back to Kauaʻi.

The mother of one of the boys in my class often drove us all to the basketball and football games. At this time in my life, I was enrolled in dancing class. I don't know how it happened, but, suddenly, my brother Charles and I were told to go take dancing lessons. Our dancing school was in the Waiʻalae-Kāhala area, about two blocks toward the mountains from Kāhala Avenue. The pigpens were located just behind the dancing school. Sometimes the smell was pretty ripe. After we got to know the girls, class got to be fun. Most of the girls and boys went to Punahou, so we got a lot of razzing but most of it was good-natured. We didn't become a threat until later when we were in high school.

I got into quite a few fights in the first year and a half that I was at ʻIolani. Most of the time, the older boys would stop us, then take us down to the locker room and lace on the boxing gloves, and let us fight until one of us had had enough. The fights were regulated, so we fought three-minute rounds with a one-minute rest in between rounds. No one ever got hurt, and we were made to shake hands after the fight was over. Every spring, we would have boxing tournaments at school. These were held during the nine-thirty recess on Friday mornings. There were seven different weight classes, and I always fought in the lightest class. I never won a championship in my class, but I won a lot of fights.

One time, I got into a fight with a classmate during the morning recess. One of our teachers pulled us apart and took us to the headmaster's office. We sat there for over an hour when the headmaster came in, looked us over, and said, "So, you want to fight?" Then, he walked out leaving us for another hour. When he finally came back to his office, he took us to his house and down into the basement where he put boxing gloves on us and took us out into his back yard where no one could see us. He then said, "Fight until one of you has had enough." So we went at it until the other boy decided that he had had enough, and we stopped fighting. The headmaster made us shake hands and then let us get cleaned up. Then, we went to the dining hall and had lunch with him. The three of us sat at a table by ourselves and had a good time while everybody else wondered what had happened. That man knew how to handle wild, young boys. My opponent and I became good friends and never got into any more fights.

My roommate after the first year was Rex Glaisyer, and we roomed together for three years. After that, he went to Punahou for his last three years of high school. After high school, he went on to college and veterinary school and then came back to Kaua'i and took over his father's practice. He later became our ranch's veterinarian. The year that Rex left 'Iolani School, our football and basketball coach, Father Bray, invited me to stay at his house. His house was on Judd Street, the third house down from the school's front gate. There I stayed until the start of World War II.

Father Bray was an Episcopal priest for the Hawaiian congregation at St. Andrew's Cathedral in Honolulu, in addition to being the football and basketball coach for 'Iolani School. He also served at St. Marks in Kapahulu. Occasionally, he would wake me at five-thirty on a Sunday morning and explain that his regular acolyte was sick and ask if I would come and assist him. The carrot for this service was breakfast at the Young Hotel Coffee Shop in downtown Honolulu. After breakfast, he and I would go to the nine-thirty service at St. Andrew's where I would join the rest of the 'Iolani boarders. We liked this service for two reasons—one, it was fast because there was no music, and, two, the girls from St. Andrew's Priory attended this service. However, all we could do was take a quick glance across the aisle, since the Sisters would always sit in the aisle seat to keep us separated. Betsy Christian, who had been in my class at Līhue, and I were never allowed even to say hello.

Up until 1953, 'Iolani School was located on the corner of Nu'uanu Avenue and Judd Street where Craigside condominiums are today. 'Iolani purchased the twenty-five acres on the Ala Wai where the school is currently located. Father Bray went to Kaua'i several times to raise money and try to find big boys for the football team. On one occasion, he brought back two pheasants that my grandfather had shot and given him. Like the good Englishman he was, he hung them by their tails (just like you would in England). Well, England and Hawai'i are definitely in two different parts of the world. By the time they dropped to the floor, there were maggots in them and they smelled to high heaven. Father Bray made me promise that I wouldn't tell my grandfather about this, and I didn't until after Father Bray died. My grandfather got a big laugh out of this tale. Father Bray had served in World War I and had gotten shell-shocked, so there were times that everyone in the house would be very quiet and try not to irritate him. After you lived there for any length of time, you got to know by walking past his office when it was time to disappear. At any other time, he was a kindly father figure to all of us.

Once a month, we seven-day boarders were able to have a weekend off campus if we had family who would have us. The first two years at 'Iolani, I spent some of those weekends with my paternal grandmother who lived in the Dowsett tract in upper Nu'uanu Valley. Those weekends weren't much fun for an active young boy. All we did was to sit around the house or in their formal English garden with my father's sister, Aunt Catharine, and her husband, Reginald Carter, who was the organist at St. Andrew's. So, needless to say, we went to church on Sundays. He also got me to sing in the boys' choir. I had to sing at the eleven o'clock service and miss lunch when I wasn't off campus for the weekend. I only sang in this choir for two years because my voice started to change and my services were no longer needed.

The highlight of my singing career was the opportunity to sing for the memorial service for King George V of England when he died in 1937. We wore purple cassocks with white surplices and cute, little, stiff white collars with a small, stiff, purple bow ties. There were twelve of us in the choir, and we all had to sit in the front row. So we were on our best behavior throughout Bishop Littell's hour-long sermon. Sometimes there would be a clergyman returning from missionary work in China who would deliver the sermon. The stories of work in China were fascinating, and we would be all ears with no fidgeting. You must remember that there was no trans-Pacific air travel in those days, and Honolulu was a welcomed rest stop after a long boat ride.

On weekends, off the Halekulani Hotel was my Honolulu home. Mrs. Juliet Clifford Kimball was the sister of my grandmother Grace King Rice. She and her husband, Clifford Kimball, started the Halekulani Hotel in the nineteen twenties after moving from Hale'iwa on O'ahu. They ran the Haleiwa Hotel for a number of years until an opportunity came to move into town. I was welcome every weekend that I was free to leave campus for the weekend. I had already learned how to surf on Kaua'i but was able to hone my skills with the beach boys who worked with the Halekulani guests. It was fun learning the finer point of surfing from those professionals. I could also walk to the Waikiki Theater and see the latest movies in town. There were never any grade B movies at the Waikiki Theater.

Aunt Juliet had two sons who were away at college when I first started going to the Halekulani. Later, when they returned from school, I used to go out with them to Kapiʻolani Park and help them exercise their horses. It wasn't very exciting riding around in circles. Walk, gallop, walk, and gallop around the track that surrounded the polo field. After chasing cattle on Kauaʻi, this was boring. Another pastime was watching the girls go by on the beach—sport for the young boy, but not as much fun as it is today. The bathing suits in those days were not as revealing as they are today.

The Halekulani was a series of small bungalows and one two-story building. There was a one-bedroom building that was called the Bridal Suite, but it always seemed to be occupied. The rest were nice two and three bedroom buildings. I don't know how many rooms there were, but they were always full. The Matson ships would arrive from the mainland once a week, bring in new guests, and leave with those who had been in Hawaiʻi for two or more weeks. In the winter months, there were guests who would stay for two months. These were all older and wealthier people. The Halekulani was known as the home of the "newlyweds and nearly deads." In the main dining room, guests reserved tables and would sit at the same table year after year. Aunt Juliet would have a new waiter wait on her table until she felt that they were capable and wouldn't make mistakes. I remember one rookie who couldn't get things right. Did he ever have a hard time! This was during the depression, and jobs were very hard to find. So there was hardly any turnover. Furthermore, the tips were good.

After the Kimball's younger son Richard (or Kingie, as he was called) finished college, he came home to work in the hotel. Aunt Juliet built an apartment over her cottage for her two boys. I loved it because then I could stay upstairs with Kingie. George, the older brother, was away at law school, so he wasn't around while I was there. One thing I learned early on was that, if I wanted a good night's sleep, I had to get to sleep before Kingie. He had the loudest high-pitched snore that I have ever heard. If he got to sleep before you did, he kept you awake for a long time. All in all, it was a fun time, and I had many good times there at the Halekulani.

During one Easter vacation from school, I took Goro, Takuji, Noboru Kinoshita, John (Honey) Makanani, and Raymond (Oopu) Ellis over to Kīpū Kai for an outing of fishing and diving. We caught enough fish in the first afternoon that we didn't need to use any of our canned goods. One night after we had all gone to bed, about one in the morning, Oopu came and woke me up. He was trembling like he was really afraid. He said that he had heard Hawaiian music in the room where he and Honey were sleeping. We all got up and went into the room, and, sure enough, we did hear music. In those days, there was no electricity or any battery radios over there. We were never able to find out what or who was making the music.

The next day, we dove and speared fish right in front of the house and did very well, enough so that everyone had plenty of fish to take home. While we were cleaning up before leaving, one of the boys looked at the ocean and, right where we had been diving that morning, big as life, was a twelve-foot shark. I guess that shark was drawn to the spot by the smell of the blood from the fish we had speared.

In 1938, we stayed in Hawai'i for the summer instead of going to Oregon. Most of my memories of that summer are being with my grandparents. This was the last summer at Koke'e with my grandmother, for we were back in Oregon in 1939 and she died in the spring of 1940. The biggest event of the summer was the arrival of Dr. Carl Skottsberg and his assistant, Olof H. Selling from Uppsala University in Sweden and Lucy Cranwell from Christchurch, New Zealand. They were botanists and were in Hawai'i to collect plant samples for their university herbariums. In those days, there were no four-wheel drive vehicles, so all travel through the forest was by horseback or by foot. I was assigned to be the groom for the scientists. Every once in a while, I was asked to climb a tree for a flower or a fruit for them. After returning to the house in the evenings, I would watch them prepare their samples for drying and preservation. One day, Mother and I took them down the Nualolo Trail and showed them a large Kaua'i Koki'o (*Kokia kauaiensis*) that was in full bloom. They were thrilled. Mother brought home a couple of flowers and even painted a picture of a flower. This picture was then used as a cover for a copy of the Garden Bulletin of the Pacific Tropical Botanical Garden. I am now the proud possessor of this original painting.

Another highlight of the summer of 1938 was when my grandfather received a letter from the Ford Motor Company in Detroit asking if he would entertain Louis Ferdinand, the grandson of Kaiser Wilhelm of Germany, and his bride, Kira, who was the niece of one of the Russian Grand Dukes who had escaped the Revolution of 1917. Several years before, Louis had been sent to America to learn about mass production assembly lines. What better place than the Ford Motor Company, the home of the modern-day assembly lines? The bridal couple had been given a trip around the world as a wedding present by the Kaiser. When they arrived in Hawai'i, they came straight to Kaua'i and up to Koke'e. They were put up in a cottage in the Rice compound, which was called the Bridal Suite.

The next afternoon, it was my job to take them to the Kalalau Lookout. In those days, there was no vehicular road to Kalalau, so we went by horseback. On the way, I started to whistle the tune to "Glorious Things of Thee are Spoken" not knowing that it was the tune to the German National Anthem "Deutschland Über Alles." Louis Ferdinand wanted to know how

I had learned this tune, and I told him that it was from a hymn we sang in church. It was an hour's ride from the Rice Compound to the Lookout. There were no clouds to obstruct the view, so they were able to take in the wonderful sight. They were both thrilled at the view all the way down to the beach. It was an hour's ride back home, and that was all the riding for the day. After dinner that evening, Kira showed us how to fold a piece of paper into a bird whose wings would flap when you pulled its tail. I still remember how to make that paper bird. Little did we know that, by the same time the following year, the world would be embroiled in World War II. After the War, I learned that he survived, and he and Kira had a family and were living in Germany.

After all the guests had left that summer, Rex Glaisyer, my roommate at 'Iolani, and I did some goat hunting. We would go riding on the ditch trail overlooking Waimea Canyon and look for goats. We had thirty-thirty rifles, which were pretty high powered for us, but that was all we had. When we would find goats in places too dangerous for us to retrieve them, we wouldn't take a shot. Sometimes we got lucky and shot one, but most of the time we came home empty handed. We picked Friday afternoons to hunt because Saturday and Sunday the grownups from Waimea and Kekaha would come up to hunting the Canyon. After five days with no hunting, the goats would venture into places where the grazing was good and there hadn't been any hunters around for several days. Our timing was good. Our aim was so-so.

The summer of 1939 was the year of the San Francisco World Fair, which was held on Yerba Buena Island in San Francisco Bay, half way between Oakland and San Francisco. Just before the fair opened, my grandfather and I had our pictures taken while standing next to the twenty-eight-millionth Ford car to come off the assembly line. Unfortunately, the picture of this event was lost in the tsunami of 1946 when we were living in Nāwiliwili. We attended the fair for the better part of two days. One thing that disappointed me about the fair was that I wasn't allowed to get in to see the Sally Rand Fan Dance show because I was too young.

After getting our fill of the fair and before going north to Oregon, we went south to Los Gatos where we met the George Bakers who had a home in the hills above the town of Los Gatos. The house overlooked the valley, and one could see all the way to San Jose. We spent three days with them. They had a big cherry tree in their yard and also a swimming pool. The cherries were the Queen Anne variety. The Bakers didn't really care for them, but we Hawaiians went wild. Fortunately, none of us got sick from eating too many cherries. Mr. George Baker was a Baker of the Baker Chocolate

Company, and his wife was Carmen Ghiradelli of Ghiradelli Chocolates. Their children were George, Jr., who was a little older than I; Jerry, who was my age; and Carmencita, who was a little younger than my brother Charles.

We had some excitement in our dad's new Lincoln as we were on our way north to Oregon from San Francisco. Somewhere south of Redding, the back door of the car ahead of us flew open and a young child of about three years of age fell out onto the road ahead of us. Fortunately, our dad was quick enough to turn off the road and into a grain field that had just been harvested. The boy was not seriously hurt but was pretty scared. When his father saw that his son was not seriously hurt, he asked us to take the boy and his mother to a doctor in the next town because he had to get to work. You must remember that we were still in the Great Depression years and jobs were hard to find. The father just couldn't risk losing his job with a diversion to the doctor when he had a family to support. We dropped the mother and child at the doctor's office and continued on our way.

When we finally arrived at Madras, Oregon, we found the road east to Hay Creek was too muddy to proceed without chains. So, we went another ten miles on the main highway and then took an alternate route. When we neared the ranch, the ground was all white with hail. It looked almost like a light snowfall.

After arriving at Hay Creek in the early part of the summers of 1939 and 1940, my first job of the year was bagging wool at the shearing barn. The fleece was tied in little bundles for packing. I would place a large burlap bag in a holder on the floor and throw the bundles of fleece into the bag. Before putting the bundles into the large bag, I had to separate the coarse wool from the fine wool. After eight to ten bundles were dropped into the large bag, I would jump into the bag and stomp the fleece as tight as I possibly could, and, then, start all over until I could add no more fleece. I would, then, loosen the top of the bag from the holder and drop the bag to the floor where I would sew up the open end of the bag. Finally, I would brand the bag with the ranch brand and a number. Then, the process would start all over again. I continued this procedure for ten long days or until the shearing was done.

(Note: Nancy and I visited the island of Hawai'i where we saw the remains of an old shearing station between Hualalai and Mauna Loa. This station was in operation in the 1860s and 1870s. They had a mechanical press for what I was doing with my own weight in 1939. Have we progressed or regressed? I am very glad that I am not in the sheep business. Sheep are not very intelligent animals.)

In late August 1939, we left Hay Creek for San Francisco for a week or so before boarding the *Lurline* back to Hawai'i and school. While in San Francisco, we spent another three days with the Bakers in Los Gatos. While in Los Gatos, I met a girl, whose name I have forgotten. She told me that she knew a girl in Honolulu by the name of Clare Rolph and that, if I should ever meet her, to say hello for her. Well, to make a long story short, Clare was a friend of a third cousin of mine and a few of the other girls that I had been with at dancing school. I got to meet Clare shortly after that, and, for the next two years, we went steady. The Punahou boys didn't like the idea of an 'Iolani boy dating a Punahou girl, but there was never any trouble. In 1941, my senior year at 'Iolani, Clare was sent to finish her last two years of high school at Katherine Ransom's school for girls in California. We corresponded for about three years when, suddenly, I got a "Dear John" letter saying that she was marrying a dashing Naval officer. I didn't hear from her again until 1948 when we saw each other at a cocktail party in San Francisco that my dad and his new wife Marjorie hosted. This meeting took place after Nancy and I were engaged. We had a friendly chat and nothing again until 1989. In the middle of 1989, I got a letter from her asking for some advice about where she and her family should stay on Kaua'i. I suggested Kiahuna Plantation. When they arrived in June of 1990 for their vacation, Nancy and I had dinner with them, and we met her husband and children. In the car going home after dinner that night, Nancy said, "Hobey, you have good taste and I approve." I have since learned that Clare's husband died, and she has remarried and is very happy.

After we returned to Kaua'i and before school started, I went up to Koke'e with my grandfather and the Jack Plews'. While we were up at Koke'e, the Germans invaded Poland. Uncle Jack and I went over to Mickey Christopher's house to listen to his shortwave radio, and we heard Neville Chamberlain declare war on Germany for Great Britain. It was scary to think that, just a year ago, we were entertaining the Kaiser's grandson at this very place. Little did we know how soon we would be embroiled in this conflict.

My grandmother, Grace King Rice, had hypertension for most of the 1930s. After the trip to Oregon in 1937, her health deteriorated. She died on March 4, 1940, when I was a sophomore in high school. As I remember it, I heard about her death on a Monday. George Kimball, my cousin, picked me up on Monday evening from school and we boarded the interisland steamer *Hualalai* for the overnight trip to Kaua'i. We arrived at Nāwiliwili at about six in the morning and went directly to Kalapaki for breakfast. After breakfast, my grandfather and I went to Kōloa and the mortuary to see my grandmother. This would be where I would have my first look at a dead body. It was a very traumatic experience for me.

After a short time, we went back to Kalapaki for lunch and, then, back to Kōloa again. After closing the coffin, we followed the hearse all the way to Kapaʻa and All Saints Church for the funeral service. When the service was over, there was the viewing of my grandmother's body for the last time. My grandfather and I were the last ones there to watch the closing of the coffin. I cried all through the ride to the Lihue Cemetery and all during the committal service. When a Hawaiian choral group started singing "Aloha Oe," my grandfather broke down and started crying. I was now cried out, so I led my grandfather away to the car and we drove back to Kalapaki. After dinner, the Kimballs and I boarded the *Hualalai* for the trip back to Honolulu. Up until that day, I had never been to a funeral and the episode made a very strong impression on me. Ever since that day, I have always hated funerals. I even get teary-eyed even at funerals of people I hardly knew.

In the summer of 1940, when my grandfather and I got back to Hay Creek Ranch, he left me and said that he was going to drive around and see the country. What he actually did was to visit Patricia Smith, my grandmother's nurse and persuaded her to marry him. Later on in the year, they were married and she moved back to Kauaʻi with him.

The summers of 1940 and 1941 were spent on the ranch in Oregon doing pretty much the same routine as the year before. The only thing different was fighting forest fires. In the summer of 1940, we were in the forested part of the ranch, staying in an old homesteader's cabin. Right after we had lunch, it started to rain, and with it came thunder and lightning. After the storm passed, we went outside and could smell smoke. We found a large fir tree that had been struck by lightning, which had torn a twenty-foot splinter out of the tree. The splinter was not burning, but the needles under the tree were smoldering. We were lucky to reach to the tree as soon as we did. There were no flames, and we soon contained the fire. In the meantime, we found four more hotspots that were smoking in the immediate area. These fires were easy to put out since there wasn't a thick layer of needles under those trees. The first fire took the rest of the day to put out.

In the summer of 1941, we had to go to the Merritt Place and check on the cattle about once a week. It was an hour's ride across the prairie from the rest of the ranch's summer range. The Princeville Land and Cattle Company owned the land in the middle of the prairie. We always called it the Muddy Company because their cattle kept the stream's water roiled and muddy most of the time. I liked the Merritt Place because of the clear trout stream that ran through it. There were lots of beaver in the stream, and the water from their dams kept the grass nice and green all summer. There were also crayfish in the stream, and we would catch them and eat them. Another meat that the cowboys taught me to love was wild duckling. Just before they could fly, we would catch them to eat. We would never pluck them, but just skin them. They were fat, juicy, and tender, though slightly illegal.

Toward the end of my summer stay, another cowboy, Frank Foster, and I were on our way back to the headquarters from the Merritt Place when we saw a bolt of lightning hit a big dead pine tree. Smoke soon started to rise from the base of the tree. Frank said to me, "I hope we get home before the rangers come to investigate." We still had over a mile to go before we could get off the road, and, sure enough, the rangers arrived and asked the two of us to help them put out the fire. We couldn't refuse because there was a law in Oregon that you had to go fight a fire if asked by a ranger of the Forest Service. We put out what fire we saw, but the rangers wanted us to stay and watch to see if the fire had traveled along the underground roots and might surface somewhere else. Frank and I spent the night by ourselves while the other cowboy took our horses back to headquarters. The rangers had other fires to attend to, but they did bring us food and water. With our meals that night, we had the first instant coffee I ever had. It was called George Washington Powdered coffee, and it was horrible! The next morning, the ranger came and checked on the remains of the fire and that took us back to our headquarters. Both of us got paid forty-five cents an hour for our work—a grand total of eight dollars and ten cents, which wasn't bad because I only got fifty dollars for two months work at twelve hours a day six days a week from my dad.

The return trip to Hawai'i was lots of fun. I had an inside stateroom with a bathroom and a shower to myself. There was another single room between my room and Frank Burns's room. Frank Burns, who I knew quite well, was the son of the manager of the Lihue Plantation Company on Kaua'i. A young woman from Honolulu had the room between us, and, every night, we could hear her pushing her trunk against the door to make sure no one could get into her room while she was asleep. However, she wasn't that good-looking, so neither of us cared for her. There were two young female college graduates who were going to Hawai'i to work as schoolteachers. They were both just out of college, and this was their first trip away from home. We all sat at the same table, and they wanted to find out all they could about Hawai'i before they got there.

After dinner, on the first night out at sea, the three of us went up to the bar to watch the slot machine players. The girls had never seen gambling of any kind and were fascinated. Soon, the barman came to our table and asked if we wanted a drink. We declined. A little while later, he returned and said that the Filipino man near the dance floor would like to buy us a drink. I told the girls that he was a wealthy man from the Philippines who controlled a large group of Filipinos in Hawai'i. We agreed to have one drink. Before we had finished the drink, the barman appeared again with an invitation to join our rich Filipino friend. The girls needed no further encouragement and accepted his invitation. His name was Dr. Hilario Moncado, the head of the Filipino Federation of America. It was a semi-religious group of individuals who didn't eat meat or cut their hair. Each member also donated one dollar a month apiece to the Federation.

We danced until two in the morning and had a great time. This was the last I had anything to do with the two schoolteachers because Dr. Moncado got them to change their table seating to his table. Later, on Kaua'i, when he was leaving after a visit to Kaua'i, he saw me at the pier. He came over and shook my hand and thanked me for the nice American girls. I didn't care much about losing the company of the teachers because there were a lot more interesting young women on board and the full moon at sea was so romantic. That trip was the best and last voyage on a Matson Liner I ever had.

Back at 'Iolani as a senior in high school, things began to take on some urgency regarding college and plans about where to go. I had almost all my requirements for graduation by now, so I had some time for extracurricular activities. I was the sports editor of the school paper and co-editor of the yearbook. Our football team had not done very well that year, and, for the first time, we didn't make the Thanksgiving Day game. School was winding down for Christmas, and the news was all about the problems with Japan and how long it would be before we were at war with Germany.

In November, Mother came to visit but spent most of her time on Kaua'i with her father and sister Edith Plews. She was booked on the Matson Liner *Lurline* on the fifth of December, 1941. She and I had dinner together on the night of the fourth, and she left for San Francisco the next day. The following day I spent working on the sports page of the school paper for Monday morning's deadline. I had planned to finish the layout on Sunday morning.

On December 6, 1941, I was a senior at 'Iolani. That evening, a few of my friends and I went downtown to see what was happening because the fleet was in at Pearl Harbor, and the town would be crawling with sailors. We toured the River Street tenderloin district until about ten at night and then headed for Waikīkī. Being haole and looking, maybe, like we were either sailors or soldiers, we were able to get a drink of hard liquor with no trouble at all. The last place we stopped at was Lau Yee Chai's at around midnight. We had one last drink and headed back to school. We didn't know it then, but that night was the end of our carefree childhood.

CHAPTER FIVE

World War II 1941–1945

On the morning of December 7, 1941, we were on our way to breakfast when we heard sounds like thunder to the west of us near Pearl Harbor. We thought that, maybe, there was practice-firing going on. By the time we got to the dining room, we heard Webley Edwards saying on the radio, "This is the real McCoy. Pearl Harbor is being bombed." After breakfast, we were told to go to church at St. Andrew's as usual. We got dressed and went downtown to church. Being that it was early, we thought that it might be fun to go to the waterfront. Just as we got to the Hawaiian Electric Plant by Aloha Tower next to Irwin Square, we saw a plane flying toward us and another one right behind it firing its machine guns. When the first plane was directly overhead, we could see the Rising Sun insignia on its wings and the U.S. and Star on the plane behind. We got scared, and, needless to say, we got out of there and back to church in a hurry.

At church, we heard our football coach, Father Bray, try to persuade Henry Giugni, who later became Dan Inouye's administrative assistant in Congress, to stay in church and not try to get to Pearl City, where his family lived, until things quieted down a little and it was safe to travel about. While this was going on, an unexploded antiaircraft shell fell and exploded about two hundred yards from St. Andrew's on Beretania Street almost killing an old Chinese man.

After church, I went to the Young Hotel to see my grandfather, who was in Honolulu for the sugar planters' meetings. We went up to the roof garden, and all we could see was heavy black smoke coming from Pearl Harbor. It was not an encouraging sight.

On my way back to school, walking up Nu'uanu Avenue just above School Street, I saw where another antiaircraft shell had fallen and exploded. When I returned to Father Bray's house, all of us who lived there were recruited to go to Kawananakoa School to assist the Red Cross in caring for families of the servicemen from Wheeler Field and Schofield Barracks who had been evacuated because of damage to their homes. We helped in the preparation of the meals and in serving them for three days. In our spare time, though, we practiced stretcher bearing and basic first aid. Several months later, Mother, who was on the mainland, saw, on the cover of *Life* magazine, a picture of some young men training for stretcher bearing and swore that one of them was me.

Before the bombings, whenever we ʻIolani boys would walk through Pauoa Valley, we were always at the mercy of a group of Portuguese boys who would try to pick fights with us. They would stand on the opposite side of the street and make snotty remarks at us. If we didn't rise to the bait, they would send their younger brothers across the street to harass us into hitting them or telling them to get lost. As soon as the little brother would act like he was being abused in any way, the bigger boys would cross the street and accuse us of hitting the little kid. Sometime we could talk our way out of trouble, and sometimes we had to run for it. One way or another, they never seemed to hold a grudge, it seemed like this was just sport to them. On the night of December 7, I was on my way to Kawananakoa School for my shift feeding the wives and children of the service men from central Oʻahu. That's when I met one of the toughest of the Pauoa Valley gang, and he showed me a large knife. He told me that we white people better watch out for the Japanese. Suddenly we were friends.

On Tuesday December 9, when we got back to our house, we saw some men across the street working near a long deep trench in the Nuuanu Cemetery. They were placing large canvas bags in the trench. We then realized that they were burying the dead from Schofield and Pearl Harbor. The enormity of what had happened on Sunday hit us pretty hard. The trench must have been one-hundred feet long.

On Wednesday December 10, 1942, my cousin George Kimball, who was in the Naval Intelligence Service, called to tell me that Mother had gotten home safely. I was relieved to know that her ship had made it back to San Francisco safely and that Mother was okay. We heard later that the *Lurline* and another ship had switched lanes and that a Japanese submarine had torpedoed the other ship. After the War, however, we learned that this information was not true. There was no ship sunk between Hawaiʻi and the mainland during the entire War.

On Wednesday December 10, my grandfather told me that he would be picking me up early the following morning and that we would be on the first plane back to Kauaʻi. The school had closed, and all the boarders were supposed to find other arrangements. The school didn't open again until April of 1942, and, by then, I was making more money than some of my teachers. On the way to the airport, we could see a little of the damage but not Pearl Harbor. The windows of the plane were blackened so that we couldn't see anything from the air. That was the end of my high school education, as I went to work at Kīpū Ranch the next day.

After my grandfather, Pat, and I returned to Kaua'i from Honolulu, the first thing we had to do was to make a room secure for a blackout room. Luckily, there was an interior bedroom that we could modify with minimal effort. We needed to make it light secure so we had some place to spend the evenings. Every night after dinner, we would go to the blackout room and talk about the day's doings and listen to the radio or play cribbage. Most of the time, we would go to bed by nine o'clock because we had to get up at the crack of dawn. After a few weeks of this, I started to bring home ears of corn that had a few kernels of flint corn in them. I would remove and save the kernels of the flint and, later, grind it up in the coffee grinder and made corn meal out of it. We made a pretty good corn bread out of the corn meal. In 1942, all of our corn was a sweet corn variety, but, later, we got some seeds of a new variety of tropical flint corn especially developed by a Dr. Mangelsdorf at the University of Hawai'i and called "Marribello." This variety became our staple variety from then on.

On the evening of December 30, 1941, I went to bed at about nine o'clock and fell right to sleep. I was dreaming I was in an airplane and was bombing the enemy somewhere in the South Pacific when I heard my grandfather's voice saying, "Get up. We are being bombed." In those days, I didn't sleep with any clothes on. I scrambled around and found a shirt and a pair of pants and put them on and went out to the front of the house. My grandfather's house was on the beach at Kalapaki in Nāwiliwili. It was a bright moonlit night, and we could see two star shells on parachutes slowly descending over Nāwiliwili. Every so often, we would hear a booming sound from out to sea and would soon see columns of water rising out of the bay. The bombing went on for about half an hour; then all was quiet. We did not count how many shells were fired at Nāwiliwili at that time, but, later, we found out that there were twenty-two in all. Except for the two star shells, all the rest were duds. A star shell is one with a fuse set to go off at a certain height and is filled with phosphorous and set to burn at a given elevation. It would slowly drift to earth giving off a bright light so the enemy fighter could see what he is shooting at.

The next day, we learned that one of the shells had hit one of the bulk gasoline tanks of the Shell Oil Company. The shell entered the tank about two feet from the top, piercing the tank and falling to the bottom of the tank where it stayed until the tank was emptied several months later. The tank was three quarters full of gasoline when it was hit. On the road next to the Shell Oil Plant the next morning, another shell was found unexploded.

About a year later in the cane field directly behind the Shell Plant, another shell was found when that field was being harvested. This shell was picked up by a Filipino worker and taken to the home of the plantation manager and placed on his doorstep. Several other shells were found later in the Niumalu area, all unexploded.

January 1942 was when I really started to work at Kīpū Ranch. Some of my first jobs were to weigh and sew up bags of either cracked corn or whole corn for sale as chicken feed. With the War on, there was no chicken feed to be had in any of the stores. At Kīpū, my grandfather had the foresight to have planted several fields in corn, some of which were ripe and being harvested. Another job was to dig fence postholes for the new fencing around the old sugarcane fields. Kīpū was in transition from a sugar plantation to a cattle ranch. As a cane field was harvested, it was plowed and either planted with corn or had furrows cut between the rows of cane where sprigs of Kikuyu grass were planted. By the time the young cane shoots were four feet high, the grass was well enough established so that the cattle could be allowed to graze. The cattle would first eat all the young cane, and, after the cane was gone, they would start on the grass.

My grandfather's surname, as you know, was "Rice," and the staple food of most of our workers was rice. Consequently, it was said that everything on the ranch was done "on rice power." All the postholes were dug by hand. There was one other young man my age, and we were put with eight other middle-aged, Japanese men who were paired in teams of two—one man with a shovel and one man with an ʻōʻō. An ʻōʻō is an adaptation of the old whaling flensing knife. We made our own on the ranch from old spring steel, which was shaped in the blacksmith shop and usually fitted with a handle made from a piece of three-quarter-inch, galvanized water pipe. The postholes were dug to a depth of thirty inches. The two young boys were a team, and the old men pushed us for all we were worth. We soon caught on to the system and eventually would be digging six holes to their five. We very soon earned their respect. But, my being the boss's grandson meant that I had to work harder than the rest. After the postholes were dug, the posts had to be set and the wire strung and stretched. We young fellows were not allowed to do this work.

In January of 1942, the ranch was successful in acquiring a contract for supplying sweet corn and sweet potatoes to the submarine base at Pearl Harbor. The sweet potatoes were of the Nancy Hall variety. When the corn got to the stage that it was ready for eating, a group of Japanese women would pick the ears, and we young guys would be the pack mules for hauling the corn out to the edge of the field. There it was counted out—ninety-six ears to the bag. When we had accumulated one-hundred bags, the bags were loaded on to a truck, taken to Nāwiliwili, and shipped to Pearl Harbor on a sampan. We made shipments every Monday, Wednesday, and Friday for about a year and a half. We also raised sweet potatoes and shipped twenty one-hundred-pound bags along with the corn.

In early March of 1942, I was sent out into the sugar harvesting field to work with a group of men, called the Kakalaka Gang, who hauled the loaded cane cars out of the field and put the empty ones back in for the next day's loading. There were four men and a team of horses who laid the portable track for the cane cars. Each piece of track was about ten feet long with the two rails held together by four small steel ties. Each length of track had fishplates securely fastened to one end and loosely fastened on the other so that the next piece of track could be fitted onto the loose ends. These loose ends were just loose enough for a man with a crow bar to ram the two pieces of track together. When all the cane serviced by a line of track had been loaded on to the cars and removed from the field, the track was pulled apart, loaded on to a small flat car, and moved on to the next area where the cane had been cut and was ready to be loaded. After two weeks of this work, I went back to being a cowboy, meaning that I was available for any job that had to be done. One of these jobs was to swing a twelve-pound sledgehammer to straighten out bent portable track. This type of work really built up one's muscles.

In the first week in April of 1942, we had finished harvesting all of our sugarcane, and we were now a full-time cattle ranch. My grandfather contracted our harvesting crew out to Grove Farm Plantation where they had fallen behind in their harvesting. By the middle of April, our crew was harvesting Grove Farm's field thirty-two, which was adjacent to the Grove Farm-Kīpū boundary, when our foreman was diagnosed with stomach cancer. Without any warning, I was put in charge of the harvesting crew. Imagine an eighteen-year-old boy with no experience getting this kind of call. I was supposed to know where to cut the fire breaks for burning, when to burn, how far apart to lay the portable tracks, and how far apart to place the empty cars for loading so each car could be filled with about four tons of cane.

Kīpū headquarters was so close to the harvesting field that my grandfather could ride out every morning and check on me. Ricardo Alonzo, the cane cutting luna or foreman, would help me most of the time. However, most of the time my grandfather didn't like the way we were doing the job and would yell at me saying, "You god damned fool kid! Don't you know anything?!"

Ricardo would wait until the old man left and then say to me, "No worry, Mr. Hobey. I help you." Then, we would go right ahead and do what we were doing in the first place. All the men in the crew knew what they were doing and what was expected of them. So everything would just buzz along and everybody was happy. Throughout the process, I learned a great deal from the experience.

We were just finishing harvesting field thirty-two when the Battle of Midway took place. Suddenly, we heard the air raid sirens go off in Līhue. There we were in the middle of a cleared field with this long line of cane cars, a D7 Caterpillar, and no place to hide, when a lone plane came flying over us. At first, we didn't know whose plane it was. But, when it got directly over us, we saw the stars on the wing and knew it was ours.

From the end of June until the end of September, we were far enough away that my grandfather couldn't ride over every morning, and life became a breeze. Those were pretty good months for me as I went from sixty dollars a month to one-hundred-twenty dollars a month with a fifteen percent monthly bonus. This made my monthly check one-hundred-thirty-eight dollars per month, and I learned a lot in those five months. I tried every job in the harvesting field except laying track. I tried cutting cane and loading cane into the cars, and I even drove the locomotive for short distances. It didn't take me long to realize that this was not what I wanted for my life's work.

After we got through with the harvesting for Grove Farm, we all went back to Kīpū. The Filipino cane cutting and loading gangs were all given their releases from Kīpū so that they could get jobs with the U.S. engineers. Getting a release meant you had clearance to work elsewhere. During the War, nobody could just quit his or her job without a release or they would be arrested and given any job that was going begging whether they liked it or not. We were under martial law and at the mercy of the military. Writ of habeas corpus had been abrogated for the duration of the war. So the Filipinos got their releases, and I became a full time cowboy. This meant riding herd on the cattle, branding, weaning, slaughtering, and, most of the time, fixing fences.

One of my jobs was riding around the pastures looking after newborn calves. Often, in the winter months when it had been raining heavily for some time, some of the cows would not clean their calves properly and the flies would lay their eggs in the unclean spots. The eggs would hatch into maggots, which meant we had to catch the calf and then wash it with a Lysol solution. This usually did the trick, if we got to the calf early enough, otherwise we had to make repeat treatments. Sometimes we couldn't save the calf. Another case of calf mortality was when we had unusually heavy rain and everything would flood. The cows always tried to keep their newborn calves in a spot sheltered from the wind, but, in doing so, they had their calves in the gullies where the water would come rushing down in heavy rain. After one particularly bad winter, I asked my grandfather if we couldn't start a seasonal breeding program. After much explaining, arguing, and shouting, he finally came around. With a seasonal breeding program, our cows had their calves starting in April. The newborn calves were born in warmer and drier weather, and the cowboys didn't have to pack a gallon of Lysol solution on their saddles.

In early 1943, the Army contracted to set up a small sawmill in the upper part of pasture number ten. They were going to use eucalyptus to make rough lumber for bridges and other heavy construction work. They used a team of our draft horses and a thirty horsepower tractor for the next two years or more. The Army took over two-million board feet of lumber out of the forest. Eucalyptus is a tree that will sprout from a cut stump and grow into a useable log in about fifteen years. After five years, you could hardly tell where any trees had been cut. One bonus for us was the huge pile of sawdust, which the Army didn't want. We normally used sand for bedding in the stalls for the horses that we kept in the stables. We started using the sawdust and soon found that we didn't have any flies around. Another bonus was there were fewer bugs when the manure that came from the sawdust treated stalls was used in the gardens for fertilizer. It was a sad day when we had to go back to shoveling sand again.

During the years of 1943 to 1945, Kīpū Ranch had the lease for the mountain range opposite Nāwiliwili. The island was under martial law, and the field artillery unit based mauka of Puhi wanted to set up an observation station on the hills above Nāwiliwili. They asked my grandfather, Charles Rice, for permission to set up on the peak called Kalanipuʻu. He gave permission and the Army did some investigative work on the access and location of the camp. They came to the realization that the GIs could not transport the supplies that they would need for a week's stay. The Army made a deal with my grandfather to haul the supplies for them on our pack mules. Every Friday morning, two of us cowboys would saddle up six pack mules and our horses and head for the inside end of the breakwater. There we would meet up with the coming week's contingent of men with thirty gallons of water in five-gallon cans and twenty gallons of gasoline for their stove on three mules, and always enough food and other accessories to load up the three other mules. The GIs would head up on foot, while we took a little longer, less steep route and hauled the supplies up to the camp. The GIs would always feed us lunch, and we, then, would load up the mules with the empties and start for home. We would load the mules with the empty water and gasoline cans and deliver them to where we had picked up the morning crew.

One cool Friday morning, as soon as we reached the upper reaches of tide water in the river, we noticed a shimmering in the water. We soon realized that this was a vast school of nehu, also known as anchovy (*Stolephorus purpureus*). Nehu is a small fish of about two inches in length that the tuna fishermen prize for bait. There were millions of the small fish. As we continued down the river about two miles to the mouth, the fish did not diminish in numbers. This phenomenon lasted for about three weeks, and, then, the fish disappeared. To my knowledge, there has never been another bloom of nehu like that since then.

Another extraordinary happening was the appearance of a school of huge manta rays in Nāwiliwili Harbor in early 1944. One day, when we had packed the supplies to the Army Camp up on the mountain ridge, one of the soldiers asked me what the big black things were in the bay. When I went to the edge of the hill and looked down into the bay, there were about a dozen huge black shapes in the water. I looked at them for a little while and finally decided that they were manta rays. From our height, it looked like the largest ones had a wingspan of about twelve to fifteen feet across. One of the soldiers wanted to shoot one of them, and I told him that they were harmless and not to shoot them. We never saw another congregation of rays since that day. You wonder what they were doing in the bay.

In early 1944, the Coast Artillery decided that they wanted a lookout, and they chose Unalau Point for their lookout post. So here was another day trip for the Army. The Coast Artillery wanted to dig a hole on the top of Unalau Ridge, so we had to pack construction supplies. Unalau Point is the second point on the south side of the entrance to Nāwiliwili Harbor. One day, I led a string of six mules loaded with four cases of dynamite, thirty gallons of gasoline, a portable gasoline jackhammer, some water, and food. On my saddle, I had a box of number three electric blasting caps. I was a veritable walking bomb. The soldiers tried blasting out the lookout hole, but the rocks at the top of the ridge were too soft and porous for the dynamite to do much good. So they finally gave up after about four feet.

The next project for the Army at Nāwiliwili was to haul sand and gravel for a pill box the Army wanted to build about five hundred yards toward the point from the inside end of the breakwater. Again two of us were told to go to the site with two mules, and, in the course of a morning, we hauled all the sand and gravel they needed and then went back to the ranch. The pillbox is still there today.

Right after the War started, a ship was sunk by a Japanese submarine somewhere north of Kaua'i and things began to float onto the beaches at Wailua. My grandfather sent Solomon Malina and myself over to Kīpū Kai to see if anything interesting had floated ashore. At Wailua, lots of cases of motor oil, potatoes, and onions had come ashore, but, at Kīpū Kai, all we could find was a bale of raw rubber. As we were going around the point to the east of the house and just as we arrived at the most exposed spot of all, a huge black thing arose out of the ocean about five hundred yards from us. Needless to say, we were scared out of our wits. We kept watching and finally realized it was a humpback whale. When we got back to Kīpū and told the rest of the cowboys and grandpa what had happened, everyone had a good laugh.

Another little story had to do with a pipe-like object that looked like a bomb or small torpedo that washed up on the beach at Kīpū Kai sometime after the whale incident. We reported this find to the Army headquarters, and they sent a demolition team to Kīpū. We, again, went over the mountain on horseback. This time, all I had to carry was ten pounds of some kind of plastic explosive but no caps. After we got to the object and the soldiers saw what it was, they knew that it was a practice bomb and a harmless one at that. They suggested, "Since we've come this far and are going to be sore when we get back from the ride, let's have some fun and blow it up." They asked me if I wanted to blast some fish, and I told them no because it would attract sharks. They, then, used the whole ten pounds to blow up the bomb. That was probably the loudest noise ever, except for thunder that was heard at Kīpū Kai. When we finally got back to Kīpū, they were a sore bunch of guys, but they'd had their fun.

In 1944, we took a group of airmen who were on Kaua'i for rest and recreation to Kīpū Kai for a day of round-up and branding. Some of these guys knew what they were doing and helped make our day a lot easier and faster. After a big beef-stew-and-rice lunch, we took the airmen around the point where we had seen the whale and to a small valley beyond that to look for goats. We ran across a band of about twenty goats in a somewhat open area, so we tried to rope some. One of the airmen was of Mexican descent and from the southwest. He took off after a goat, and, when he got near the goat, it tried to jump out of the way but only jumped into a lantana bush and got tangled. Our boy just leaned over in the saddle and grabbed the goat by the horns, and, before any of us knew what was happening, he had the goat in the saddle in front of him. You should have seen the looks of the cowboys; they couldn't believe their eyes! The Hawaiian cowboys then realized that they were not the only ones who could ride horses, do cattle work, and catch goats bare handed.

One of the extras of doing cattle work was going over to Kīpū Kai for branding. The whole cowboy crew would go over early in the morning and drive all the cows and calves into the big double corral. Then, the cows would be separated from the calves. When this was done, we would start a fire to heat the brands. We used two brands, one was the "Ranch WR" brand, and the other was the year brand. This brand was the last digit of that particular year. After the brands were suitably hot, the real work began. Usually, there were two teams of ropers—one who caught the calf by the neck and pulled it out of the crowd, and the other who caught the hind legs. Then, the ground crew would throw the calf to the ground, hold the front legs in their hands, and sit on the shoulders to hold the calf still for the branding. If the calf was a male, it was castrated right then. Then they would release that calf and another calf would be brought out of the crowd of unbranded ones. When all the calves were branded, they would be reunited with their mothers and released into the pasture again. Sometimes there were calves that had been branded before and were big enough to be weaned. These calves would be separated out and driven to a pasture as far away from their mothers as possible so they could not get back to their mothers to nurse anymore. After all the cattle were let loose, the branding fire was raked out and all the "mountain oysters" put on to broil. When cooked, the mountain oysters were eaten by the hungry cowboys. Before putting the oysters on the fire, they were counted and the total divided by two so we had a count of the number of males. This count was then subtracted from the total and the number of females was known.

While all this was going on, my grandfather was up at the house cooking up a beef stew for lunch. He would always bring large amount of beef ribs, which he would brown, in a huge stewpot. After this came chunks of carrots, onions, and potatoes. Most of the time he wouldn't peel any of the vegetables, so, sometimes, you would get the outside onion skin in your serving. When the meat was tender and the vegetables almost cooked, he would also add several cans of stewed tomatoes. There would also be a large pot of rice for everybody.

After branding and before lunch, some of the cowboys would go down to the sea for throw netting. Some would go after 'opihis, which were quite abundant since no one could go fishing by boat during the War. After the fishermen returned, we would attack the stew and rice. If time permitted after lunch, those who wanted to take a nap could do so before riding back over the mountain. You've never heard snoring as loud as that which came out of those Hawaiian cowboys.

Before the road over the mountain was built by Jack Waterhouse in

1949, one of the disadvantages of raising cattle at Kīpū Kai was getting the young steers and cull heifers out of the valley. We would usually spend the night at Kīpū Kai so we could get an early start the next morning. The evening before, the cattle would be collected and held in a small pasture overnight. The next morning, we would start pushing the herd against a fence that ran straight up the hill to the cliffs. About halfway up the hill was a gate to push the cattle through, and there would be the trail over the mountain. One cowboy would lead the way, and the rest of the cowboys would push the herd from one side and behind. This was the hardest part of the whole expedition. Once we got to the top of the pass and the cattle pushed through the gate at the top, it was every man for himself. The cattle had the right of way, and the cowboys had to keep the cattle on the trail. We would scramble over huge boulders trying to keep the herd on the straight and narrow. Eventually, we all ended up at a corral at the upper Nāwiliwili corner of field number eleven. The young cattle would then be trucked to the fattening pastures. A couple of times we weren't successful and the cattle broke back as we started up the hill. We would let them rest for a couple of weeks and then try again. There were always some that repeatedly got away. These we would let go, and, when we had time, we would slaughter them over at Kīpū Kai, salt the meat, and then haul it out on pack mules. This meat would be divided up among all the employees and retirees of the Ranch.

Sometimes my grandfather craved fish, and he would send a couple of cowboys over to Kīpū Kai to catch moi for him. Moi is a member of the threadfin family, and, in ancient Hawai'i, it was reserved for the ali'i. During those times, any commoner caught eating moi would be summarily killed. When there was to be a lū'au, we would go over to Kīpū Kai and surround fish at night. These fish were predominately nenue or rudderfish and were used to make poke. The poke made with nenue or mullet was different than the poke found in the markets of today. It was chunks of either fish, usually with the skin on, seasoned with salt, limu kohu, 'inamona, and green onions. 'Inamona is roasted kukui nut ground up with salt and used as a condiment in Hawaiian cooking. Another fish that was plentiful when conditions were very rough was the āholehole. A small, silvery fish of about eight to nine inches in length, it is found in large schools. I once caught one-hundred-twenty-five āholehole with one throw of my throw net. Another delicacy is the wana or sea urchin. Wana is an acquired taste, and one must be careful not to eat too much at one time as it is very rich.

Others animals we raised at Kīpū Kai were turkeys, peacocks, and chickens. The chickens were raised for their eggs, and, when they got too old, for stewing hens. The turkeys were for Thanksgiving and Christmas. The best way to catch a turkey was to slip a noose, which was attached to a long bamboo pole, over its head as it roosted at night in the kiawe trees. This was a thrill a minute because the War was on and the island was in complete blackout at night, so we had to be very careful that we didn't show too much light. We knew where the turkeys roosted because we had scouted the forest looking for lots of droppings. We always wore raincoats and old hats for this job. The turkey would let loose their droppings as soon as they were the least bit disturbed. Turkey droppings don't smell good, and the smell persists for a long time afterward. That was the reason for the raincoats. After we caught one, we would tie his legs up and put him in a burlap bag and cut a hole for his head so he could breathe. After we caught enough turkeys for the family, we spent the night at Kīpū Kai. The next morning, we would load all the turkeys on pack mules, and over the mountain we would go. After unloading the mules, we would deliver the turkeys to the various families who would be hosting either a Thanksgiving or a Christmas dinner. The turkeys were rather skinny and tough and not like the full breasted ones of today. We tried a peacock once, but it wasn't as good as an old turkey. It was even tougher and drier than a turkey.

The Kīpū style of ranching required a variety of skills—horse shoeing, carpentry, plumbing, horse training, grass planting. You name it; we did it all. The grass we used at Kīpū was all Kikuyu grass, a native of Africa. It was the favored grass for any rancher who wanted a good, hardy, palatable grass for their cattle. We planted all of our pastures using stolons between the rows of sugarcane or rows of corn when the cane and corn got to be about a foot high. The cowboys or the older Japanese men would cut the stolons by sickle, and the grass would be trucked out to the field to be planted. The wahine gang would walk down the rows, place the stolons in the furrows, and cover them with their feet. When the corn was harvested, the cattle would be let into the field, and, by then, the grass had established itself. The only trouble with this method was that the field would be very bumpy if you drove a truck across the furrows. Later, in the fifties, we would change this method to a more suitable one of scattering the stolons over the field, then harrowing the field and, lastly, planting the corn. This eliminated the furrows and made for smooth pasture, when the corn was harvested, we could put the cattle in the pasture immediately.

Slaughtering cattle for market was all in a day's work. As I remember it, the first slaughterhouse was in Nāwiliwili approximately where the Marriott Hotel's employee parking lot is. We kept the steers for market in the valley across the road from the slaughterhouse. Then, we would drive them across

Nāwiliwili road to a corral, separate out the ones we were going to kill the next day, and drive the rest back across the road. The cowboys would slaughter the animals and deliver them to market. This slaughterhouse was closed in the middle of 1942, and our operation moved to the Grove Farm slaughterhouse in Puhi. This facility was a lot more modern. When we started to use the Grove Farm facility, we started the slaughtering at about one-thirty in the morning because it was cooler and there were no flies to bother us.

The other two non-contiguous pieces of property that we would use for pasture were opposite the Wailua Golf Course and a piece at Pāpaʻa. The Pāpaʻa piece would only carry about eight head of cattle and was not very cost effective. The Wailua piece was a better one. It would carry about fifty head of young animals. It was directly opposite the golf course next to the Montgomery Hotel, as the jail was known in those days in honor of the warden Kalei Montgomery.

We ate a lot of steaks in those days, and my grandfather always liked his steaks well done. After a while, my tastes changed so that I didn't want shoe leather steaks anymore. As soon as the drugstore in Nāwiliwili reopened and I knew that we were going to have steak for dinner at home, I'd go to the drugstore for a hamburger dinner. This complex was a hotel, appliance store, repair shop, barbershop, pool hall, and a drug store. At this drugstore you could get a hamburger, soda fountain service, and nonprescription medicine. All this was on a lease from the Territory of Hawaiʻi for ten years duration. While there at the drugstore, I started to play pool and learned how to gamble with cards and dice. Curfew was at eight o'clock, and we had to be off the streets and at home or the Military police would arrest us if they caught us. After 1943, the curfew was changed to ten o'clock, and the theaters started showing movies at night again. This was a welcome change of pace.

In the early part of 1942, the Japanese community wanted to show their loyalty to the United States in whatever way the Army would allow. They formed what was called the Kiawe Korps. Every Sunday, this group of Japanese would be furnished transportation by the Army and would be taken to Mānā to clear away lantana and low kiawe branches. The purpose of the clearing was to give our troops a clear view of the beaches in case of an invasion. One Sunday, several Hawaiian boys and I joined our friends and went out to work with them at Mānā. After the day's work was done, we loaded up the trucks and headed back to whatever town we had come from. As we traveled in convoy through Kekaha town, there was a young Hawaiian boy standing on the steps of the theater and counting the trucks.

When he spotted me, he shouted for everyone to hear, "Hey look! Get Portagee too!" It took me many years to live that one down.

After work, one of my pastimes was to take my throw net and try to catch mullet for dinner. I would go along the rocks under the space where the cliff cottages at the Marriott are now. There was a coconut tree that grew out from shore over the water, and I would climb it and watch for the fish. Mullet are a fish that are seaweed eaters and, when feeding, turn on their sides so that they shine a bright silver color. Thus they are easy to see. When I would see a school of them, I would scramble out of the coconut tree and get my net ready. Then, I would slowly creep to about where I had last seen them feeding. If I could to see the fish in a favorable spot, I would sneak up and, at the right moment, cast my net over them. If I caught one or more, I would go back to the house and clean the fish. Then, I wouldn't go back to the beach for a day or two. I would catch two or three fish a week, so we always had fish for dinner at least one night a week. Another delicacy that I used to catch was lobster. The lobsters at Kalapaki were small, but I could catch six or seven of them occasionally. Lobsters are caught by diving down and looking under the rocks or in holes in the reef. One of the best places for lobsters was at the edge of the reef just outside of the big rock at the mouth of Nāwiliwili Stream. The one drawback was that there was a unique seaweed there that, when you touched it, would make you itch like crazy. To get the lobster in that hole, you had to lie on the ocean floor and reach in for them. And you had to lie right on that bed of seaweed. One had to be pretty desperate to go after those lobsters, and that's probably why there were always lobsters there.

The Ranch also owned a dairy, and the dairy barn was located in what is now a parking lot opposite where Hamura's Saimin Stand is today. The whole block was the exercise pasture for the cows. Our milk wasn't pasteurized so that we couldn't sell it to the schools or the Army, but we had plenty for the regular customers and our family. Our Ayrshire and Guernsey cows gave high quality butterfat milk. After being bottled, the cream would rise to the top of the bottle, and, after a day in the refrigerator, you would have to use a spoon to get the cream out of the bottle. All the extra milk was run through a separator to save the cream, and we would then give the skim milk to the calves being raised for veal. With all this cream on hand, we were able to keep my grandfather's household and several friends supplied with butter all through the War. Basically, we lived off the fat of the land while everybody else was rationed. After being raised on raw milk all my life, I couldn't bear the taste of pasteurized milk.

(A little aside about the cream—after Nancy and I were married, we had some friends in for dinner, and, when it came time for dessert, Nancy went into the kitchen to finish the preparation. After quite a while, she came back into the dining room and asked me to return the kitchen with her. When I got there, she had tears in her eyes. I asked what the matter was, and she said that, every time she tried to whip the cream, it would turn to butter as soon as she started to whip it. I told her to just spoon the cream onto the dessert—serve it that way, and let it go at that. This she did. The dessert was terrific, and nobody said a word.)

The dairy was finally sold to the Nishida family of Wailua Homesteads who operated the Hilo Dairy.

Hawai'i had a food-rationing program for most of the War, but we were not inconvenienced by it. As already mentioned, we had all the butter and milk we needed. The butter was not the bright yellow that you see today but a very lightly tinged yellow color. Still, the flavor was good. At Kīpū, we also had a large vegetable garden, so vegetables were no problem. Because of being in the sugar growing business at Kīpū, my grandfather always got a one-hundred pound bag of washed sugar every year, and that, too, was all we needed for everyday use. We only used white sugar occasionally like when we baked a cake, and that didn't happen too often. Meat was no problem because the ranches on Kaua'i could supply all the beef needed for the whole population. All during the War, Kīpū supplied the Lihue Supermarket, which was opposite Kress Store. The old market is now the office of Tad Miura's Kauai Realty.

Starting in early 1944, we started to deliver one steer a week to the Lihue Hotel, which belonged to my grand uncle, William Henry Rice, the sheriff of Kaua'i. His son-in-law, Wayne Ellis, leased the operation from his father-in-law. Wayne started a Thursday night special steak dinner for the soldiers. This was because he had heard complaints from the soldiers about how the Army cooked their beef. The whole animal was cut into steaks, and, if I remember right, the biggest night was two-hundred-forty-nine dinners.

In those days, a great many of the families at Kīpū kept pigs in their back yards. We raised pigs and sold the piglets to the families to raise. Every month, we would kill and cut up one of the pigs that was ready for slaughter, and it would be sold to the neighborhood. My job was to weigh out the meat and collect the money. The price was three pounds for a dollar, with no charge for the owner of the pig and my grandfather. The owners would then buy another piglet and start over. The pig raisers loved this setup because they didn't have to collect from their neighbors.

In late 1943 after the War had settled into a known road to victory, martial law was relaxed a bit, and some of the more mundane things in the life of a community began to happen again. Things like the movies at night, a relaxing of the early curfew, no blackout, and of all sorts of sports. In 1944, the blackout and curfew were lengthened to ten o'clock and the movie theaters started having movies in the evenings. We boys from Nāwiliwili used to go to the Royal Theater in Līhue on Sunday evenings. The theater was on Rice Street just below Kress Store where the Kawamoto Barber Shop is today. One of our favorite meals on Sunday evenings was to get a loaf of bread fresh from the oven at Tip Top Bakery, slice it down the middle and fill it with a stick of butter and a can of pork-and-beans. We would then wrap the bread back up in its wrapper and take this into the show for our dinner. The bread in those days was unsliced and came out of the ovens at four-thirty in the afternoon. Not the most healthy diet, but filling for a young man.

I guess I have been remiss referring to all the boys and the gang. So I will fill in their names and add a few comments about them. First off, here are the names of my classmates from Lihue Grammar School—Goro Sadaoka, Takuji Fujimura, John (Honey) Makanani, Raymond (Oopu) Ellis, and Roiji Tanaka. Roiji left Lihue School the same year I left for ʻIolani in 1937. His parents sent him to Japan for high school, and he never came back to Kauaʻi. We have heard that he served in the Japanese Navy in World War II and survived and is still living in Japan. Others were Noboru Kinoshita, brothers Lawrence, Ralph, and Joe Makanani, Henry (Daffy) Panui and the Ah You boys—John, James, and Kenneth. The younger two Ah You boys made rather dubious names for themselves later on in their lives. James was convicted of armed robbery and spent many years in the Oʻahu prison. I haven't seen James since before I went into the Army in 1945.

Kenneth was the more infamous one. He was in the Montgomery Hotel at Wailua for a parole violation. One night, he pushed the bars of his cell apart and got out. He then pushed the bars back to their original shape and took off for Nāwiliwili. Once reaching Nāwiliwili, he found the keys to Jack Sheehan, Sr.'s boat, started it up, and left for Honolulu. It wasn't until mid-morning until anyone noticed the boat missing. By that time, he was off Oʻahu and the Coast Guard was out patrolling for him. When they came alongside, he ignored them and drove the boat ashore on the beach at Waimea Bay on Oʻahu's North Shore. This event happened in the early 1960s. One day, in 1978 or 1979, Jack Sheehan, Jr. and I were at a lūʻau at the Black Pot Cafe at the pier at Hanalei. Kenneth, who was now out of jail and working as a heavy equipment operator at Princeville, came by and said hello. We talked for about half an hour, and, when he left, Jack asked me who the man was. You should have seen Jack's face when I told him, "He was the guy who stole your dad's boat."

Under martial law, the Army had taken over the gym at Kaua'i High School and a medic company was stationed there. Our group of Nāwiliwili boys got to know some of the medics and started to play basketball with them. We got along very well with them and had games almost every weekday evening. The whole division was eventually sent to the battle of Saipan, and the gym reverted to Kaua'i High School. After a couple of months, a league was formed. We got our own team together and entered the league. We called ourselves the "Surfriders." I don't remember the names of all the team members, but here are a few of them—Daffy Panui, John and Lawrence Makanani, John Ah You, Ralph Makanani, and myself. We made the letters and stitched them on our uniforms ourselves. The uniforms were blue with white lettering and numbers. We did pretty well but were never contenders. The team to beat was the team from Kekaha. This team was made up of Herbert Kauahi and Benny Holt, who were originally from Nāwiliwili, Tommy Hayselden from Kapa'a, Ambrose Smith, Pointer Robinson, and others whose names I have, of course, forgotten. When we played them, the games were always close because they didn't want to embarrass us. When I left for the Army in 1945, the league was still going strong and so were the Surfriders. We called ourselves the Surfriders because most of us surfed at Kalapaki.

In 1944, baseball was revived and I joined the Grove Farm junior league team. I tried pitching but couldn't throw strikes, so I ended up as a first baseman. This league only lasted one year and folded for lack of interest. The next year, I joined the Līhue Town team, which was in the senior league. I was a pretty raw rookie against the veterans. There were three brothers from the old Kīpū team—Memo, Buster, and Yutaka Matsumura. The team used me mostly as a warm-up catcher and sometimes I played in the outfield when the outcome of the game was never in doubt. I learned a lot about the finer points of the game from the coach, Chicken Sadamitsu. One of these points was how to bunt, and that skill served me in good stead later on when I played for Menlo Junior College after I got out of the Army. Chicken encouraged me to bat left handed, and, in one game, I got two hits in two times at bat swinging left-handed. The most fun was warming up pitchers. Our best pitcher was Lefty Hirota. He was easy to catch because all of the balls he threw came right where your mitt was. We also had a couple of minor league players from the Army on the team. They were awfully fast, but you had to be on your toes because sometimes they were also very wild.

There was another sport I took up briefly during these years. On

Wednesdays, I would go out with Wayne Ellis and caddy for him. This was my first introduction to golf. One particular Wednesday, they didn't have a fourth, so they made me play. I didn't play again until 1959.

When World War II broke out, all bird hunting came to an end, and no one was allowed to have a gun unless you had a permit. My grandfather was one of those who had all the permits he needed. On Kīpū Ranch, we grew corn and sweet potatoes, which the pheasants loved better than a kid loves candy. So, without anyone hunting them and with an abundance of their favorite food, they multiplied rapidly. One day, Mamoru Matsumura and I walked up to the fence of a two-and-a-half-acre field of sweet potatoes and just stood there and watched the pheasants fly out of the field. We counted forty-two birds leave the field by flying away. We figured that many more scurried out of the field between the rows, and even more just hunkered down and waited for us to leave. This just set the stage for what came next.

From the beginning of wartime hostilities, Kīpū supplied the submarine base at Pearl Harbor with corn and sweet potatoes. One day in October of 1944, my grandfather informed me that he wanted me to take a couple Navy men hunting. When the Navy men arrived with their shotguns, I found out the men were Admiral Furlong, the commandant of Pearl Harbor, and his adjutant. We had no hunting dogs, so we had to flush the birds by walking through the pastures. We started next to the nearest sweet potato field, and, before long, we had eighteen cock pheasants in the bag. The Admiral said that this was enough, and we quit. I was happy because I was the bag boy and had to carry the birds as they shot them. We, then, went to Kalapaki to my grandfather's home and had a couple of cocktails before they left to go back to Honolulu. Thank god they took all the pheasants home with them, so I didn't have to clean them.

However, the story doesn't stop here because, in about a month, an invitation came from the Admiral for my grandfather, his wife Pat, and me to be his guests at the opening game of the Service World Series of Baseball. We made reservations, flew to Honolulu, and stayed at the Alexander Young Hotel between King and Beretania Street on Bishop Street. On the day of the game, a Navy car with driver appeared for us and drove us out to Pearl Harbor to the baseball field now known as Furlong Field. I can't remember all the players' names, but a few stand out—Joe DiMaggio, Bob Feller, Johnny Mize, Schoolboy Rowe, Johnny Bernadino, and Peewee Reese, among many others. One name that is not so well known is that of Walt Judnich, who played with the Seventh Air Force and once hit four home runs in one game at the old Honolulu Stadium. After the War, Walt played for the St. Louis Browns for a couple of years. Later, Johnny Mize,

Schoolboy Rowe, and Mike McCormick came to Kaua'i and teamed up with a group of Army men who were stationed on Kaua'i. They played a game up at Kukuiolono Park against an all-star group of Kaua'i players. I don't know who won the game, but, that evening, George Votmann, the manager of the Kauai Soda Company, gave a party for some of the locals and the three major league players. Mize and Schoolboy put on a skit that had us all in stitches.

In September or October of 1944, my grandfather and I flew to Moloka'i to see if we could buy some young steers from Molokai Ranch and some bulls from Paul Fagan's ranch on the east end of Moloka'i. We had purchased bulls from Mr. Fagan's ranch previously and had good results. When we got to Moloka'i, we found that they were in the throes of a serious drought and were glad to see us come. We bought two-hundred-fifty yearling steers from Molokai Ranch and made preparations to have them shipped to Kaua'i. However, we were not able to get a barge to ship them until January 1945. While unloading them at Nāwiliwili, I was helping a steer that had slipped and fallen to the ground. I twisted my back and couldn't work for a month.

In 1944, just before we left for Moloka'i, we had an offer from the Army to buy some of our unbroken colts. By then, they were five or six years old and hardly anybody wanted to tackle them because they were big, rangy animals. The Army in Honolulu, however, wanted them for rodeo animals. We had five animals that we were willing to part with, but they were not halter broken to lead. One of our oldest cowboys, Robert Keuma, said that the quickest way to get them to lead was to ride them. Guess who had the honor of riding them. The older cowboys would rope one of them, blindfold it, then saddle it and say, "Okay, Hobey, get on." I'd get on, the blindfold would come off, and away we'd go. I would ride the horse until it stopped bucking and someone would catch it. Then, I would get off and have a cigarette while they caught and saddled another horse. I would get on that one, and the whole process would be repeated until all five had been ridden. This process continued for a week. I did pretty well and only got thrown off about four times. We got them to lead and got them shipped off to Honolulu for the Army. We heard later that they did very well as bucking broncos. In my case, I considerably developed my riding skills.

One day, when I returned to Kalapaki after work, I found the harbor filled with LSTs and other ships. There were maybe five-thousand marines on the beach all looking for coconuts. One of our gardeners, Charles Hada, was climbing the trees and knocking down coconuts. It was thrilling because the marines wouldn't wait for the whole bunch to come down. Instead, they raced for the first one to fall. I joined Charles in climbing trees.

We climbed every tree on the place. There must have been twenty or more trees. I climbed one tree, which had a bend in it, about thirty feet off the ground. I not only had to climb up but I also had to climb around the trunk. When I look at that tree today, I think I must have been a little crazy. In those days, we climbed coconut trees without the benefit of climbing spikes or any other assistance. The Marines were appreciative, and you wonder how many of them had the runs the next day. We learned later that their flotilla was bound for Peleliu and an incredibly bloody battle. After the War, we learned that these Marines were the Fifth Marines, and they went from Peleliu to Iwo Jima and then on to Okinawa. I have always wondered how many survived the battles to return home alive.

In 1944, a company of Marine artillery arrived on Kauaʻi for further training. They came from Funafuti in the South Pacific. They built their camp where the third, fourth, and fifth holes are now at the Wailua Golf Course. The camp also extended south to the beginning of Hilton Hotel and where the Kauai Beach Condominiums are today. The commandant was Colonel Corson. He and my grandfather played a lot of cribbage at Kalapaki. When he heard that I wanted to go into the service, he tried to get me into the Marines. I went down to the camp one day and was given a physical, but I flunked because I was slightly colorblind. I think he was trying to get me into officer's school, which I didn't want. Military regulations prohibited the colonel from driving his own car, so he had to have a driver. It was my job to entertain the driver when the colonel came to play cribbage. Sometimes the games lasted until quite late, and I would have liked to have gone to bed for I had to work the next day. The driver was a second lieutenant by the name of Frank Fasi, who later became the mayor of Honolulu. He married a Japanese girl from Hanamāʻulu and went into the junk business in Honolulu after the War.

At about the same time, Mother was able to get back to Kauaʻi from the mainland. Since I was no longer working at Kīpū, I stayed with Mother at the Lihue Hotel until she could find a place to live. She didn't want to live at Kalapaki because she knew that Pat Rice, my grandfather's second wife, was pregnant and she didn't want to be a bother to her.

While at the hotel with Mother, I went out with Bill Moragne and Wayne Ellis looking for monkeypod trees that could be used for making wooden bowls and straight logs for paneling. At that time, these two men and Samuel Wilcox were in the process of forming Hale Kauai. Bill, Wayne, and I went all over Līhue and Kōloa looking for trees that could be acquired. Bill Moragne was the assistant manager of Grove Farm Plantation, but he never once said anything about the monkeypod trees that were growing in the Hule'ia Valley on Grove Farm land. Later on in the fifties, I asked Bill, after he had become manager of Grove Farm, why he didn't harvest the silver oak (*Gevillia robusta*) that were growing in the valley. He really didn't give me a good answer, but he said it wasn't time yet. Hurricane Iniki took care of the silver oaks. They are now all broken and dead.

CHAPTER SIX

The Army 1945–1946

In March of 1945, I asked my grandfather if I could go into the Army because all the other young men my age were already in the service. In Hawai'i, if you were employed in agriculture, you were considered essential to the war effort. You needed your employer's permission to be drafted. My grandfather begrudgingly gave his permission. He told me to go to the Selective Service Board and tell them that my employer said it was okay for me to be drafted. I notified the board in April and was told that I would be called up in the first part of May. I received my call and was told to report to the National Guard barracks at Hanapēpē for processing. After two days of one word, we were notified that we would grandfather until the summer of 1947.

The next afternoon, we were trucked over to Nāwiliwili and boarded the Wai'ale'ale for Honolulu. As we boarded the ship, I was given an envelope containing all our records and the instructions to give them to the sergeant who was to meet us at the dock. We left Nāwiliwili, and, the next morning, we were in Honolulu. When we got to Honolulu, a sergeant took control of the group, and I handed the envelope over to him. We were bused to Schofield Barracks and quartered in a large barracks building. Then, it was lining up and learning close-order drilling until lunchtime. Lunch in the Army was the usual—stand in line and move forward as the people in front of you are being served. Finally, when you get there, the food would be slopped onto your tray as fast as the servers could do it without throwing the stuff on the floor. Then, it was to a table, sit down, eat as fast as you could, and get out of the mess hall.

The afternoon was a blur of orders that sometimes seemed to conflict, but the Army knew what they were doing even if we didn't. After an afternoon of marching, we had a little time to ourselves, then dinner, and more time for relaxing. There was no place to go, as we were restricted to the barracks. Then, it was to bed at taps.

The second day, the first order of business was to get our shots. We all stood in line, and, when we neared the medics, we were each told to put our right hand on our hip and receive the tetanus and typhoid shots. After that came another order, "Take one step forward and put your left hand on your hip for a smallpox vaccination." The next thing I remembered was lying on a cot with an orderly holding an alcohol-soaked gauze to my chin. The orderly told me that I had passed out and made a perfect three-point landing on the floor with my two feet and chin.

Soon a doctor came along, looked at my chin, and said to me, "Do you think you can stand it? I have to sew up your chin?"

I had been stitched up before, so I said, "Go ahead."

The doctor got his kit together and immediately started sewing me up without the benefit of Novocain. I could feel every bump on the thread as he pulled it through my skin. Either his needles were dull or my skin was tough because, in no time, he was sweating profusely. It took four stitches in my chin to close up the gash. Then he left and I never saw him again. I found out later that I was not the only soldier who had passed out but the only one who had to be sewn up. One of the other fellows who fainted was a professional wrestler and a great big man. That afternoon, I was taken to the quartermasters for my uniforms. All my buddies had gone in the morning after the shots while I was being sewn up. There was a great deal of good-natured banter about my passing out, but there was also consolation for not getting any Novocain. A week later, when it was time for our next typhoid shot, the orderlies sat me down when they gave me my shot. This treatment followed me all the way to California where I got the third typhoid shot. The next few days were spent learning to march in step, in addition to all the other close-order maneuvers.

One weekend, there was a picnic for all the recruits and their families, but this meant only O'ahu men. I was lucky because Hina, who used to work for my grandfather at Kīpū Kai, had a son who had also been drafted at the same time I was. He invited me to come with him and see the rest of the family. It was a great day talking about the old days at Kīpū Kai and all the fun we had fishing and chasing goats and getting into mischief when we were much younger. It was also good to get some local cooking and food like musubi with ume inside. I also found out why Hina had quit Kīpū and come to Honolulu. But that's between Hina and myself, so let sleeping dogs lie.

By the end of the next week, we knew that we were to be shipped to the mainland some time the next week. On Sunday, I got a pass to go into town. I knew that Mother was in Honolulu, but I didn't know where. So, I went to the Halekulani Hotel to see if my Aunt Juliet might know where she was. When I got there, Aunt Juliet said that Mother was out at the Von

Holt's at Lā'ie, and that she was going out to the party there in a few minutes and that I could go along with her. Aunt Juliet also said that I could find a ride back to Schofield when we got to Lā'ie. We had a nice ride out to Lā'ie, and I had a chance to talk to Aunt Juliet before getting into the big crowd. When I got to the party, Mother was thrilled to see me and introduced me to a classmate of my father's from the Naval Academy. He had been a Rear Admiral. When it was time for me to think about returning to Schofield, Admiral Zachary offered to take me back. Mother thought that this would be fun and readily agreed. So, off we went, a buck private in the Admiral's car. He told his driver who I was, and that made it okay, I guess. All the way back to Schofield, he told me about the four years he and my father spent at Annapolis together and the fun time they had. When we got to Schofield, he insisted that he drop me off right in front of my barracks. I wanted to be dropped off some distance away so that no one would see me drive up in an official car with a flag with one star flying from the front bumper. But he would hear none of it. And who was I to argue with an admiral? When I got out of the car, thanked him for the ride, and saluted him, he returned the salute. He said he hoped that we would meet again after the War.

When I walked into the orderly room to report in, the sergeant wanted to know what the hell I was doing in an admiral's car. When I told him the truth—that he had gone to the Naval Academy with my father, no one wanted to believe me. That really made my day because, after that, the entire cadre treated me a little differently.

On Wednesday evening, we were told that we would be shipping out the next day and to have everything ready to board the buses after breakfast. The buses came at ten in the morning, and off we went to Honolulu Harbor to board a Navy troop carrier for San Francisco. The trip took about six days, and the weather was nice and calm. We were given jobs to do on board. I was with five Portuguese boys from O'ahu. Our job was to keep the after part of the main deck clean. Around three times a day, loudspeakers would sound out the orders, "Sweepers man your brooms. Clean sweep down fore and aft." After the morning sweep down, there wasn't much to sweep up. So we had a lot of time on our hands. One of the fellows had a guitar, and he played mostly cowboy songs. He couldn't speak English very well and used a thick "Portagee" pidgin in his everyday conversation. But, when singing cowboy, songs there wasn't a trace of an accent.

One day, a life raft was spotted. Our ship came to a stop, and a lifeboat was lowered and sent out to picked up the raft. It was empty, and there was no sign that of it ever having been used. Some of the sailors on deck were really ticked off. They said that this was a common trick the Japanese submariners used to lure a ship into stopping so it was easier to torpedo. We were lucky that there was no submarine around. While we were stopped, about a dozen of the largest mahimahi I had ever seen swam up to the ship, checked us out, and swam away. I wished that I had had a hook and line to try and catch one.

We arrived in San Francisco early one morning, and, as soon as our ship was tied up to a dock, we were marched off and onto a ferry to Angel Island. Angel Island was a quarantine station for all incoming troops from the Pacific. There were a few Japanese prisoners of war on the island. Every time they saw the Japanese/Hawaiian troops go by their windows, they would scream obscenities to them. I think they were telling them that they were traitors to the Japanese race. Our guys who knew a little Japanese would give it right back to them in spades. One thing good about Angel Island was that there was no KP duty for American troops because the mess hall was staffed with Italian prisoners of war. The Italians thought that they could bankrupt the U.S.A. by over feeding us. We never had such good food, and plenty of it. They were a happy bunch and seemed glad to be in America.

While on Angel Island, there wasn't much for us to do except take competency tests. When the time came for us to be shipped out, all the Portuguese boys were sent to Camp McQuaid, which was called "Ignorance Hill." Soon, the rest of us boarded a train to Marysville, California, and Camp Beale for further processing. This was another gravy train assignment, but again more tests. This time, though, it was more math testing. I must have done pretty well on all my tests because two of the officers in charge of our group put the move on me to volunteer for Officer Training. I politely refused to go out for OCS. After that, I wasn't hassled anymore.

While we were at Camp Beale, we were sent out into a large field for exercise. There was no formal exercising, so we were on our own. Some of the boys from Hawai'i had never seen a rabbit before, and someone scared one up. The boys from Hawai'i went wild and started to chase the poor rabbit. There were enough men there that they could run in relays until the rabbit started to tire. As soon as the rabbit started to slow down, several black troops who were watching the goings on moved in and caught the rabbit. The first thing they did was to cut the four feet off the rabbit and let the Hawaiians do what they wanted with the rest of it. All the mainland men laughed at the Hawaiians for being so stupid to let the blacks get the feet for good luck charms.

We were at Camp Beale for about two weeks when our orders came to move out. A mixture of Hawai'i men and some mainland types were ordered to Camp Hood in Texas. I was one of them. We left Camp Beale in the late afternoon and were in Salt Lake City around midnight. That was the only place where I ever got hot coffee and a roll, from the American Red Cross, in all of my travels in the Army. We were on a combined military and commercial train. There were young mothers with little children, plus some older people. When it was mealtime, we soldiers always got to eat first. It was kind of hard for me to look them in the eye because I had been brought up to wait until the women and children had been fed first.

From Salt Lake City, we traveled to Grand Junction where some of the civilians changed trains. We continued along the Denver-Rio Grande route through the Royal Gorge. In the middle of the gorge, the train stopped. We were able to get out and look up to the top of the gorge and see the bridge that spans the gorge. I promised myself that, someday, I would cross that bridge and look down on the river. That promise was fulfilled in 1969 when Nancy and I did it. Our route now took us through Arkansas, Oklahoma, and into Texas. The first stop in Texas was at Fort Worth where we changed trains and left for Killeen. That's where south Camp Hood and the Infantry Replacement Training Center was located. We were, then, bussed to our barracks and started being processed.

The first order of business was to get organized into squads. Then came the collection of bedding and uniforms and fatigues, along with our rifles and gas masks. By then, it was time for lunch. After lunch, drills started in earnest and free time was a thing of the past. Our sergeant was a tough, old guy but fun to be around if you didn't screw up. Our lieutenant couldn't get through inspecting our squad before the captain inspected the other three squads. From then on, we would double-time one mile every day for four months.

One day, early into our training, our sergeant was showing us a little judo. I had learned how to fall, so, after the second throw, the sergeant let me alone and picked on a small Japanese fellow by the name of Shimabukuru. I said to one of my new friends, "Watch this." When the sergeant went to throw Shima, Sarge didn't know what hit him. He had found himself on the ground, and he didn't know what to do. Luckily, the captain was watching, so the sergeant couldn't do much in retaliation. The judo lessons stopped right then and there, and we went on to other forms of exercise.

One afternoon, we were out in the field on some project. The temperature must have been over one-hundred degrees when about five of us found the shade of a pecan tree. We got caught and were told that, after supper, Sarge had a job for us. After supper, we assembled with Sarge for our punishment. He took us to the back steps of our barracks and told us to dig out the mud from under the steps and then fill the hole with rocks. I had done this kind of work on the ranch so we started right in. We dug out the mud and even made a ditch for the water to flow into a drainage ditch. Then we filled the hole and the ditch with rocks and told Sarge that we were done. He couldn't believe that we had done the job so fast. At the next inspection of the barracks, the captain commented on the good job. We thanked our lucky stars that Sarge never told him why and who had done it. Apparently there were other barracks with the same problem.

Basic training continued, and we soon got into a routine. The days came and went with not too much change. One day, when we were out in the field doing some kind of outdoor training, we were given a break. We all sat around on the ground. All of a sudden, a Mexican fellow said to a large farm boy from Minnesota, "Don't move; stay very still." Then, we saw what was happening. It was early June, and there was a rattlesnake crawling up the farm boy's arm. The snake crawled up to his shoulders and started down the other side. As soon as the snake's head touched the ground, the Mexican smashed the snake's head with his rifle butt. That was a little excitement for our morning break. After that episode, we were always careful to look around before we sat on the grass.

We could get 3.2 beer at the PX and regular beer in the town of Killeen. If anyone wanted hard liquor, one had to go to Belton in the next county. Most of the whiskey you got in Belton was pure rotgut, so we stuck to beer. Most of the beers available in Killeen were brands made in Texas, and they left a lot to be desired. To the west of camp (about twenty miles distant) was the small town of Lampasas where, every Saturday night, there was a dance for the soldiers. Lampasas was in the middle of Angora goat country, and, after a rain, the whole town smelled of goats. The girls in town weren't the best looking or very good dancers, and we were chaperoned very closely. I went to Lampasas only once in the four months that I was at Camp Hood.

On my first tour of KP, the mess sergeant offered us a variety of jobs. I took the job doing pots and pans that were left by the bakers who had worked in the evening. Nobody else wanted to help me, but, finally, one timid soul said he would. We started right in, and, before the serving crew had finished sweeping and mopping the mess hall, we were done with the pots and pans. I called the mess sergeant over, and he inspected our work and complemented us. I asked him what he wanted the two of us to do next, and he told us to go to the back of the mess hall and smash all the cans to be recycled. This took us about half an hour, and we were back looking for more work. The sergeant asked me if I knew how to use a knife because all the bread for lunch and dinner had to be sliced. I told him that I had worked with a knife before and that I would do the job. Here I lost my assistant and never found out what he did for the rest of the day. The sergeant gave me the knife, showed me where the bread was, and told me he wanted slices one-half inch thick. I started to slice the bread, but the knife was dull. So, I asked the sergeant for steel so that I could sharpen the knife. He was quite impressed with how I sharpened the knife and cut the bread. After I got through, I had very little to do for the rest of the afternoon.

A couple of times after that, when the company was having lunch out in the field, the mess sergeant would find me and take me to the area where lunch was to be served. Then, he would ask me to supervise the digging of a trench for the fires to heat the water to wash our mess kits. When our company was going on a two week's bivouac, the mess sergeant asked me if I wanted to sleep in the barracks and help him with getting the meals out into the field and then serve them as well. I jumped at the chance and was the envy of all my friends. The rest of basic training was a lot of the same thing over and over. One part of it that I enjoyed the most was working with explosives. I volunteered one morning when we were supposed to go through an invasion exercise and proceed through a minefield. We set one-quarter-pound charges of nitro starch into preset holes that were filled with water from the rain the night before. When our company's turn came, we waited until our lieutenant came through and made sure he got a blast that covered him with water. After the exercise was over and we all joined up, our squad thanked us for the bath we gave the lieutenant.

VE day came while we were still in training, and there was a lot of whooping and hollering. Most of the guys thought that the War was over, but they didn't consider the Japanese. Those of us from Hawai'i knew better, and we knew that they were still a nation not to be taken lightly. When the A-Bomb was dropped on Hiroshima and later Nagasaki, we all felt better. When the Japanese surrendered and sued for peace we all breathed a sigh of relief. By now, we had only a couple of weeks before we would be assigned to either combat units or something else. The Army never told you what they were going to do with you. They would tell you where you would be going in the States. But overseas was still secret, and you didn't know until you were on a ship.

One form of relaxation was card playing, and for me this was mostly poker. One Sunday, just before the Japanese surrender, a friend of mine and I got into a no-limit poker game. Neither of us had very much money, but we stayed in the game for about an hour when my friend went broke. I had been doing pretty well, so he said he would stay with me until I wanted to quit. After about an hour of give and take, the houseman dealt a game of five-card draw, jacks or better to open. I was dealt a pair of aces so I stayed in the game and drew two cards. I got two more aces giving me all four. The betting was hot and heavy, and I stayed in the betting until all my money was on the table. Three other fellows kept on betting on the side, and. when everyone called, I found that there was a straight, a flush, and a full house against me. I raked in about five hundred dollars as my share of the pot. After about three rounds at the table with the houseman dealing again, it was the same five-card game again. This time, I got three aces and drew two cards and got another ace. The same thing happened as before, but the betting stopped before all my money was in the pot. Again, there were three good hands against me but I won. By now, I had won a little over one-thousand dollars. After a couple of rounds, my friend told me that he was going to the bathroom. I took the hint. When we got outside, he told me that the houseman was setting me up, and, after he had cleaned the other guys out, he would work on me. I never went back into the game and my friend and I had all the money we needed for beer for the rest of our time in camp. The houseman cleaned out the rest of the players and went over the hill that night. He was finally found in California and brought back to Texas with a little Mexican with a carbine who followed him wherever he went for the rest of our stay in Texas.

When we were on the firing range, we learned that several of us had had experience shooting rifles. We had heard that you didn't want to qualify as an expert though, as you would be asked to be a sniper. The word was that the life of a sniper was a short one, so we made sure that we never made expert. One day, we were issued the new carbines to familiarize ourselves in their use. Then, we were given nine bullets and were to engage in rapid fire. When the order to commence firing was given, I loaded and started firing pretty fast. Our lieutenant kept tapping me on the helmet and said, "Soldier, you are firing too fast." When the scores came up, I got nine bulls eyes and the lieutenant was long gone. He never said another word.

We drank a lot of beer whenever we had time off from training. One day, the PX had a shipment of Budweiser on hand. Three of us started at two o'clock one Sunday afternoon and, by eight at night, when the PX closed, there were four cases of empty bottles under our table. Needless to say, the next day we perspired profusely. But it was fun while it lasted. You must remember that this was all 3.2 beer instead of the normal 5.6 beer, so the alcohol content was way less.

About halfway through Basic Training, it was announced that there was going to be a swimming meet. I signed up to swim for our Regiment. There were several Hawai'i boys who had been swimmers in high school in the islands, so we had a pretty good team. I swam in the fifty-yard and hundred-yard freestyle races. I won the fifty-yard freestyle race, but didn't do too well in the hundred-yard race. I was out of condition and ran out of gas. I got a nice little medal for my win though. Our Regiment won the meet handily.

When Basic was over, I was held back in camp for about a week along with several others who had volunteered for Airborne training. We soon found out that we were no longer needed for the jump troops. To keep us busy, we were put on guard duty—two hours on and four off. One Sunday afternoon, I had the four o'clock shift. Since it was still summer and nice and warm, I was dressed in khakis. About an hour into my shift, the wind changed to the north and it got cold. I had no jacket to keep me warm, so I had to keep walking. After my two hours were up, no one came to relieve me. My relief finally showed up at nine o'clock, and guard duty was called off for the night. Everything on base was closed for the night, so I didn't get any dinner that night.

After a week of loafing and pulling guard duty, we got our orders to proceed to Fort Ord in California. We had ten days furlough before reporting to Fort Ord, so I took off for Hay Creek Ranch in Oregon to see my dad for a few days. The trip from Texas to California was a grueling one. We were three days on the train with no place to lie down to sleep. In other words, we had to sit up all the way. After a week with my dad, I got back on the train in Portland, Oregon, for Monterey, California, and Fort Ord. At Fort Ord, it was back to training during the day and some challenges like map readings and such in the evenings, but nothing very strenuous. Every afternoon, we had to assemble for the Retreat Parade. This got to be fun trying to show off our company's marching skills against the other companies.

One day, we were taken to a swimming pool and, one by one, we had to jump off the one-meter board and swim to the other end of the pool. Some of the fellows had a hard time making the distance. There was a lifeguard showing off as he was jumping on the three-meter board. But, every once in a while, when someone had a hard time swimming across the pool, he would stop. He never once jumped in, and you knew that he didn't want to. When my turn came, I got on the board slowly, went to the end, jumped off the board and sank to the bottom. When I saw the splash in the pool next to me, I kicked off and swam under water the whole length of the pool. The lifeguard was not pleased, but there was nothing he could do.

After about three weeks, orders came down for us to proceed to Fort Lawton in Seattle, Washington. We knew we were going overseas, but we didn't know where. In Seattle, we were issued winter uniforms, so we knew that we were being shipped someplace where it would be cold. The mess hall at Fort Lawton was manned by German prisoners of war. When they served us our meal, you got the impression that they (like the Italians on Angel Island) thought that they could bankrupt the U.S.A. by over feeding us. They also were a happy lot and very pleasant to talk to. Finally, we got our orders that we were boarding a ship the next day. But still no destination.

The next day, we were taken by truck to the docks and loaded on a rather small coastal steamer. We had one stateroom for ten of us. We were split into two shifts—one from five in the morning to noon and one from noon to about seven at night. The name of the ship was the *Cherikof*. I also learned that the ship's original name was the *Lurline*, one of the many Matson Line *Lurlines*. Everyone was given a task while we were on board. I got latrine duty. As we were pulling away from the docks, a soldier whom I had met on the train on the ride north asked me what my job was on board. When I told him, he asked me if I would like to work in the galley, since one of the soldiers chosen for that job had gotten seasick. I said that I would love the chance of getting away from the toilets. The deal was made, and I became a second cook.

The first afternoon, I had to make mashed potatoes for nine-hundred men. After I was about done, an officer came in and tasted the potatoes and told me to put more milk and butter in them. He stayed around until I had the potatoes the way he wanted them and then left me alone for the rest of the trip. The first cooks were all Ilocano Filipinos, so I had a good rapport with them because I knew a few Filipino phrases. I got to eat white rice every night, and I was in heaven. My experience at cutting meat on the ranch served me in good stead. When we were going to roast beef, we would get cases of frozen beef, which would be steamed until done and then browned in the ovens. I was able to pick out the loins for us. We would slowly thaw them, and, then, I would slice them into steaks that we would pan fry. We had to be careful not to get caught by an officer, though. We learned how to make scrambled eggs by the five-gallon batch and bacon by the bushel. One evening, I was heating up about ten gallons of sauerkraut, and, when I went to check on whether it was hot enough, I almost scalded my arm. It was a little red but no damage done. We didn't have to peel potatoes, as there was a special detail for that purpose. Up until then, this was the most pleasant part of my army experience. We had two steam kettles, which could hold at least twenty gallons of vegetables or three cases of frozen meat. There were also four small steam ovens where we cooked the potatoes for mashing.

Our trip lasted ten days and we landed at Attu, which is at the western end of the Aleutian chain of islands. Then we were flown over to Shemya, an island about thirty-eight miles away. Welcome to the Aleutian Islands!

When we finally got to Shemya, we found it to be four miles long and two miles wide. It was about two hundred feet in elevation on the northern side and sloping down to sea level on the southern side. There were about seven thousand men on the island and seven women. Our shipload of men were scattered around the island in separate units. I was assigned to the Port Company, or stevedores to the uninitiated. Since it was winter no boats were expected until late spring so there was not much for us to do. I was able wrangle a temporary transfer to the PX warehouse crew. There were five of us there and we lived in a Quonset hut with all the amenities. We scrounged food from the Mess Hall so we had eggs, with bread for toast and even some unsliced bacon. We never had to get up early because we had all the makings for breakfast. Our job was to keep the PX stocked with whatever they needed. This meant going to the Quartermasters for things like cases of candy, cigarettes, and toiletries and other food like crackers. The PX sold all the beer to the different units and it was our job to deliver the beer from the Quartermasters to the cashier of the PX. Needless to say, we got our share off the top. We had a six-by truck at our disposal, and I learned how to drive the vehicle, double clutching. There was also a two-lane bowling alley as part of the PX complex, and we would get there just at closing time. After everybody was gone for the night, we would bowl until about three in the morning at least three times a week. There were no automatic pinsetters in those days, so we would take turns setting pins while the others bowled.

This gravy train lasted for about one and a half months. I was then called back to the port company and put to work taking inventory of all the steel in the engineer company's yard. By now, it was February and there was about three feet of snow on the ground, and it was cold. This job lasted for one week, and, after the inventory was done, there wasn't much to do. I wanted to get back to the PX, but our CO didn't like the exchange officer. So he asked me if I would like to try the post office. I figured that I wouldn't have to go out in the snow and cold, so I agreed to go. After three weeks, I was asked if I wanted to stay, and I said yes. As soon as my transfer was official, I was promoted to corporal, then, in another six weeks, I was promoted to sergeant, and, then, in another six weeks to staff sergeant. I started by sorting incoming and outgoing mail and delivering mail to the various company mail clerks when there was mail to hand out. I found out after Nancy and I were married that, almost every day, there was mail to be distributed. I probably handed the quartermasters company's mail to Art Shaw, who later married Dot Gillin of Poʻipū, one of Nancy's childhood friends. From that rather menial job, I moved to the parcel post window for about two and a half months and then to the first class window. Here I sold stamps and handled other first class mailings. My final move was the money order window. The largest single money order at the time was one-hundred dollars. If a person came in with more than one-hundred dollars, we had to write in increments of one-hundred dollars. One payday I wrote thirty-five-thousand dollars worth of money orders. I started at eight in the morning and didn't finish until after six in the evening.

The two outside chores we had were to deliver the outgoing and pick up incoming mail at the airport and to pick up money for the finance office when it arrived at the airport and deliver it to the finance office. This required us to wear side arms for the job. None of us had ever had any training in pistols, so we never loaded the guns. During the winter, there were mornings that we couldn't start our truck because the engine compartment would be full of snow. I should mention that when the winds were only sixty miles per hour nobody blinked an eye. When it got to seventy and over, sometimes the road would be drifted so badly that no one could move until the snowplows did their work.

On the morning of April 1, 1946, I was sitting in my money order cage when our Postal Officer called me into his office and closed the door and made me sit down. Then he told me that there had been a terrible tsunami in Hawai'i and that many people had been killed. I said, "Don't pull that April Fool stuff on me." He replied, "Sit here and listen to the report on the radio." When the radio started to tell about the wave, I couldn't believe such a thing could have happened. When they started telling about the loss of life in Hilo and Kaua'i, he pulled out a bottle of whiskey and shot glasses for himself and me. Then he poured the whiskey into the glasses and told me to drink the whiskey. Now this was a no-no in the service, but he did it anyway. After that date, news was scattered and there wasn't much meat in it. It was three weeks before I learned from my grandfather what had happened.

I found out that the house at Kalapaki was no more. I also found out that Charles Hada died trying to get Pat out of the house and had the car in the Porte Cochere with the engine running so she and Robin could get away. Before Hada could get to high ground himself, he was caught by the second wave and that's what killed him. He left a wife and two very young children. In the meanwhile, Pat was having trouble getting Robin out of his crib because there was something holding the cover of the crib down. By the time she got the baby loose, she was caught by the second wave and almost swept out to sea. The sash of her bathrobe was snagged by a branch and ultimately kept her tethered and safe. In the lull between the second and third wave, her neighbor John Ah You saw her, raced into the stream, and got her and the baby to high ground before the third wave came ashore. My grandfather requested that the Red Cross get me home immediately to assist him in the clean up, but they wouldn't do a thing. So I stayed in the Army until I was finally discharged. I am glad for that because I probably never would have gotten together with Nancy.

Fog was another bit of weather that we had to contend with. We would play softball in the evenings starting at eight, and, when the fog was so thick that the catcher couldn't see the second baseman, the game would be called. We played on a corner of the runway. There were a couple of times when no incoming planes could land because they couldn't find the island. One night in early June of 1946, a B24 bomber from Nome, Alaska, was trying to land but couldn't see the field lights at all. They finally ran out of gas and the crew bailed out. Most of them landed in the ocean, and only one person landed close enough to shore to make it to land before freezing to death. The pilot was found in late September under the pier in an almost perfect state of preservation. The plane crashed into a warehouse full of blankets and Coca-Cola. Boy, was that a mess.

After it warmed up a little in the summer, we would go fishing on the north side of the island below the post office. We would catch cod, Atka mackerel, Japanese perch, and others that I never got to know. They were all white-fleshed fish and were delicious.

One other sport we played was basketball. The finance office and the post office combined to form a team. We did pretty well in our division, winning about as many games as we lost. One of the teams that we always had a lot of fun with was the Quartermasters. They were an all black team, and it was a laugh a minute every time we played them. They were constantly teasing and laughing all through the game, and nobody got upset or angry. There were other teams that had no sense of humor.

Finally, on the second of October, I, along with a couple of the post office crew and about three hundred others, boarded a ship for Seattle for discharge. We stopped at Adak, Alaska, to pick up two-hundred more troops all going home. After leaving Adak, we hit a real North Pacific storm. The waves must have been thirty- to forty-feet high, and we couldn't sleep in our bunks for three nights. One man was actually washed out of his bunk by a wave and broke his shoulder when he hit the deck. Three other soldiers were also very lucky to have survived what happened to them. They went to the fantail to look at the waves, when a large wave swept over them and covered them with water. Lucky for them, they were able to hang on to the rail and didn't get swept into the sea. After the storm subsided, the rest of the trip was uneventful and we landed safely in Seattle. We were transferred to Fort Lawton to wait for transportation to Camp Beal in California for discharge. Fort Lawton was the same as when we were there last. I have yet to see any sun or the "bluest skies you've ever seen" that Seattle is famous for. The German POWs were just as pleasant and generous with their servings as when we were last here. We finally got word that the next day would be the one when we would head back to California.

After an uneventful train ride, we offloaded at Marysville and were bused to Camp Beale. I checked into my assigned barracks, found an unoccupied upper bunk, threw my duffel bag onto it, and headed to the PX for a beer. When I returned to my digs, I was met with, "Hi Hobey!" from my lower bunkmate. He was Yukio Kinoshita from Nāwiliwili on Kaua'i who had been one of the regulars in our group before any of us went into the service. We spent some time talking about where we had been in the service and then decided to get something to eat. While having dinner, we continued our reminiscences and finally went back to the barracks and bed. The next day, Yukio was separated and left for Minnesota where he had a girl friend. After that, I only saw him on Kaua'i two times. He had a wife and family in Minnesota and just didn't want to come back to Kaua'i anymore. I have since learned that he died in 2003 while still living in Minnesota.

Soon, I got my own discharge, after signing my life away, because I wanted to leave the Army in California and not be sent back to Hawai'i where I had been inducted. The Army was responsible for returning you to where you were inducted but would not give me cash instead. As soon as I could, I left for Hay Creek Ranch in Oregon to see my dad. When I got to the ranch, I found that he had to go to Portland for about a week to see his accountant. I was left alone. But J. Hudson White, who had been the ranch foreman when I was there in the late thirties and early forties, had a contract with the old man to haul his wheat into the town of Madras to the railhead. I signed on as a swamper and made a few bucks helping him load and unload his truck. After a week in the city, my dad returned to Hay Creek, and, in a day or two, we left for San Francisco where I was to meet Mother.

CHAPTER SEVEN

Menlo Junior College & Return to Kaua'i 1946–1948

After arriving in San Francisco, I went to the Fairmont Hotel and checked into Mother's suite. She had the car of my brother Charles, and our first order of business was to get me outfitted with new civilian clothes. In the next few days, we traveled down the peninsula to Palo Alto and Menlo Park to look for clothes for me. After she got what she thought were satisfactory clothes for me, we could relax and have fun. We visited the Allied Arts Guild where she had worked during the War. She had a good time revisiting old friends whom she hadn't seen in about three years.

My brother Charles was a freshman at Stanford University, and my brother Bruce was at Menlo Junior College. Both were getting A's in school. Charlie had gone to Menlo High School, which was affiliated to the College. I applied to Menlo Junior College for the spring semester and was accepted on probation without a high school diploma on the strength of my two brothers' records at the school. Charles had gone through high school at Menlo with a straight A average. In the two semesters that I attended Menlo, I only earned a B average.

Before entering school on February 1, 1947, there was Christmas and New Year's to tend to. Mother had made friends with a Russian woman by the name of Irina Roublon, who was a milliner. She made some fabulous women's hats, not only for Mother but also for a lot of high society people. She also made a hat for Nancy after we had become engaged. She asked Nancy what she liked, and Nancy said she liked music. Irina then made a hat with musical notes on it.

One night, Irina, Mother, and I had dinner in the Tonga Room of the Fairmont Hotel. The Tonga Room was on one of the lowest floors of the hotel, and there was a swimming pool in the center of the dining room. There was a raft floating in the pool with a trio playing Hawaiian music while the raft was pulled from one end to the end of the pool to the other. The Lead singer of the band was Solomon Bright, of Hawaiian Cowboy fame, and his Surf Riders. I can't remember what the conversation was all about, but suddenly Irina leaned across the table and said to me, "What you need is an affair with a thirty-five year old woman." All this in front of my mother. I didn't know what to say or do, so I just played dumb and let the whole thing pass. Later, when Mother and I got back to our rooms, she said to me, "Be careful. Her husband is a Cossack and is very jealous."

Christmas was quiet with the three boys and Mother but New Year's Eve was another matter. Charlie knew some girls at Stanford, and we were invited to several parties in the city and in Berkeley. This turned out to be a lot of fun. Every party was a black tie affair. Tuxedo every night! No wonder I hate the damned thing today.

After the holidays, when everyone was back in school, Mother and I drove down to Carmel for the rest of January. Mother was doing some serious writing, and I just went along for the ride. This was right in the middle of Bing Crosby's Clambake at Pebble Beach. This was also the time Tommy Bolt had a fight with one of the other golfers at the Pine Inn in Carmel. The papers were full of this news for a week. One day, Mother and I went over the hill to Monterey to look for the materials to make a throw net. In one of the fishing stores, I got all I needed. I also found out that one of the clerks had originally come from Hanamā'ulu on Kaua'i. I started on the throw net immediately but didn't finish it until I was back on Kaua'i and married.

Some time during our second week at Carmel, a woman friend of Mother's (who was a physical therapist) asked me if I would like to help her with a patient with whom she was working. I jumped at the chance to do something different. The young man she was working with had hit his head on a rock after diving off a pier. He was paralyzed from the waist down. What the nurse wanted me to do was to help him get to his feet so that he could start trying to take a few steps. I helped her three days a week for the next two weeks and saw a good amount of progress. I found out later that he was able to walk without any support at all. This gave me a feeling of satisfaction knowing that I had had a small hand in his recovery.

Soon it was time to go back to start school and book learning. My high school career had been cut short by the bombing of Pearl Harbor, so I was a little apprehensive about starting formal schooling again. In my first semester, I took accounting, English, typing, and business math. My business math teacher was a man by the name of Charles Winterbottom. He was an old football coach who had either played with or worked with the likes of Pop Warner and other famous old time coaches. I had only one afternoon class three days a week, and I would help him with the afternoon P.E. classes for the high school boys until baseball practice started later in the afternoon.

A couple fellows on the baseball team and I lived in barracks left over from World War II. All of us in the barracks were veterans and over twenty-one years old, so we could go into a bar and have a drink. There was a nice restaurant across the street from the school where we would go for dinner quite regularly. It was called the Stone Cellar and the steaks were superb. The guys were a lot of fun, but we got into trouble a couple of times. One time, we swiped a marble statue from the high school gardens and brought it back to our barracks. I was never implicated, but Dick Brooke and Ole Olson were nailed right away. They had gone to Menlo as high school students and had gotten into all kinds of mischief, so they were the first ones accused. They were told to return the statue that night and nothing more would be said about it. The statue sure was heavier when we had to take it back where it belonged.

Our baseball team at Menlo started out with over twenty players, but it was finally whittled down to ten players because the rest of team quit. I don't remember the name of all the players, but ten of us persevered throughout the season. We won only two games out of twelve. I played centerfield most of the time and spent a lot of time out there with my back to the infield running after balls. One day while we were playing Marin County Junior College, a ball was hit between the right fielder and me. I got to the ball first, but I just stood and watched it while everyone was yelling at me to pick up the ball and throw it back to the infield. The ball had come to rest against a six-foot long rattlesnake, and he was quite unhappy. The right fielder wouldn't even come close at all. Finally, word got back to the coach. So, soon, a couple of men with sticks came out and did away with the snake. Another time in Vallejo, California, they had a short right-field fence, and it was only a double if you hit the ball over that fence. I hit a ball over the fence in right field, and, when I rounded first base on my way to second, a beer bottle sailed past my ear. The beer bottle had come from the stands behind first base.

The same team invited us to a dance after the game. We politely said that we had to get back to Menlo. Dick Brooke, Ole Olson, and I stopped in San Francisco on our way back to school and went to a Chinese restaurant on Grant Avenue. While eating dinner, a guy came up to our table and tried to proposition us, but we said no! He was quite insistent, so we finally said that we knew where there were several young boys who might be interested. He jumped at the idea, so we took him back to Menlo and turned him loose in the high school dorm. Then we got the hell out of there. We returned to the barracks and jumped into bed as fast as possible. Sure enough we soon heard the sirens and knew the cops were on their way. The next morning, everybody was talking about this mini-drama, and we pretended to be interested.

On our team, Ole Olson was our clean-up hitter but never cleaned up anything. George Mason was our shortstop and had a .500 batting average. I was the second batter because I was the best bunter on the team. I had a .435 batting average and several of my hits were bunts. Our leadoff batter almost never got on base. I think he had two hits for the season. Once, we played Santa Rosa Junior College at Santa Rosa where it was rumored that the New York Yankees were scouting their pitcher. I went three for four at bat against him and about seven-hundred yards chasing after well hit balls. I can say that I lettered in a college sport, for I made my letter in baseball while at Menlo.

The wild threesome of Dick, Ole, and Hobey went to quite a few San Francisco Seals baseball games in the old Seals Stadium. A couple of times, we went down to Fillmore Street to listen to Dixieland and jazz music. We were a gutsy bunch going into the heart of the toughest street in the city. One time, when we were playing a baseball game in the Mission District of San Francisco on Harrison Street, the crowd was definitely not very sociable. There was one old crone in the stands who could hardly walk because she was so drunk, but that didn't seem to hurt her language a bit. Some of the younger boys on the team learned some new words that afternoon. After this game, it was get in the cars right away and get out of there pronto.

When the baseball season was over, it was time to focus on the books and finish the year. After final exams, it was time to head home to Hawai'i for the first time in two years. The flight home to Hawai'i was on a DC-4 and took fourteen hours from San Francisco to Honolulu. Once in Honolulu, I joined up with Mother and stayed a few days with the George Moodys on Old Pali Road. I returned to Honolulu just in time for the Kamehameha Day Parade. George Moody talked me into riding in the parade with a group of horse people from Honolulu. After the parade was over, I had to lead the Grand Marshall's horse back to the starting point at 'Iolani Palace. The Grand Marshall stayed with the King and Queen while the rest of us had another forty-five minute ride back to the start where transportation was waiting for the horses. I was less than thrilled.

A couple of days later, we headed back to Kaua'i and home. My grandfather's house at Kalapaki was gone because of the1946 tsunami, and my grandfather was living in a little house on Rice Street in Līhue. Mother got the house opposite Yoneji Store. This house was where her sister Edith Plews and her husband had lived before they moved back to England when the War was over. The house and lot were owned by Garden Island Motors, and Mother, being a director of the company, got to stay in the house. Mother got one of the first fancy Ford convertibles, which had woody sides. My grandfather let me have an old 1941 Ford woody station wagon for the summer. The Kauaʻi Airport was located at Barking Sands at Mānā, and not in Līhue as it is today. It took more than an hour from Līhue to the airport. I hadn't been back home for more than a day when my grandfather took me up to Kīpū to say hello to the cowboys. After about fifteen minutes of talking with them, my grandfather said, "You sound like you haven't been away from pidgin English at all. I guess the old language doesn't die easily."

After Charlie, Bruce, and I got back to Kauaʻi, the evening round of parties started in earnest. Most of the kids were a little younger than I, so I was making a lot of new friends. One day, I got a call from my cousin, Eleanor Boyden, Anna Sloggett's sister, asking me to take Nancy Sloggett home from a party she was giving at Hanamaulu Cafe. It seemed that her son was having his high school girlfriend down for a while, and Eleanor didn't want any unattached boys around, and I was one of them. Nancy was eighteen years old. She had just graduated from Punahou that June and was on her way to Pine Manor Junior College in Wellesley, Massachusetts, in September. The night before the Hanamaulu Cafe party, I saw Nancy and told her I was taking her home the next night. She got a little ticked off at that because she didn't want to be told what to do. But, the next evening after the Chop Suey party, she said to me, "The party's over. You can take me home now." I told her it was only seven o'clock and that Charles K. L. Davis would be singing and playing the piano. So we went to the Moir's home in Poʻipū and listened to Davis play and sing Hawaiian songs. During the evening, Nancy and I talked about what we were going to be doing during the summer. She said that her parents were going out to the family house in Hanalei, and she was going to learn how to cook. I told her that Mother had just bought some property in Hāʻena, and I would be out in that neck of the woods during the summer and maybe she could cook something for me!

On the way home, I asked Nancy, "In that big house, what room is yours?" She told me, and, then, I asked where the bed was and which way did it face?

She said, "You sure are nosy," but told me anyway. Then I told her that the way it faced was the right way because her room had been my room and that's the way my bed faced when I lived in the house from 1929 to 1937. Her father had bought the house and ranch in 1939.

The time I went over to get reintroduced to Nancy and met her parents Dick and Sue Sloggett, I almost blew the whole deal. I told Nancy's mother that her mashed potatoes were lumpy and that I would help her with them. I also told Nancy and her parents about my first attempt at mashed potatoes in the Army and everybody had a good laugh.

There were several young people staying at Hanalei for varying parts of the summer, so there were activities almost every evening. One evening, Dick Sloggett told me that the Rotary Club was going to honor Reverend Wiley from All Saints Church in Kapa'a in two weeks from the coming Sunday. I told him that I would like to go with him. Thankfully, Nancy had forgiven me for the mashed potatoes episode, and we were getting to be pretty good friends by now. One night, she told me that the man she would marry would have to give her an emerald cut diamond ring for an engagement ring. I just said "good luck." Her three aunts had all received emerald cut diamond rings for their engagements, and that's where she got the idea. We continued with two more weeks of seeing each other and were getting very close. On the Saturday evening before we were to go to All Saints to honor Reverend Wiley, I asked Nancy to marry me. She hemmed and hawed for about ten minutes and finally said okay. I told her not to tell anyone until I had a chance to ask her father. The next day, Nancy, her father, and I went to church and then back to Hanalei.

That afternoon, I was eating lunch at home with Mother, and she said, "Hobey, I hope you won't be too disappointed if Nancy won't marry you. But your going to church with her family is a dead giveaway that something is up."

I said, "Is that why Dr. Kuhns laughed so much when he saw us drive in?" Then I told her that Nancy had, in fact, said yes, and that I was going over to Hanalei that evening to ask Dick for her hand.

I spent the afternoon making a double plumeria lei for Nancy's mother. When I got to Hanalei, the Sloggetts were just finishing dinner. Dick went into the living room to listen to the evening news. After a few minutes, I went in and we talked for a bit; then, I asked him if I could marry his daughter. He said, "Sure!" But he wanted to know how soon. I told him that Nancy and I wanted to go to school for another year. He said he thought that this was a good idea. Then he started to tell me about how he had to write a letter to Sue's father in Michigan for her hand, and how he had agonized over the wording of the letter. He then said goodnight and went to bed. Nancy and her mother were on pins and needles waiting to know what had gone on. I told Nancy that everything was okay. Sue asked where Dick was, and I told her that he had gone to bed. Sue went to the bedroom and made Dick come out and have a glass of champagne with us. Nancy had told her mother about my proposal and they had the champagne already chilled.

On Tuesday morning, I flew off for Honolulu and Grossman-Moody for an emerald cut diamond ring. I was back that evening and the ring fit perfectly. I really made a hit.

The rest of the summer was spent getting Mother's house at Hāʻena habitable and planning our wedding for the following June of 1948. I would be going back to Menlo Junior College, and Nancy was headed for Pine Manor Junior College in Wellesley at about the same time. Also, there were parties almost every night, but it was a lot more fun now that I had Nancy to myself and no more competition.

But life wasn't a big party all summer long. I got a first class sinus infection and it felt like my head would split. When I finally went to the doctor, he stuck some cotton probes up my nose, which had been soaked in cocaine to anesthetize me. When he thought the moment proper he stuck a hollow needle through the bone into my sinuses and started to flush them out. At first, the pressure was quite painful, but, when the blockage broke loose, the relief was wonderful. I had this procedure done twice a week for the next two weeks. After this, the doctor said that I couldn't put my head under water for the rest of my life. That didn't last long, and I started body surfing again before the summer was over. I am thankful that I have never had a recurrence of that problem.

One day, Nancy was with me when we were branding calves at Kīpū. She was a rancher's daughter, so she knew what was going on. Solomon Malina offered her some mountain oysters, which had been broiled over the coals of the branding fire. Without batting an eye, she took a couple and said, "I like these" and ate them. The rest of the cowboys teased Solomon a little because he was trying to embarrass her. She was accepted as a proper wife for me.

Summer vacation finally came to an end and it was off to the mainland for Nancy, Charlie, Bruce, and me. Charlie and I flew to Honolulu and saw Nancy off on the *Lurline*, and, the next day, Charlie and I flew to San Francisco and were at the dock to meet Nancy when her boat arrived. We escorted her to her hotel, the St. Francis, and Charlie and I went to our hotel, the Fairmont. The three of us had a couple of days in San Francisco together before taking Nancy over to Oakland on the Ferry and putting her on the train to Massachusetts. Then, it was down the peninsula for Charlie and me.

During the year, I lived in the boys' dormitory with a roommate, Jack Wallace from Pasadena, California. We had the end room of the building with the fire escape stairs for a back door. On the left corner of the building were Dick Brooke and Jimmy Pflueger, while on the right were Jerry Ober and another boy. I mention these names because they will come into the story a little later. School started, and it didn't take long to get into the swing of things. There was no baseball in the fall, and I didn't play football. But we did go to the games. One game was down in Pasadena. So my roommate took me with him, and down to Pasadena we went. Jack Wallace had a car, and we drove down on Friday afternoon, got into Pasadena late that night, and went right to bed. We were staying at his parents' home, but I barely got to meet them because they were going south for the weekend. The next day, Jack took me shopping (mostly window shopping, but I did get a few things). The game was at the Rose Bowl, and I got to walk on the field after the game. It was somewhat of a thrill. The next day, we headed back to Menlo. On the way back north, we stopped in Buellton for some split pea soup at Andersen's. I have never forgotten how good the soup was, and, after my daughter Joan moved to Santa Barbara, we went there for a bowl of soup. The place wasn't the same. It has gotten very touristy and commercial. But the soup was still good.

At Thanksgiving, Charlie, Bruce, and I flew up to Oregon and had Thanksgiving dinner with Dad and Marjorie. Marjorie was a nice woman who later became known as "The Elephant Lady" of Portland, Oregon, for her work in making the elephant enclosure at the zoo a better and more comfortable place for the animals. We had three days with a little snow to make things just cold enough for us California softies and, then, back to sunny California.

After Thanksgiving, it wasn't long before Christmas vacation. I took the city of San Francisco train to Chicago and, then, caught a bus to Flint, Michigan, and spent Christmas vacation with Nancy at her grandfather's home. Nancy's grandfather, Dr. Reynolds, was a family-practice physician and was still practicing. Nancy had a great time seeing her old friends again. She had been sent from Hawai'i to her grandfather's during the War to keep her away from the soldiers.

Everybody knew who I was. But, at every party we went to, there were at least fifty young people, and I had to remember them because I had met them the night before. All the parties were formal, and most of them were black tie affairs. Luckily, I brought my tuxedo with me, so I was okay as far as dress was concerned. For New Year's Eve, I had ordered a white carnation lei for Nancy. It arrived right on time, and she was the hit of the party. If I remember correctly, the New Year's party was at the home of Red Curtis, who later became the head of General Motors. For my return trip to San Francisco, I was booked on the same train that I taken to get to Chicago. Nancy persuaded me to stay an extra day and fly to Chicago to catch the train. It snowed that night and most of the next day, so I missed my train connection but was able to get on a plane to San Francisco that evening.

On our way, we stopped at Omaha, Nebraska, and almost didn't get to leave because of the snow. This was an overnight flight, and, when I awoke the next morning, we were over the Rockies at thirteen-thousand-feet elevation. On my way to the toilet, one of the flight attendants told me to move slowly because of the high elevation. On my way back to the seat, as I was passing the flight attendant, a woman was on her way to the toilet and the stewardess warned her about taking it easy. She didn't listen and passed out just as she was going by me. I caught her and eased her into an empty seat. When breakfast came, I had an extra sweet roll from the girls.

Fred and Marjorie were on the train that I was supposed to be on, and they were alarmed that I wasn't on it with them. I got to San Francisco before they did and left a message at their hotel that I had returned to San Francisco safely. After they got in to San Francisco, they had a cocktail party for some of their friends and invited me to come. I met my old high school flame there, who I had not seen since 1941. She was now married and had two children.

During the months of January and February, a couple of funny things happened at our end of the dormitory. One evening, I had gone to the bathroom and had just taken a shower. Being an all boys dorm, I just threw my towel over my shoulder and was walking back to my room when I heard footsteps behind me. When I looked back, there was an old lady walking behind me. I was quite embarrassed and put my towel around my waist and apologized. But she just laughed and said that she had raised a family of five boys and not to worry. She was Jerry Ober's grandmother, and, after this, we went to her home in Oakland several times. She kidded me about my nice round bottom.

One day, Jimmy Pflueger and his roommate Dick Brooke were out for a ride down the road next to the school when he hit a quail. They stopped and picked up the bird, brought it back to the dorm, and plucked and cleaned it. That evening, they decided to cook the bird and tried to use a metal wastebasket to cook it in. They started their fire and were about to start broiling the bird when another fellow came in, somehow picked up the waste basket, came into our room, went to the fire escape, and threw the whole basket down to the ground. Jimmy and Dick went downstairs and had to start all over again. Then, they finally cooked the quail and ate it.

The last episode was right after New Year's. Dick Brooke and Jimmy Pflueger were studying in their room when someone threw a lighted firecracker into their room. When the darn thing exploded, Jimmy jumped up and dived under his bed. He was not a happy camper, and I wouldn't have wanted to be the person if he ever was caught. Jimmy had been in the Marines during the War and had seen some pretty bad things and didn't take kindly to sudden explosions. When school started up again after the Christmas break, my heart wasn't into bookwork. I wanted to get home and get the house we were going to live in ready so we could move right in after we were married. I stayed with my studies until the semester break; then, I left school, moved back to Kaua'i, and started working on the ranch. My grandfather came all the way to Barking Sands to pick me up at the airport. I got a lot of good-natured kidding but I didn't mind. Now, I could get busy and fix up our new home.

Nancy in 1946.

In the Army on the island of Shemya in the Aleutian Islands, 1946.

Hobey in 1947.

Nancy in 1947.

Wedding on June 14, 1948.

Wedding portrait.

CHAPTER EIGHT

Marriage and Children 1948–1962

After returning to Kauaʻi at the end of the fall semester at Menlo Junior College, I went right to work at Kīpū Ranch. One of my first jobs was to see that the house where Nancy and I would be living was fixed up in a suitable manner. The house where we were to live needed a lot of work because no one had lived there for over fifteen years. During World War II, my grandfather had used the house for the storage of some of the things from the house at Kalapaki that had been salvaged after the tsunami of April 1, 1946. Everything I owned up to the time I was twenty-one was lost in the wave. It was now early February 1948, and we were to be married on June 25, 1948. So there wasn't much time to get the place prepared for us.

We had a set of plans for the inside of the house, especially an inside dressing room and closet for both of us. Once the plans arrived, we had a contractor, Mori Morishige, start building all the shelves and drawers. All the work was done just in time for us to move in. The house was painted inside and out so that it looked like new. It was a big house with three bedrooms and two full baths, a large living room, and a screened lanai on the west side of the house. There was a good-sized kitchen and, later, a lean-to laundry after the children started coming.

Nancy finally got itchy feet and wanted to come home and help get things ready. Before Nancy came home, I changed my name from Holbrook March Wichman to Holbrook Wichman Goodale. I had been getting pressure from my father's sister, aunt Catharine Carter, and other old timers here on Kauaʻi. Aunt Catharine asked that I change my name to Goodale so that the name would be carried on. Luckily, I asked Nancy's mother and father and the wedding invitations had not been ordered. My change of name document was the first one that my cousin George Kimball's Law Firm had ever done. I met an attorney from the firm about ten years ago, and, when he heard my name, he came over and introduced himself to me and said that he had seen my name many times and was delighted to put a face to the document. He told me that they were still using the original form.

All this time up to the wedding I was working on the ranch. By now, there was no more sugar to worry about, just the cattle. My grandfather was still riding horseback every day and continued to do so until he was seventy-five years old. My brother Charles once cajoled him into stepping on the scales, and, before he could get off, Charlie had him weighing three-hundred-thirty-five pounds. The old man wasn't too happy about being weighed. On the days we slaughtered cattle for market and days when we were fixing fences, he would ride around the pastures and check on the cattle. If anything was not right and needed attention, he would tell us to fix it.

After Nancy returned home, things got more exciting. We could then decide on the colors for the house and start to assemble furniture and all the other things we would need to furnish the house. I would have dinner with Nancy and her mother and father several nights a week and go over the progress of the house. The Sloggetts would always make me go home at ten o'clock in the evening because I had to go to work the next day. I got to know the road up to Wailua Homesteads like the palm of my hand. Mother was, at this time, working on the house at Hā'ena. Nancy and I would go out and help her whenever we could, but, the closer to the wedding, the more parties there were and the fewer weekends off. One party that I wish I never had to go to was my bachelor's party. It was held on Tuesday evening before the wedding on Saturday. It was at the home of my cousin Tommy King on Royal Drive in the Wailua Homesteads about a mile from the Sloggett home. Upon my arrival at the party, I was given a large mug filled with bourbon and a little water. I did my best to nurse it, but people were always coming up to me and wanting to have toast with me. I finally finished the mug off and tossed it into the river gorge. No sooner had I gotten rid of one mug than another appeared, and there we went again.

Finally, around two in the morning, someone said, "Let's go to the Sloggetts and have Nancy cook us some breakfast."

I said, "Sure, I know the way to her bedroom."

When we got to Nancy's house, I had started up the stairs to her room when Sue, her mother, appeared and said, "Hobey Goodale, get out of this house and don't come back until you are married." I got out of there as fast as I could, but the guys never let me forget about it.

One party that was held in our honor was a kitchen shower. But there were no appliances or any kitchen equipment, only canned goods that had all the labels removed. We had a great time after we were married trying to figure out what we were having for dinner that night. One group of four fairly large cans looked very suspicious, as the cans were too bright and shiny. This was when the pineapple cannery in Kapa'a was still in operation and the American Can Company made all the cans for the pineapples right there in Kapa'a. This fact was an indication that something was fishy because not only were the cans too shiny but they were too light also. It seemed to me that they didn't weigh enough for anything good to be inside them. Furthermore, one of the persons at the party was Bob Morton, the manager of the can company, who was a great practical joker. The next day, Nancy, her parents, and I opened one of the cans. It was lucky that we did because had we not opened the cans they would have exploded and there would have been horse you-know-what all over our kitchen.

Uncle Philip and Aunt Flora Rice gave another big party at their home in Kukui'ula for Nancy and me, along with Lois Robinson and her fiancé Larry Somers as honorees. It was a sit-down dinner, and Nancy and I had to sit on a small bench at one end of the table while Lois and Larry had to sit on a similar bench at the other end of the table. We had to balance our rear ends on those small benches, while the other guests had comfortable chairs to sit in. This dinner was one of those old-time, formal affairs that are no longer done today.

A few days before the wedding, I asked Nancy if she had any ideas about what we would like to have for meals on our honeymoon and what we should order. This question caught her by surprise, for she had never thought of food. We were going over the mountain to Kīpū Kai for our honeymoon, and all supplies had to be packed over the mountain on pack mules, preferably the day before. We finally got our heads together, made a list, did the shopping, and had everything ready to go the day before the wedding.

Finally, June 24 arrived, and it was time for rehearsal for the wedding. Nancy had her sister Sally for her maid of honor and five bridesmaids: Polly Ward, Mary Fewell, Bebe Moody, Addie Gibb, and Budge Horner. I had my brother Charles Wichman as my best man and Sam Wilcox, Bruce Wichman, Doug Pratt, Dick Sloggett, Jr., and Donn Carlsmith for groomsmen. The rehearsal went okay, and we had to do the walk only one time. It was then off to an early dinner and off to bed to be bright eyed for the next day. Nancy's mother ran a tight ship, and everything ran right on schedule.

The next afternoon, our wedding was at four-thirty in the afternoon. It is supposed to be good luck to start a wedding while the hands of the clock are rising. When Charles and I got to the church, of those who were already there, the women were seated in the church and the men were all out by their cars listening to the heavyweight championship boxing match between Ezzard Charles and Joe Wallcott, the champ. For me, the ceremony is still a

111

daze. As soon as it was over, Nancy and I were herded off to the reception at the Sloggetts in Wailua Homesteads. As soon as we got into the car, I asked my brother Charles to turn on the radio so that we could hear the end of the fight. No sooner did the radio come on than Jersey Joe was knocked out. I didn't want to hear any more of the recaps.

The receiving line was very long, and it seemed to go on forever. But we were lucky that my brother Charles kept us well supplied with champagne. What are best men for, anyway? After the last person went through the line, Nancy and I had only a few minutes to circulate and be sociable before we had to cut the cake, change into our going-away clothes, and leave for our honeymoon. Nancy's mother wanted us out of the way so the old folks would go home and the party could really start. In those days, it was not polite to leave before the bride and groom left. On the way out to the car, I got a good underhanded throw of rice in my face and then cut my hand when I reached under the car to see if there were any cans tied under there. The cans had been tied with wire. Charlie told me to get in the car and drive out of the yard, and he would meet me with a pair of wire cutters to cut off the cans.

At the ranch, we had started a seasonal breeding program with our breeding cows. During the reception, the cowboys who were there had funny smirks on their faces whenever they looked at me, so I knew something was up. They finally told me that the bulls had gone in with the cows that morning to see who would have a baby first. The cows won by five months. My grandfather thought this would be a lot of fun, especially if the great grandson came first.

We spent our first night together in our house at Kīpū. Fairly early the next morning, we left for Kīpū Kai on horseback. It was lucky that we left the house early because some of Nancy's aunts came to Kīpū, and, while checking the house, they peeked in the windows. Wouldn't it have been fun if we had been caught in bed?

After getting settled in the house at Kīpū Kai, we went swimming, and, then, I went to the fishpond, caught a couple of mullet, and told Nancy that I would make chowder for her. Boy! Have I come a long way in fifty years? I don't know what I cooked, but it wasn't chowder. I can't remember what plan B was, but we got by. In the kitchen was a little mouse that sat and watched us eat the whole time we were there. We would feed it, and it got quite tame. One night, I decided to hang live bait off the limestone rock opposite the house called the Turtle. After dinner, we went out to the end of the Turtle and set a line with a live fish swimming just under the surface and a heavy line attached to the hook. Soon, Nancy said that she was getting hay fever from the old Army blanket that I had brought to keep us warm and that she was going back to the house. I said that I would go back with her. The next morning, when we checked the line, we found that something big had taken the bait and that the hook had straightened out, so much for that kind of fishing. We couldn't have eaten that much fish anyway. Solomon Malina would come over the mountain every other day to check on us and see if we needed anything. When he got to the top of the pass, on his way over, he would start cracking his whip so that we would know that someone was coming and wouldn't be caught by surprise. I had heard stories of other members of the family who were honeymooning at Kīpū Kai and were seen by people working over there.

We had a lot of fun all by ourselves at Kīpū Kai. We finally came back to civilization in time for the Fourth of July Celebration at the Yacht Club. Everybody there teased us, but it was all good-natured. At this gathering, ten-year-old Linda Cunningham, who had always called me "Hobey," suddenly called me "Uncle Hobey" and did it ever make me feel old! Suddenly, I wasn't Hobey anymore but now it was Uncle Hobey. Nancy and I now settled into a routine, which would modify from time to time as situations changed.

After Nancy and I settled into our new life together, I took up casting for bass in our reservoirs at Kīpū. There are four small reservoirs on the ranch. They are a carryover from the days that Kīpū was a sugar plantation. Later, it was casting over at Kīpū Kai in the ocean. My tackle was a short rod and a small level wind reel with ten-pound test monofilament line. This was in the days before spinning reels. Our rods were shorter than those used in spinning tackle today. For bass, we used artificial lures, and, for the ocean fishing, it was strips of cuttlefish. The bass at Kīpū never got over about three pounds, but the reservoirs were close to home and easy to get to. Getting to Kīpū Kai was more difficult. It took a lot longer, but the ocean fish were much better tasting than the bass. The most numerous fish of the ocean fish were the pāpio. There were other fish, too, but most of them were not as good eating as the pāpio, so we threw those others back into the ocean. One day while casting, I got an 'ō'io or bonefish on my line. When I finally got the fish to shore and weighed it, it weighed five-and-a-half pounds. Boy, was my wrist ever sore and stiff! It was the biggest fish I had caught on light tackle up to that point.

I have talked about Kīpū Kai so much I had better give you a description of the ocean front at Kīpū Kai starting at the southwestern end. Out to the end of Black Mountain Point from the end of the beach, there are several holes where moi could be caught with a throw net. The rocky shoreline was good for getting 'opihis or limpets. From the start of the beach and heading east, the beach is around a mile long. At about the half-mile point, there is a small reef with several good moi holes. The beach ends at the "Crocodile." This spot is a low, sandstone formation running east to west. To some, it looks like a crocodile and, to others, like airplane wings. At the east end of the Crocodile is a short beach of about three-hundred yards running north and south called Wild Beach. It's called Wild Beach because the prevailing surf comes pounding onto shore there, and the reef that fronts the length of the beach drops off to about fifteen feet. This is not a swimming beach, but the shelling was good when we were young. From the north end of Wild Beach, there is a large sandstone formation that culminates in a high rounded hill. This formation looks like a turtle and is rightly called the Turtle. From the base of the Turtle, there is a nice sand beach stretching about a half-mile semicircle in front of the house. Immediately in front of the house, there is a small barrier reef where the swimming is good and safe for small children. Beyond the house, there are two cliffs that come right down to the water's edge. For the next mile, there are several beaches fronted by large reefs. At one place, the reefs form a barrier and a nice lagoon inside where we frequently caught octopus. There are a couple of moi holes on this stretch of coastline. Here the target fish were manini or convict tang, nenue or rudder fish, and āholehole. Kīpū Kai was a wonderful place to grow up. In the days before 1950 and the vehicular road over the mountain, you had to walk or ride horseback wherever you wanted to go. There were also wild goats in the hills that sometimes would come down to the edge of the beaches. Here they were easy marks for a young boy with a twenty-two long rifle.

The best and most productive casting spot was the western end of the Crocodile. I would cast and retrieve with cuttlefish bait while Isao Ishida and Hiram Matsumoto would cast out with long surf casting poles and 4.0 reels and forty-pound test line. They were looking for the large ulua. I always had more fun because I got more action. One late afternoon, I was fishing of the end of the Crocodile and the fish were not biting. So I let my bait sink to the bottom at about twenty feet deep. There it got caught on the bottom, or so I thought. When I looked into the water, there on the bottom was a small lobster about where my line was. I pulled on the line and felt a slight jerk, so I kept as tight of a tension on my line as I dared. Soon, the lobster let loose from the bottom, and I reeled in as fast as I could. The lobster got bigger and bigger looking the closer he got to the surface. When I finally landed him and got him home to a scale, he weighed five-and-a-quarter pounds. He was pretty tough to eat. After that, I perfected a method to catch lobsters with hook and line. I would go out and catch two or three in an evening and then go home.

Later, I got myself a heavier surf casting rig for 'ō'io and moi. I also caught several pāpio up to about ten pounds but never any of the big ulua. One day out at Hā'ena, when my son David was about eight, he took my outfit to try his luck. Within an hour, he was back home again with a nice pāpio, which we had for dinner. I asked David about the weight, and he said that it was more than five pounds. He also said he had felt deflated when his mother asked him if someone had given him the fish.

Dove shooting was another sport. For this you didn't have to walk all over the countryside. Above the stables, we had sheds as shelters for the sows that we kept for breeding. There were usually four of us who would go out on a Sunday afternoon to shoot doves—Pat Cannon, Wayne Ellis, Dr. Jay Kuhns, and me. We would sit just inside the cover of the sheds and wait for the doves to fly in to feed on the grain we fed the pigs. At first my grandfather didn't like the idea of us shooting around the pigs because he thought we would scare them. After about two Sundays of dove shooting, one dove that had been shot fell at the feet of one of the sows. Before we could get to the bird, the sow picked it up in her mouth and promptly started to eat it. From that point on, we had to run for our birds before the pigs got to them. The limit was twenty-five doves per man, and we would get our limits in about two hours. Doves are very easy to pluck. So, while we waited for the next bird to fly in, we would pluck the ones we already shot. This way, when we were done shooting, the doves had all been plucked. This process lasted for about five years until we stopped raising pigs. It was fun while it lasted.

On the eighth of October 1948, Nancy and I were going out to celebrate my twenty-fifth birthday. Before we could leave, Paul and Edwina Rice stopped in and Paul wanted to take a look at the stables and pigs. I took him up to the stables, while Edwina stayed with Nancy. Paul and I went all around the stables and the blacksmith shop, with Paul asking questions while I worried about being late for my birthday dinner. When Paul finally said, "Let's go back to the house," I was relieved and back to the house we went. When we got to the house, there were about a dozen cars in the yard. It was a surprise party, and we weren't going anywhere that night after all. The party, by then, was in full swing.

Another time, we invited guests over at six-thirty, but Uncle Philip and Aunt Flora appeared at the door at six. Nancy and I had just finished the final touches for the party and hadn't had time for our showers yet. We scrambled. While one of us entertained the old folks, the other showered as fast as possible. It turned out to be a very nice evening anyway. We learned early in our life together not to panic.

By the time Nancy and I were married, we were expected to be at Grove Farm for Thanksgiving and Christmas Eve to celebrate with Aunt Elsie and Aunt Mabel Wilcox. In the first couple of years, Aunt Mabel heckled me a little because of some past political differences between the Rices and the Wilcoxes. It took her about two years before she decided that I was okay. She asked me, during cocktails on my third Thanksgiving with them, to carve the turkey. She would, then, carve the ham. I readily agreed, for now I knew that I had been accepted as a member of the family. In the ensuing years, Aunt Mabel was very generous to our family.

After Nancy and I were married, we were able to join a group of recently married couples who partied and played a lot of bridge. We drank and smoked too much, but we survived. During this period we joined several service clubs. Nancy joined a sorority called the Beta Sigma Phi. I joined the Jaycees, Toastmasters, and the Kauai Cattlemen's Association. Nancy soon became pregnant, and our lives started to change with the responsibilities of raising children. Our firstborn, David Whitney, was born on September 25, 1949. The cows started having their calves in April of 1949, so they beat us by five months. The gestation period for humans and cattle is 285 days, give or take ten days. So much for my grandfather's having the bulls held back until the day we were married.

There is a saying that the first one can come any time, but, after that, they take nine months. I don't know about that because our second, Katherine Rice, came ten months to the day later. When Nancy was first pregnant with David, there were nights that I would lie awake worrying that I might not be a good father and about how we were going to educate these children. After the second child was born, there wasn't time to worry, for we had our hands full.

When I was still in high school before the War, I had a small herd of goats at Kalapaki. This herd started with six baby goats that I had caught one day when we were hunting on the mountain opposite Nāwiliwili. There were three males and three female kids, and we raised them all to maturity. One of the males I castrated, and, when he was fully-grown, we slaughtered him. His meat tasted just like tender lamb. This group multiplied until there were about sixty by the time I went into the Army in 1945. Before I left, we caught all the goats, trucked them to Kīpū, and turned them loose in one of the pastures. After Nancy and I were married, I went down to the pasture and caught a female kid and brought it home. Nancy adopted it as her first baby and named it Patsy. The kid had the run of the house and would walk around dropping little black pellets all over the floors. When David came along, Patsy was relegated to a pasture in back of the house. There I had a wild billy, and, pretty soon, Patsy had a kid of her own. We ate that one when it got big enough, and Patsy had many more offspring over the years.

Nancy and I would bet on the Punahou-'Iolani football games. The bet was usually some chore around the house. After David was born, this game was played in early November. When David was six weeks old, the bet was who ever lost would have to get up and do the two in the morning feeding for two weeks. I lost, and I said to David, "Kid, you better start sleeping through the night." From that day forward, he slept through the night. Nancy was pretty upset. The following year, the bet was who ever lost would have to do the dishes for a week. Again I lost. But, this time, my grandfather came in one morning and said, "I think the ranch had better buy you a dishwasher." So, I lucked out again. Nancy and I have never bet on the game since.

In the spring of 1949, Mother was planning to go to New York to help set up a Hawaiian display at the Rockefeller Center and would be gone for three months. Mother had a female chow that had gotten an eczema of some kind and was looking terrible. So, before she left for New York, she had the dog sent to the vet with instructions to either cure her or put her down. After about a month, the vet appeared one day with Yum Yum (as the dog was called after Yum Yum in the Gilbert and Sullivan Operetta *The Mikado*). We couldn't believe our eyes, for she was completely cured and had a fine coat of reddish brown fur. I asked the vet what he had done. He replied that he gave her a clove of garlic every day, and we were to continue to do so for another month or so. We took over the care of Yum Yum and got to be really fond of her. Knowing that Mother would be coming home soon, I started to feed her a few scraps at the dinner table. I would tap the table and she would put her paws on the edge of the table and get her tidbit. I really had her spoiled.

When Mother finally returned to Kaua'i, she wanted us to keep Yum Yum because she looked so happy with us and with all the freedom that she had on the ranch. That meant that we were stuck with a spoiled dog. After David was born and we returned from the hospital with him, the first thing we did was to let Yum Yum smell him. After that, it was as if the baby were hers and she would get nervous when he cried. We did this with all four of our children, and she treated them all in the same way. She never snapped at any of them. It was a sad day when she finally died.

In 1949, I went to Maui to attend the Jaycee Annual Convention as a delegate from the Kaua'i club. There I met Larry Haneberg, who, when he saw my name, asked me if I was any relation to the Holbrook Goodale who had been killed in an airplane crash in 1927. I told him that he was my father. Larry then told me that his father had been a passenger in the plane and had been killed also. Larry and I became good friends. At that same meeting I also met Clint Childs, who asked me all about Kaua'i and the people there. The next year, he came to Kaua'i for the convention and to see for himself whether he would like to move there. He must have been pleased with what he saw, for, within a year, he had gotten a job with the Lihue Plantation and moved there with his family. While on Maui, I drove up to Kula to see my Uncle Harold Rice and check out his pig operation to see if we could use some of his practices. I was able to drive right to the house in Kula, even though I had not seen the house since 1933. But I wasn't able to use anything they were doing with their pigs that was better than what we were doing.

Mother had bought some shares in the Haena Hui in 1947, and, by 1949, she was living out there full time. In those days, I worked six days a week on the ranch, but we would go out to Hā'ena and stay with Mother on Saturday night and Sunday. I would help around the house and in the yard. Nancy and I would also go beachcombing, for the shelling was quite good in those days. By 1951, David and Kathy were in the toddler stage, and, when Mother heard that Nancy was pregnant with another, she said, "I can't stand that many children underfoot, so I'm going to build you a house of your own." When she showed me where this was to be, I almost choked, as the jungle was almost twenty feet high and very dense. I went to work clearing and burning and soon had enough room for the house. As the house was being built, I cleared more until we had a nice area around the house. I planted some fruit trees but was never able to benefit from the fruit because Mother gave us the lot next door with a house already on it. In 1969, we finally built a driveway up the hill from the highway to the house. Before this, we had to use the back entrance where there was very little parking space off the main highway. The old house, which we added on to a couple of times, finally was blown down and completely wrecked in the hurricane of 1992.

In 1951, Nancy and I went to the Big Island of Hawai'i to attend the annual meeting of the Hawai'i Cattlemen's Association. We stayed the first three nights at the Seaside Inn on the waterfront of Kailua town, which was operated by the Roy family of Kona. After that, we moved up the hill to Aunt Steve Wichman's place until we left for Hilo. At the cattlemen's meeting, I was met by a man by the name of Wishard. His father had been an engineer on Kaua'i, and he had also been a member of the Kaua'i Board of Supervisors. His greeting to me was, "I suppose you are here to give a dissertation on the benefits of Kikuyu Grass." I knew that Kikuyu was not thought very highly of on the island of Hawai'i. He then told me that his son had gone to school with me at Menlo Junior College and that he was teasing me about the Kikuyu. After the drought of 1953, those ranchers who had Kikuyu were able to survive in better shape than those who relied on the more succulent mainland grasses. Mr. Wishard was a gentleman and introduced me to many of the Hawai'i ranchers in attendance.

While in Kona, I was fortunate to visit Parker Ranch where I met Richard Penhallow, the assistant manager of the ranch. He showed me around the headquarters and sent me off to see the rest of the ranch with Charlie Kaua'i, a foreman. I had a very memorable day touring Parker Ranch. The next day it was south to Honomalino with Bobby Hind. Bobby was a cousin of Bob Engelhard of Kaua'i, one of my good friends. Bobby's father and grandfather were old time friends of my grandfather. At Honomalino, we saw how they were reclaiming 'a'ā lava land for grazing by pulling a heavy anchor chain across the lava and lantana bushes. This was being done below the main road toward the ocean while up in the land closer to Mauna Loa they had fenced off a large tract of land between two old lava flows. This land was fenced into two large paddocks that were used to trap wild cattle. The wild cattle were then taken down to the lower pastures, where they were tested for tuberculosis and had their horns tipped so that they couldn't gore the horses. They were then put out to pasture to fatten up a little and then shipped to Honolulu for slaughter. With the most mauka gates opened, more wild cattle were suckered into the lush grass, and the process would repeat itself. I went back in 1954, and Bobby Hind told me that they had shipped about twenty-one thousand head of wild cattle to market. We also visited Pu'u Wa'awa'a Ranch, the hind ranch in the shadow of Mount Hualālai.

Our next stop on the way was at Pāhala to pay our respects to an old poker-playing friend of my grandfather, Jack Ramsey. Mr. Ramsey had been the manager of Kilauea Plantation on Kaua'i and had moved to Pāhala two years before. While at Pāhala, I was able to have a short visit with Leslie Wishard, my Menlo classmate. It was then on to Hilo for a visit with my brother Charles. While in Hilo, we visited the Lyman House Museum and were treated like newlyweds. The docent who took us around the house played an old copper record of the "Wedding March" for us. The museum was only one building in those days. In Hilo, we also met the widow of Charles Hada, who had been killed in the tsunami of 1946 at Kalapaki. It was a bittersweet reunion. Then it was back to Kaua'i and the raising of two little livewires.

In 1951, I was elected to the board of directors of Garden Island Motors.

And, in 1953, I was elected treasurer, a position I held until 1968 when I became manager. I would go to GIM every Tuesday morning and work in the office all day. Tuesday was the day that we slaughtered cattle, and the cowboys would be off work as soon as they had delivered the meat to the various markets. The slaughtering would start at about one in the morning, while it was still cool and there were no flies. After delivering the meat, the cowboys would go home, get some sleep, and have the rest of the day off. I spent my Tuesdays at Garden Island working with Roy Yokomoto, our credit manager, going over the collection accounts and writing letters trying to collect outstanding accounts. I didn't do any car selling until I quit the ranch in 1962.

The staff at Kīpū included six cowboys—Solomon Malina, Mamoru Matsumura, Hiram Matsumoto, Robert Keuma, Sr., Isao Ishida, and me. John Cravalho did the plowing and mowing of the pastures. Robert Keuma, Jr. and Fuji Matsumura were the stable men. Larry Andrade, who was the liquor law inspector, would come and help us any time he could get off. He loved the cowboy life almost as much as riding his motorcycle. With this crew, we took care of two-thousand head of cattle, forty horses and about fifty pigs. We didn't just ride on horseback, but would also fix fences, do carpentry, plumbing, blacksmithing, and handle all the other chores associated with a ranch. By 1949, we had installed all the new fencing around the old cane fields, so the tedious work of building new fences was over. Then, it was only routine work of a working cattle ranch to take up our time. From 1948 to 1956, August was the time of the year that we did all of our branding of calves. Every Saturday morning in August, there would be several cowboys from different ranches and small farms who would come to Kīpū to help us. After the branding was done for the day, there would be a lot of beer, soft drinks, and pupus for everyone. Some of the Portuguese fellows would bring their 'ukuleles and guitars and play music and sing. It was amazing how a person who could only speak with a thick pidgin drawl could sing cowboy songs in perfect English. Anyway, everyone looked forward to the Saturdays in August.

Ranching is an occupation for which the routine is the same from year to year, with small but exciting happenings every so often. Wild pigs would come down into the open pastures, and we would go out on horseback and try to rope them. We got pretty good at roping pigs. Then we would put them with our tame pigs to fatten so that we could eat them. Every so often, my grandfather would say on a Friday morning, "Let's have kalua pig tomorrow." We would get the imu ready that afternoon, and, first thing the next morning, we would slaughter the pig and put it in the imu. There was a spring on the ranch where some really good luau taro was growing. So we used to get a big bunch of the young, tender leaves and cook them along with the pig. Once the pig was safely covered and cooking, we would go about our regular Saturday chores until about eleven-thirty when the pig was fully cooked. My grandfather would always get poi for everyone, and we would divide the pig and the cooked luau leaves among the cowboys. Everybody would have some food to take home for supper that evening.

Jack Waterhouse bought Kīpū Kai from the five Rice brothers in 1947. The eldest brother had died, and the heirs couldn't get horses to ride over the mountain and were not happy with the situation as it existed. Around 1950, Jack started to build a vehicular road over the mountain to Kīpū Kai. After the road was finished, he had the road builders do more work at Kīpū Kai. At a point just about four hundred yards from the house where they were working, there was a spring right at the water's edge. Very soon after the road builders had blasted their way around the point and had covered the spring, Jack had a pretty severe heart attack. The older Hawaiian cowboys said that the spring was one that the demigod Kamapua'a had dug when he first came ashore on Kaua'i. Kamapua'a was supposed to be able to change himself from a shark into a pig or a human being at will. The Hawaiians blamed the heart attack on this legend. After Jack was recovering and before the doctors would let him fly back to Kaua'i, he asked me to look after the place for him. He had two men working for him over at Kīpū Kai, so my work was just checking on them. Before Jack had gotten the green light to travel again, there arrived on Kaua'i a ten-month-old bull calf from the mainland. Jack had bought him at auction before his heart attack. The bull, named Larry, was from the famous Carnation herd and was supposed to be hot stuff. He finally grew up but was never the size we felt he should have been. After he started breeding cows I got a call to go over to Kīpū Kai and check on Larry the bull. When I got there, I found that Larry had gotten lazy and had not withdrawn his penis into its sheath after servicing a cow, and it had gotten scratched and infected. It was extended to its full length and was so swollen that there was no way he could draw it back in. So it was over the mountain and call the vet and back again over the mountain and get the treatment started. Larry recovered and spent the rest of his life being a little more careful. Larry was the first bull that Jack Waterhouse bought for his ranch.

Just before Jack died, many years later, he bought another bull. This one tuned into a beautiful, big bull. After Jack's death, my son, David Goodale was called to go over to Kīpū Kai and appraise all of the rolling stock for estate purposes. I knew why David wanted me to go over with him. It was that there were seven gates that had to be opened and closed, once going over and again coming back to Līhue. After the appraising was completed, Lindy Sutherland, the manager, wanted to know if we would like him to take us around the ranch. Since I hadn't been over to Kīpū Kai in twenty-two years, I quickly said, "Yes!" When we got to a paddock with some cows and a bull we stopped. Lindy told us that the bull was the last bull that Jack had bought before he died. As we were watching the cattle, the bull tried to mount a cow but nothing happened. After a bit, he tried again but again failed. I said to Lindy, "I think something is wrong with the bull." I happened to be in on the troubles of the first and last of Jack Waterhouse's bull purchases. Again the vet had to be called, but this time the ranch had a cell phone and they were able to talk to the vet while they were standing next to the bull. I heard later that the bull had hurt his back but recovered to sire more calves.

We started playing polo in 1951 and continued until 1953. It was too expensive and time consuming. We played the indoor game with an inflated ball about the size of a softball. Our polo playing skills were not the best, but, in 1952, Manduke and Haku Baldwin from the Haleakala Ranch on Maui brought four of their cowboys to play us in August. We got our pants kicked. That night, though, we had a lū'au for them at our house and had a great time. David had noticed that the Maui men all had polo spurs and we had none. Haku invited us up to Maui for a rematch a month later and had a pair of polo spurs for each of us. Solomon, Hiram, Mamoru, and I went to Maui and played them, and this time we won. It was hot and dusty on the field, and sometimes we couldn't see the ball.

While we were gone, Nancy was at home with David, Kathy, and Joan. Joan had been born in June of 1952. One morning when Nancy was feeding Joan, there came a terrible noise from the laundry room. Nancy rushed to see what the noise was all about, and she found two little children looking terrified. They had put a whole case of empty Coca-Cola bottles in the dryer and turned it on. Needless to say there were no unbroken bottles left. Nancy cleaned the mess up as best she could and then put some old towels into the dryer and let if run for a few minutes. This cleaned out all the broken glass. The dryer ran without a hitch until we moved into our new house in Līhue in 1963.

In 1953, the price of coffee was higher than it had been for many years, so I started looking into going into the business. There were many coffee trees of the Guatemala variety in the Hule'ia Valley. This variety was considered one of the best at this time. I bought a pulper and started picking from the wild trees. By the spring of 1954, I had a couple of hundred pounds of dried parchment coffee in storage. On April first of that year, Nancy and I went down into the valley after work to clear around some of the better trees. I was using a cane knife with a hook on the side opposite the cutting edge. While I was taking a swing with the knife, the hook caught on a branch and deflected the flight of the blade so that, instead of cutting the tree, I cut the back of my hand. I looked at the cut and said a few choice words because I could see that I had cut the tendons on two of the fingers on my left hand. Nancy and I got back into the car, and, while she drove, I wrapped my hand in a towel, and into the doctors we went. I thought that this was it for my fingers. But, when Dr. Wallis saw my hand, he said, "No problem. We can fix this up in no time at all." He used woven stainless steel sutures on the tendons and regular sutures on the skin. The stainless steel is still in my hand, but it doesn't bother me at all. They don't even set off the buzzer when I go through security at airports. However, that was the end of the coffee plantation. I sold the pulper and got a few dollars for the already processed coffee.

The manager of the fertilizer company, now known as Brewer Chemical, was a man by the name of Douglas Baldwin. His assistant was Bob Engelhard, a good friend of mine. Bob was a frustrated rancher, as most of his family members were ranchers on the Big Island. He recommended that we do some fertilizer testing on the ranch. I got my grandfather to agree, and the test plots were put in. When the results were in, we had the information that we needed to make our pastures more productive. Our basic grass was Kikuyu, but, in the middle fifties, we were able to get starts of Pangola grass, which was a higher producer of bulk matter and more palatable to the cattle than the Kikuyu grass.

In 1954, Nancy and I went back to Maui for another Jaycee Convention. This time, because I was a director of Garden Island Motors, I was able to get a car from Valley Isle Motors, the Maui Ford Dealer, for my use while I was on Maui. One day, Nancy and I went to Lahaina and then back to Wailuku by way of Kahakuloa. The road was a narrow, winding one with no guardrails. There were places where I could look out the window and see waves breaking against the rock three to four hundred feet below me. Kā'anapali had not been developed at that time, and the area was all kiawe trees and some sugarcane. Kā'anapali was not started until 1962. I remember returning to Kaua'i from Kona in 1961 aboard Wayne Ellis's boat the Welakahao.

The next day, we had lunch with my grandfather's brother Harold Rice. He said that we should go over to Hāna and look at what they were doing on the Hāna Ranch. He called the manager of the ranch, John Hanchett, and arranged for Nancy and I to meet him and tour the ranch the next day. Uncle Harold also told us that we should go by Kula and 'Ulupalakua and then on to Hāna so that the wind would be blowing into our faces and the dust would be behind us. This was good advice, for it was very dry and dusty. You must remember that this was in the days when very few cars had air-conditioning. Once we got to Hāna, we were met by John Hanchett, who had been a classmate of mine at 'Iolani during high school. John asked if we would mind going to the airport first. His boss, Paul Fagan, was on his way back to Honolulu. So we had a nice drive to the airport. On the way, Mr. Fagan grilled me about what we were doing on Kaua'i with our cattle and what grasses we were using and such. I guess that I gave the right answers because John was very excited after Mr. Fagan had left and we were alone. I found out that some of the things we were having good success with were some of the very same projects John wanted to get started in Hāna. As Mr. Fagan left, he told John to take us to lunch at the Hāna Inn as his guests. After lunch, I had my first go at the infamous fifty-four bridges to Hāna, or, in our case, to Wailuku, as we were starting the other way.

That evening was our stag party of the convention. At the party, there was a stripper, and all the guys were yelling and having a good time. The stripper turned out to be a lady of the night, and she really got into her business after the show. Someone started a craps game and I got in. In those days, we didn't have much money to spend, but I had twelve dollars in my pocket. I watched the dice go around the table twice before I put any money down. On the third time around, when the dice came to me, I bet five dollars on my roll. Thirteen passes later, I finally crapped out. While I was putting my money in order, I was eased out of the game and never went back. When I got back to the hotel, all the wives and some of the earlier returnees were dancing to juke box music. I had a couple of dances with Nancy and then wanted to go to our room. Nancy didn't want to go to bed right then; she wanted to dance some more. But I persuaded her to come with me. When I got to the room and locked the door, I started to pull money out of my pockets. First, I gave her the equivalent of one month's salary to deposit in our Kaua'i bank to our account. Then, I gave her over one-hundred dollars to spend on herself and the children. The rest I kept for myself. I have never gotten into another craps game.

When I first started with Garden Island Motors, the Ford Dealers in Hawai'i, they would have an annual softball tournament on Labor Day weekend. Every year, it was on a different island. I started to play for GIM in about 1953 and continued until 1956 when the tournament was discontinued. In 1954, we went to Kona for the tournament. While at one of the games at Konawaena High School's field, where we played all of our games, I met my ninth grade English teacher, William Buttles. He invited me to his home after the game and proceeded to get me drunk. We had a great time reminiscing about the days at 'Iolani before the War. He was, by this time, vice-principal of Konawaena.

I was the catcher for our team and loved it because I didn't have to run around the outfield like I did when I played centerfield for Menlo Junior College in California. I also played softball in a church league on Kaua'i. One can't believe how the men of the cloth can argue with the umpires and among themselves. It was sure an eye opener for me.

In 1954, a group of Kaua'i farmers started forming a credit union and asked me to join. I agreed and took the lowest member number that was available. It was number thirteen. No one else wanted it because they thought that the number thirteen was bad luck. It sure wasn't for me. I was immediately appointed to the credit committee. The committee was made up of George Kawakami, Richard Wong, and myself. Our job was to approve, disapprove, or make additional restrictions on all the borrowing applications. I spent twenty-five years on the committee and then six years as a member of the board of directors. I saw the credit union grow from its inception to an organization of about one hundred million dollars in assets and several thousand members. We helped a great many people save money, get started in business, and finance the purchases of automobiles and household appliances, among other things. One of our most important lending operations was the college loan program with the federal government. We helped send many of Kaua'i's children to college, those who might otherwise not have gone at all. I was defeated for a third term on the board because I deemed it more important to go to Honolulu to see one of our newborn grandchildren than stay for the annual meeting. So, after thirty-one years of service, I became a simple member where I remained until 1990 when I closed my account.

In 1955, I got my grandfather's permission to have some of the old monkeypod trees in the Hule'ia Valley harvested. Monkeypod trees have a large, black bean for a seedpod that the cattle love because it is sweet. The cattle eat the beans and pass the seeds through their digestive tracts unharmed. I have seen a cow pie with twenty-one seedlings growing in it. The valley was filled with young trees, and I wanted to get rid of the old trees so that the young ones would have room to grow. I can't remember how many board feet we were able to get out of the valley, but some of the oldest trees were beginning to have rotten centers. Foster Equipment Company from Honolulu did the harvesting. They had just finished harvesting the camphor trees at the Valley House in the Keapana Valley area and had all of their equipment on the island. I went down into the valley in 2002, and some of the young trees that I had seen in 1955 were now four or more feet in diameter and could be harvested.

At this time, Nancy was pregnant with our fourth child, and she would go walking in the evenings, with me following along after her in the car with the children. Yum Yum, our dog, would go along. One evening, Nancy was chased by a cow because the dog was with her and the cow had a newborn calf nearby. Nancy quickly scrambled over a gate and got out of the way. We had a good laugh over that one. Our son Richard was born about two weeks after the cow incident and was not in the least affected by the scramble. We now had four children, two boys and two girls, a balanced inventory.

The ranch had two noncontiguous pastures where we pastured cattle. One was in Nāwiliwili Valley and the other was near the jail at Wailua opposite the golf course. In these pastures, we kept steers, which were growing and starting to fatten for market. At Wailua, there were several times that the Lihue Plantation, while clearing the edges of their cane fields, would break a hole in the fence and the cattle would get out. We would have to go out and try to get all the cattle back into the pasture and repair the fence. One Sunday evening, we didn't get home until after ten at night. These pastures were very productive, but fencing was expensive. In both places, there was one fence for the whole area, and everything outside the fence was someone else's property. After I left the ranch, these pastures were abandoned or leased to someone else. At Pāpa'a in the Moloa'a district, we had a small pasture where we could keep eight steers. We spent a lot of time and money building a fence around the whole property. The second time we put new steers on the land, one disappeared and was never found. I suspected what had happened to the steer but was never able to prove anything. My grandfather then sold the land to the Gerbode family, who were Waterhouse cousins on my grandfather's side of the family.

When I first started working on the ranch in 1942, we were doing everything in the old fashioned ways. This meant doing a lot of roping and chasing the cattle in a way that made them afraid of anyone on horseback. After all the sugarcane had been harvested and all the new fencing had been put in place, we started being gentler with the cattle. After a couple of years, the cattle were no longer afraid of the cowboys and were easier to handle. This was true except for the branding operation, which we did in the old ways until the middle fifties. The way we did it meant roping the calves and, then, throwing them to the ground, castrating the bull calves, earmarking all the calves, and branding them with a hot iron. From then on, the calves were pretty wild, and it took at least two years before they quieted down. In about 1950, my grandfather decided that all the calves should be dehorned. This was a process whereby the young horn buds were cut out of the heads of the calves. It was a bloody and painful operation and did not do anything to make the calves any tamer.

In about 1954, I read in a cattlemen's journal about a caustic paste that would stop the growth of horns and not really hurt the calves. Not long after, we started using the paste. I read another article about docking sheep's tails with the use of a specially made rubber band that could also be used for castrating. With the caustic paste and the rubber bands and their special applicator in hand, we started using them. At first, we would go out into the pastures as the calves were being born, roping them and applying the paste and rubber bands on the newborn calves. Very soon, we noticed that some of the cows would have sores on their udders where the calves put their heads while they were nursing. We now built a small two-penned corral to hold the calves for a few hours so that the paste would not rub off on the cows. We would drive the newborn calves and their mothers into the corral, separate them and do our work on the calves. After we thought that the paste had dried sufficiently, we would open the gate and let the mothers get reunited with their calves. Then we would turn them out into a pasture with no pregnant cows. In this way, we would know which cows had not conceived and would mark them so that, if in the following year they hadn't conceived again, they would become hamburger. By using this system, our cattle became very tame and made them a lot easier to work with. We could now do the separating of the cows and calves on foot. We tried using the rubber bands on dogs to bob their tails and it worked well. The rubber bands were also used to dehorn calves without the trauma of surgical dehorning for those calves that had been missed or that the paste had rubbed off. In the late fifties, we bought some polled Hereford bulls, and then we didn't have to use so much caustic paste.

We raised and trained all of our own horses for our work on the ranch. When I first started working on the ranch, we would pick out the colts that we wanted to start working with and bring them to Kīpū. At first, we would just put a blindfold over their eyes and saddle them. Whoever was going to use that horse would get into the saddle and let it buck. Usually, when the blindfold came off and the horse saw a man on its back, it would start bucking. We would ride the young colts around in a round corral until they wouldn't buck anymore. Then, we would start the actual training, learning to turn with the pressure of the bit and reins. Some horses were easier than others to get tamed down, but some would fight you for a long time. This was the old way and was called "breaking in the horse." In fact, what you did was break the spirit of the horse. One of my best cattle horses was one who wouldn't let her original rider ride her. The man was not a good bucking bronco rider and was scared of the horse. I took over the training of the horse, and we had a love-hate relationship that was fun. Even after she was fully trained, if I got into an unbalanced position she would dump me and then stop and watch me get up and come and catch her. I would always pet her and tell her that there were no hard feelings. She would always seem to have a smile on her face every time she dumped me. She was one horse that I never had to spur to make her go, and she always gave her all. I had always thought that, if you started with a horse in a kind gentle way, you would have better luck. I tried this method on a Morgan colt and had him working in two weeks. Unfortunately my grandfather sold him to a ranch on the Big Island before I could really prove my theory over time with this horse. And because I left the ranch soon after this, I never got another chance, but I think I proved my point. This is the way the Horse Whisperer does it.

In 1956, my grandfather decided that it would be a good idea if we got a livestock scale. He got the idea from the Robinson's at Makaweli, who had been using scales on their herd for years. I had learned, by now, not to fight my grandfather about any changes in the way we operated. When I had an idea that I wanted to try, I would put the idea in his mind and keep reminding him about the suggestion. Pretty soon, he would tell me to go ahead as though the deal was his idea. We finally started using the scale to separate the steers for market by weight instead of only by eye. The most telling instance came when we were separating heifers for the replacement in the breeding herd. One day, we had done the separating by weight instead of by eye and my grandfather came along and saw a heifer that was quite a bit taller that the rest in the discard group. He wanted to know why we had culled her out. I told him that I had set the scale at a certain weight and had run the whole group through the scale, any animal that lifted the bar would go into the group that we would keep, and the rest would be fattened for market. This process of using the scale helped us upgrade our herd much more quickly and scientifically. We also used the scale to weigh our young replacement bulls for weight gains and fast growth.

Another useful addition at about this time was the purchase of a squeeze chute. We now were able to brand all our calves without having to rope them and throw them to the ground. This further helped gentle our cattle. The squeeze chute now made it possible to check all of our first-time heifers to see if they were pregnant so that we didn't have to carry any free loaders.

Before the coming of the scales and squeeze chute, we purchased a mechanical posthole digger and a front-end loader for one of our Ford tractors. These pieces of equipment made life a lot easier for us. There were still many places that we had to work under the old style conditions.

In the late 1930s, my grandfather had given a piece of land to a niece and her husband to build a home on. They never built anything on the land but held it until the end of World War II when they sold it to a developer who built apartments on the property. My grandfather was so upset about this that he swore he would never give or sell a piece of land to anyone in his family. Mother tried but was turned down, as was I in the early sixties. He sold some valuable pieces of land to friends who then, later, sold the land to developers. That didn't seem to bother him at all.

One day in early 1958, my grandfather told me he was leaving the entire ranch to his son Robin, and I was to get nothing. I told him that I had been brought up as a son and asked, "What am I to do now?" He said he would sell me all of his controlling stock in Garden Island Motors. At that time I had no idea how I could swing such a deal on my salary as ranch foreman. My brother Charles came up with a plan, which we presented to the bank. They agreed to finance me if it was okay with my grandfather.

When I presented the plan to my grandfather he said, "Okay." I now became the major controlling stockholder in GIM. The deal was that I was to pay him thirty-thousand dollars cash and another thirty-thousand dollars eighteen months after his death. This money would go toward paying his inheritance tax bill. My note of thirty-thousand dollars would be paid off with the dividends from GIM. My grandfather lived until 1964, and, by that time, I had just about paid off the original loan. Eighteen months after his death, the bank happily allowed me to renegotiate the loan for the final thirty-thousand dollars, and my grandfather was paid in full.

As part of the deal, I was to see that my grandfather was elected to the board of directors, and also to the office of president so that he could qualify for the company medical plan. The other employees of the ranch were covered under a retainer system with Jay M. Kuhns, the retired plantation doctor. My family and I could have been covered under this setup, but we opted to go to Dr. Samuel Wallis, the then Lihue Plantation doctor, at our own expense. Later, my family and I became covered under the Garden Island Motors plans. I continued to go to GIM one day a week until the end November 1962.

In June of 1960, the ranch hosted a group of mainland ranchers touring the Islands under the auspices of the Western Livestock Journal, an industry trade newspaper. We set up a big tent in our yard and fixed a Hawaiian style lunch for them. The menu was laulaus, lomi salmon, boiled taro instead of poi, and sweet potatoes. We also had sliced fresh pineapples with sodas and beer. After lunch, I gave a talk on a fertilizer and rotation test that we had employed and now use as a standard practice. I got many letters from the people who were thanking Nancy and me for the lunch and commending me on my talk. This was the first year that this tour had been held. The next year, the local ranchers were not as open hearted. In the middle of 1961, the Western Livestock Journal offered a tour of New Zealand and Australia. Nancy said, "Let's go!" My worry was how were we going to pay for this trip. "We'll, just borrow from our children's saving accounts," she said, and we signed up for the tour.

In 1961, I was appointed to be the Kaua'i member of the State Board of Agriculture by Governor William Quinn and was confirmed by the State Senate. I served until 1963 when John Burns defeated Bill Quinn in the November 1962 elections. I had been chosen as one of the democrats on the board. Dr Kenneth Otagaki was the other democrat. After the elections, we were all asked to give courtesy resignations. All but Dr. Otagaki's resignation was accepted, and we were all out of office. Ken Otagaki eventually became the director of the board replacing Admiral Chun Hoon, a republican. My place on the board was given to a member of the ILWU.

When I went to Honolulu for the first meeting of the new board, we had three full days of indoctrination into the workings of the various departments. There I met new people and some old friends, namely Ernest Willers the state veterinarian, Takuji Fujimura and Kenji Ego, classmates from Lihue Grammar School, and a couple of men from the Forestry Department. Alex Napier, a new member who was with Kahua Ranch and Slaughterhouse on O'ahu, knew more of the staff than any of the other members of the Board. So he and I had a good head start on the rest of the board. After three days of intense meetings, we settled down to the regular business of the board. Our first order of business was to elect a chairman, and George Ii Brown was so elected. The next and more controversial was the head of the department. The previous board had chosen Wayne Collins, but there was some doubt that he was qualified. He had been a radio and television announcer before coming to the department. After much questioning, we found out that he had been a forestry major in college and was just the kind of man we needed. Next it was down to the normal regular business of the board.

After about a year, when we were in Honolulu for a regular monthly meeting, we stopped by a small pool in the middle of the quadrangle that made up the board of agriculture complex. While there, I noticed some rather large, bass-like fish and asked what they were. Kenji Ego was summoned, and he told us that they were tucunaré from South America and that they had just produced a spawn of young. This was the first recorded spawning outside of South America, and they were hopeful of further spawning. Kenji told me that they were looking for a place where they could raise the young so they too might start reproducing. I told Kenji that we had just the reservoir they were looking for on the ranch, and that I would ask my grandfather if it would be okay.

When I got back to Kaua'i, I asked my grandfather about the deal and he said it would be fine. My grandfather was a very forward-looking person. He was the first to bring largemouth bass from Kīlauea to Kīpū. As they multiplied, they migrated to the Hule'ia Stream and, from there, into most of the reservoirs on the east side of Kaua'i. The largemouth bass that were introduced into the Kīpū reservoirs were called "Charley Fish" in honor of Mr. Charles A. Rice.

As soon as I could, I called Kenji Ego and told him that the deal was a go. He then told me that morning someone had entered the premises during the previous night and poisoned all the adult fish. He also told me that, luckily, the young fish had been moved to another pool and they all had survived. We, then, started to make plans for the transfer of the young fish to Kaua'i.

The first thing they did was to bring some threadfin shad to Kaua'i and released them into the reservoir where the young tucunaré were to be released. The shad were for food for the young fish. About three weeks after the shad arrived and were released, we had a very heavy rain and they all went over the spillway and were never seen again. This was no problem, for there were many mosquito fish and baby tilapia for food. Finally, the young fish, about six to seven inches in length, arrived and were released. There were twenty-two of them. The rest of the original brood was released into Lake Wilson on O'ahu. Before I left the ranch, we caught a couple to see how their growth was progressing and found that they had grown almost six inches in four months. After a couple of years, there were enough young fish to slowly stock some of the other island reservoirs. That is the story of how the tucunaré got to Kaua'i. I have since discovered that there were fifty-seven fingerlings that hatched from the original spawning and the twenty-two that were brought to Kaua'i are the only ones that ever produced any young. The other thirty-five just disappeared.

The board met once a month, mostly in Honolulu, but we also met on Hawai'i, Maui and Kaua'i at least once a year. It was on a visit to the Big Island where we saw what could happen when wild cattle and goats are excluded from an area of the native forest. We were visiting a piece of land in the Kona region of the Big Island owned by the Bishop Estate. The Estate had hired a retired state forester by the name of Bill Bryan to manage their forests. He had an area around an old koa tree bulldozed of all weedy underbrush, and, in about three months, the cleared area was completely covered with young Koa trees. It was a great example of what the native plants could do if given the chance.

On this same trip I stayed with Donn Carlsmith at Pu'u Wa'awa'a, the former Hind Ranch, which had been purchased by the Dillingham interests from Honolulu. The Carlsmith firm were their attorneys and were assisting in managing the properties. I was met at the Kona Airport by Donn's Factorum, Toshi, and taken to the Kona Surf because Donn wouldn't be over to Pu'u Wa'awa'a for several more hours. We opened the bar and had several Bloody Marys before driving to Pu'u Wa'awa'a. With Donn, we had lunch and at least one bottle of wine. So, I was in pretty good shape when the meal was over. After lunch, Donn said, "Let's go up to Hale Piula and see if we can get some mongoose bait." I should explain the meaning of Hale Piula. "Piula" is the Hawaiian word for corrugated iron roofing. Kona and the whole west side of the island of Hawai'i has no running streams, so all the water for the livestock and home consumption had to be caught and held in tanks for their day to day water needs. "Hale" is the Hawaiian word for house. Donn was the driver with Toshi and a Hawaiian man by the name of Charlie in the back seat and me riding shotgun. We had a thirty-thirty rifle for protection. On the way up the mountain, we saw a white peacock in the distance. It was one of a wild flock. In a clearing, we raised a herd of goats and Donn said to me, "Take the gun and shoot one." Just as I was taking aim on a big, black billy goat, I heard Donn say to me, "Shoot the white one." I quickly readjusted my aim and fired a shot. Much to my surprise, the white goat fell over.

I heard Toshi from the back seat say to Donn, "That guy from Kaua'i one good shot." Later, up at Hale Piula, I got another chance to shoot, and, with one shot, I knocked over another goat. Now, they had all the bait for mongoose trapping that they needed for quite a while. I gave the gun back to Donn and whispered to him that I didn't want to do any more shooting. Two goats with two shots and now I wanted to rest on my laurels.

The following day, the board had their monthly meeting at the Kona Surf Hotel. The meeting lasted for most of the day, so there wasn't much sightseeing done. The next day, the board went over to the Hilo side of the island and went to Kulani Prison to see some of the tree planting being done by the prisoners. They were planting tropical ash, and, for the most part, you hardly saw any prisoners because they were all in the forest doing the planting. They all returned to the prison at the end of the day. It gets pretty cold in the woods after the sun goes down.

In the early fifties, Grove Farm Plantation dug a tunnel through the Hoary Head Range so they could truck their cane from the Līhue side to the Kōloa Mill to be processed into sugar. After this successful venture, they planned a water tunnel from the Halfway Bridge area to Waita Reservoir at a lower level than the vehicular tunnel. Bill Moragne, manager of Grove Farm wrote to my grandfather warning him that the tunnel might have a negative effect on our water supply. My grandfather ignored the letter and never did anything about the possible problem. While drilling the tunnel they came to a dike formation, but, when they had drilled and blasted through the formation, our spring went dry. The spring was on Grove Farm land, and we bought the potable water from Grove Farm. My grandfather blamed Grove Farm for the problem but couldn't do anything about it. We were lucky that there was a drilling outfit on the island and they had just finished a well for the county. We were able to hire them to drill a well for us above the stable area. The wellhead was about four-hundred-eight feet above sea level when we started. They drilled down to sea level, and there seemed to be an adequate supply of water, so the casing was installed. While the well was being drilled, the electric line was built to the wellhead. Then we assembled a twenty-thousand gallon steel tank. When the casing was completely installed, the pump and water pipe was let down and we started the test pumping. After a day and a half, the well was dry. There was not enough water for the sustained pumping that was needed to supply the water for all the buildings and water troughs needed to water all the cattle. The drilling people suggested that we drill deeper and maybe there would be enough water deeper down. After two days of additional drilling, I was up on the hill with the drillers and one of them told me about a well that he drilled in Honolulu for a golf course. They had drilled until they hit water but it wasn't enough so they continued to drill. After going down another twenty feet, the drill dropped about ten feet. They had hit a lava tube and then there was more than enough water for the golf course. After about fifteen minutes, our drill dropped about five feet and we had all the water we needed. What a coincidence!

After this event, the pump was reinstalled and the tank filled and flushed and filled again. By now, the six-inch pipe for the main line down to the camp and headquarters had arrived, and the cowboys turned into plumbers. We got E. F. Nilson to dig the trench for the pipe we were to install, and we went right to work. It took us the better part of two weeks to finish the job, and, when the water was finally turned on, everybody was happy again. It had been over a year of living under strict water rationing, and, now, we had all the water we needed. A down side of the new system with its greater pressure was that some of the old pipes would occasionally burst and would have to be repaired immediately, day or night. The new system was finished just in time for Nancy and I to go on the trip to New Zealand and Australia.

In retrospect, this trip to the Antipodes was the reason I left the ranch at the end of 1962. We had just completed the new well, a twenty-thousand gallon storage tank, a new six-inch water line, and the water was flowing. Nancy had suggested to me that we go on this trip right after the notice came out in 1961. I had asked my grandfather for permission to go, and he had given me his okay. At the last possible minute, my grandfather's wife Pat decided that she wanted to go and got approval. my grandfather's brother Harold Rice wanted me to give up our trip and stay home and watch the ranch. But I wouldn't do it and went on the trip anyway.

After returning from the New Zealand trip, I just didn't have my heart in the ranch any more. Uncle Harold and I had clashed before. He always wanted my grandfather to try different projects that I knew wouldn't work, and Uncle Harold didn't like to be argued with. One night during the 1962 Fourth of July weekend, my grandfather slipped and fell after going to the bathroom. I was called to help get him up again. Because he weighed over three-hundred pounds and had very smooth skin, there was nothing to hold on to when we tried to lift him. Solomon Malina, one of the cowboys, was called to help get him back in bed. After we put a belt around him, we were finally able to get him on his feet and into bed. He never was able to leave his bed again, and he died in 1964 at eighty-seven years of age. Solomon Malina and I took turns sleeping at his house so there was always a man to help the nurses turn him during the night. In 1963, on Maui, his brother Harold died. After Mother and I told my grandfather about the death of his brother, we left the room and we heard him say to Pat, "Harold said we should fire Hobey." My grandfather wanted me to go to Maui for the funeral. I felt like a hypocrite for saying okay. With my November paycheck, Charlie Ishii, the bookkeeper, also handed me a letter from my grandfather listing a dozen things I was to do and not to do in the future. If I had accepted the things listed in the letter, I would have been a wimp and nothing but a "yes man." I got Nancy to ask Aunt Mabel if we could stay at her Poʻipū house while we built a new house for ourselves in Līhue. Aunt Mabel was thrilled to be one of the first one to know that I was quitting the ranch and was very happy to help us find a place to live. Once we had the assurance of a place to live, I wrote out my letter of resignation and went over my grandfather's house to give him my letter. Thus ended about twenty years at the ranch, with the exception of the time I spent in the Army and at school. In retrospect, it was the best thing that ever happened to me. From that point on, I didn't have the strain of having to work under the terms of the letter. Furthermore, I was being paid more and had time to myself and family.

Raising children in the fifties was a lot easier than it is now. Working and living on a ranch was wonderful for the kids. They could go out and catch crayfish in the stream that ran through the ranch and boil them and have a snack. For fruit they had guavas, mangos, and vi apples for the picking. Our children learned from the neighbor children to make a mixture of soy sauce, vinegar, and salt to dip the half ripe fruit into. One day, Nancy heard Kathy's plaintive call for help. When she got out into the yard, she saw Kathy up in the vi apple tree crying that she was stuck and couldn't get down. Nancy just said to her, "Your father will be home in about twenty minutes, and he will get you down." With that, Kathy suddenly knew how to get down out of the tree.

When I first started on the ranch, I wasn't paid very much and we had to scrounge to supplement our diet. I did a lot of fishing and hunting, but that wasn't always successful. So we started raising rabbits for food. It was always fun to help your dad catch a rabbit and kill it for dinner because rabbit is very tasty when it is fried. One day, just before Easter when David and Kathy were five and four years old, Nancy's mother, Sue brought some Easter presents for the kids. When the kids saw the presents, they asked where they came from. Sue Sloggett said, "The Easter Bunny." We never ate rabbit again, and I had to get rid of my rabbit farm.

The vet for the ranch was Rex Glaisyer. Remember that he had been my roommate at boarding school for three years, so we were always close. One afternoon when the children were all playing the in the yard, Rex drove into our yard with a baby chimpanzee in the car with him. The circus had come to Kaua'i, and Rex had to monitor the chimps while they were on the island. There were three chimps in the group, but he only had the little one. He got the chimp out of the car and made him shake hands with the children. After shaking hands, the chimp walked over to the fence, climbed to the top, and started walking along the ridge. My grandfather had had a small playpen built for the kids so they wouldn't run off when put out to play. Guess what? Right behind the chimp was little Kathy following along. From then on, we had to make the children wear shoes while in the pen with their shoelaces knotted so they couldn't take them off.

Joan was a child who was calm and peaceful most of the time. Whenever she did something naughty and needed a time out, she was sent to her room.

Then, she never asked to come out. Sometimes she would be forgotten for hours, but she didn't seem to mind. We wondered about this at the time, but the thought never dawned on us until we discovered her reading a book. We knew the she enjoyed reading, but never did we suspect that being sent to her room was no punishment at all. I can't remember if we devised some other punishment for Joan. Oh, yes! Joan says we made her go out into the yard and play. But she would just ask David or Kathy to throw her book out the window into the yard so she could read.

Richard, our youngest, was another easy child, for he would never argue with us when we wouldn't let him do what he wanted. He would wait a short time and go ahead and do what he wanted to do in the first place anyway. We had a stray female dog walk in one day and adopt us. She was a lovable dog and fit right into the family. She and Richard were fast friends, and they would go exploring together. One day, when Rick was about five, Nancy looked out into the pasture next to the house and saw the cattle running and then turning to look curiously back and then move forward and then turn and run again. Nancy then saw a little, blond head and the tail of the dog moving through the tall grass. It was Rick and the dog out for a walk. The cattle were young heifers that had not had their first calves, so they were very curious.

Grandpa Charles A. Rice at the Hawai'i Constitutional Convention in 1954.

Grandpa Rice and Hobey admiring new Pangola grass.

Grandpa Rice's eightieth birthday party at Coco Palms September 1956.
Left to Right: Nancy Goodale, Robin Rice, Pat Rice, David Goodale, Hobey, Rick Goodale, Kathy Goodale, Edith Plews, Jack Plews, Charles Rice, Juliet Wichman, Joan Goodale, John Plews, Wendy Wichman, Jeanne Wichman, and Charles Wichman.

South Pacific movie plantation managers and their wives at party hosted by Emile at the Birkmeyer home in 1957. Amanda Birkmeyer, Hobey, and Nancy Goodale, Brud and Shirley Larson, Fred and Louise Lawrence, Helen and Wayne Ellis, and Keith and Frances Tester.

Christmas picture–Goodale family at Kīpū, 1960.

CHAPTER NINE

The Sixties and Līhue

After I left the ranch and moved into Aunt Mabel's beach cottage at Po'ipū, Nancy and I started to look for a piece of property that we could afford to buy and build a house on. Dora Jane Cole had a piece in the new section of the Isenberg Tract in Līhue that she wanted to sell so that she could build her own home on another piece of land in the same subdivision. I had also started work as a trainee at Garden Island Motors at that time. I had already been working in the collection end of the business, and my next job was to start at the bottom of the parts department assisting with the annual inventory count. At this job, I spent two days on the floor counting nuts, bolts, and cotter pins. Later, I started to sell cars, but my first love was to work on the delinquent loan list. By 1953, we had sold so many new cars that our inventory of used cars had climbed way too high and we were having a hard time paying the bank for the new cars that had been sold. We had to mortgage the company to get cash to pay off our flooring. I was making three-hundred dollars a month on the ranch and one-hundred dollars per month for being treasurer of Garden Island Motors. The mortgage that I had to sign, as treasurer, was one-hundred-thousand dollars, and it sure scared the heck out of me. By 1957, we had paid off the mortgage, and, for some reason, I was a hero in the eyes of the bank. This worked to my benefit when I needed to borrow money to pay my grandfather for his controlling interest in Garden Island Motors.

The year that we lived at Aunt Mabel's cottage in Po'ipū was full of new things to do. We were now in an area where several of our friends lived, and we had a lot more social activity than when we were at Kīpū. The house was adjacent to Brennecke's Beach where the body surfing was good. In April of 1963, Nancy quit smoking, and, then, she got me to quit. I quit in June and have never had another cigarette. I quit cold turkey, and the kids still talk about what a bear I was.

Every afternoon when I got home from work, I would go body surfing or sharpen up on my golf game. The yard was big enough for some pretty good chipping, and there was a small sand spit in front of the house where I could sharpen up on my sand game. One of Rick's friends was Eric Toulon, who, like Rick, was a towhead. So, when they were body surfing, as long as Nancy could see two white heads, she knew that they were all right. One of the new things was a TV set, which we watched religiously. After all those years at Kīpū with no TV, it was a welcome change. One benefit of no TV was that our children were all good readers. It was a little sad when we left for our new house in Līhue, but we were able to come back for a week or two a few more times before the lot was sold to the county for park purposes.

By April of 1963, our new house was under construction. Bear Kure of Koloa was the contractor, and Hale Kauai was the material supplier. We did not have an architect, but Wayne and Helen Ellis helped us with the design plans, and Hale Kauai's draftsman drew up the plans. It turned out to be a very comfortable house, in which we lived for thirty-three years. The original plan was for a three-bedroom, two-bath house, but we added a wall on one bedroom and made it into a four bedrooms. Now each of our daughters had a room to themselves and the boys shared one room. The boys didn't matter too much because David was off to Hawai'i Preparatory Academy on the Big Island for high school and would only be home for vacations. Therefore, one room was plenty for them.

One day, when we had a gang of men cleaning the stream in the Nāwiliwili Valley, they caught one of the mud terrapins and gave it to me. The terrapins were supposed to be very high in aphrodisiac qualities. Wayne Ellis called a Chinese friend in Honolulu for the spices with which to cook the animal to make the soup. When all the spices arrived, Bear Kure had one of his friends do the honors and made the soup. The soup was good-tasting but you had to use your imagination for anything else.

For the first fifteen years, we had some pretty wild parties at our home, some lasting into the early morning hours. After that, things got a little more subdued. We really enjoyed the house but had no regrets when we moved in December of 1996. I asked Richard Tongg, a Honolulu landscape architect to do the landscape plan for the yard. I did all the planting and maintenance. I had told Mr. Tongg that I wanted something that looked nice but would not keep me so occupied that I couldn't play golf. He was a golfer also, and we played together all the time. Everybody said that I had a Chinese yard because he had only flowering trees in the front yard, while the back yard was full of fruit trees. I had a breadfruit tree and a navel orange tree in the back yard and two grapefruit trees in the side yard. The orange tree would produce fruit from November until March, and the grapefruit trees would last another month and a half more. These three trees sure saved us a lot of money over the years. The breadfruit tree was also very productive until Hurricane Iwa in 1982 when it was blown over on its side. The main trunk was cut up and hauled away, but the stump sent out sprouts from which we air-layered at least fifty starts. I let one sprout grow up to produce fruit. But the flavor of these fruit was nothing like the original tree, so I finally cut the whole thing out.

In August of 1964, my grandfather, Charles Atwood Rice, died just two weeks short of his eighty-eighth birthday. He was the last one of our family who could say that he was made an American citizen by an act of Congress. He had one of the last, big, old-time funerals with mountains of flowers. With him went the first hand knowledge of the overthrow of the monarchy in Hawai'i and much of the early history of Kaua'i. He was very reluctant to share his knowledge and was very loyal to his friends and wouldn't tell stories about them. Nancy and I got a little of what he knew when he used to stop in and have a cup of coffee before we went to work in the mornings. But if someone showed a tape recorder or any other electronic device, he would clam up and quit talking.

In 1968, Tamotsu Shinseki, our GMI manager retired, and I took over the reins of Garden Island Motors. I soon found out that I was not cut out for the daily grind and could do more good being a PR person. Ron Harker, who was the sales manager, took over and ran the company until 1984 when he retired. After another stint at running the company, I found that I was still not cut out for the grind and asked my son-in-law, Richie Richardson, if he would like to come to Kaua'i and run the company. Richie stayed on the job until the end of 1990 when he went into the real estate for himself. Then, my son David took over the running of the company. Finally, in 1998, we sold the company to Walsh Hanley of Hilo on the Big Island and we got out of the automobile business completely. What with the Internet, customers could get to see the cost of the cars and would know how much we would be making on a sale, and government regulations within the automobile business wasn't any fun. Plus, the help that we could get wasn't as dedicated as those of old. When Kazuo Mikasa our service manager, retired after working for us for forty-four years, Wally Shota, his assistant took his place. Wally retired in 1990. After that, it was one service manager after another. We had a sales manager and a salesman take us not only for quite a bit of money but a lot of good will. In retrospect, GIM was good to me. It gave me something to do and helped me send four children to private boarding school and then college. I also got to take advantage of some wonderful trips because our parts manager would not take any trips that would take him out of the country. If the trip was to Las Vegas he would be off in a minute.

Every year, there would be an auto dealers meeting on one of the neighbor islands, although never on Oʻahu. Business was at a minimum, and there was a lot of golf playing and partying. The business meetings were usually held on Friday morning and a scramble golf tournament that afternoon. The next day, there would be a tournament for both the men and the women. There would always be visiting speaker for the Saturday night banquet. This speaker was usually from one of the big three automobile manufacturers. At these meetings, we met some nice people who we still see occasionally even after getting out of the auto business.

In 1962, Tamotsu Shinseki, Ron Harker, and I went to the new car showing, which was held at the Royal Hawaiian Hotel in Waikīkī. This was when the Ford Mustang was introduced and Lee Iacocca was there to show off his new baby to the world. We all commented that Iacocca was a very motivated and ambitious young man and would go places in the automobile industry. History has proven us correct.

In 1968, Nancy and I went to San Francisco for the Ford and Mercury introductions. Ford had their cars at the basketball arena over in Oakland and was an Ice Show where all the cars were presented on ice. The Mercury show was in San Francisco proper. For the Ford showing, we all gathered at the Hilton in San Francisco for lunch and a "rah-rah" talk before boarding buses for the basketball arena. After the show, one of the Ford reps from the San Jose district office took Nancy and me to the Jack London Square for dinner and back over the bay bridge to see the Mercuries.

The next day, we had to get out of our room at the Miyako Hotel. We left the City and drove to Modesto to spend a couple of days with Mary and Bob Ballentine. Bob used to be the Jeep and American Motors dealer on Kauaʻi, and Mary is my cousin. After leaving them, we drove back to San Francisco and stayed at a motel at Fisherman's Wharf. The night before we were to leave for home, Nancy wanted to call Rick to see how everything was at home. When the operator asked him if he would accept the call he said, "I don't have the authority," and promptly hung up. The operator thought that this was one of the funniest things she had ever heard but connected us up again right away. This time we used our credit card. This was all because David had called home from college once before when we weren't home, and he and Rick had about an hour's conversation causing Nancy to scold Rick. The night before we returned, David and Rick had dinner with Dick and Sue Sloggett. Nancy's mother was not well at the time. David left for college early the next morning, and we were returning that afternoon. Nancy's mother died during the night, but Dick didn't tell David that his grandmother had died and let him go on to school. We returned home from the mainland to the sad news.

Before returning home, we stopped at Fishermen's Wharf and picked up a dozen frozen Dungeness crab to bring home for the Crab Group. Clyde French had started the Crab Group a few years earlier when he returned from a mainland trip. We postponed the crab dinner for two weeks, and then we had the Crab Group in for salad, sourdough French bread, and crab. This became a tradition for any of us who traveled through San Francisco to bring home crabs for the Crab Group. The crab was always served with several loaves of sourdough French bread and a tossed salad. The first time that Clyde brought home crabs for dinner, Clint Childs and I were in the kitchen cleaning up when we noticed that a couple of plates had the whole body of the crab untouched. We promptly got to work cleaning them out of the meat for ourselves. We found out later that those plates were the ones Jack and Patti Sheehan had had. When we questioned the Sheehans, they said that they thought only the claws were any good. Clint and I had a good laugh and full bellies.

After a long trip to New Zealand in 1962 and the month we spent in Burlingame, our next trip was with Mother to Africa. (More on the travels of the Goodales in a later chapter.) Now life settled down to high school graduations. First was David, and, then, in two years, it was Kathy; Joan was next, and Rick was the last. We attended all the high school graduations but only two of the college ones. We attended Joan's graduation from Drake University in Des Moines, Iowa, and Rick's at the University of Hawai'i. Actually, though, it was not his college ceremony but his graduation from Medical School at the University of Hawai'i that we attended. What a relief when Rick was done with school. It was a long, hard drag with four in high school or college at the same time. Just think, tuition for four and the third quarter income tax estimated payments all at once. That made for some sleepless nights, but everything ended up okay.

Nancy had started learning how to play golf while in college, so, when Rick got into nursery school, she wanted to take it up again. She signed up with a group from the YWCA to take lesson from Toyo Shirai. I told her that, when she could go out and play nine holes, I would go out with her and beat her. This we did and I beat her the first time. But, then, Nancy beat me the second time out, and we were at it from that time on. After we got a little better, we joined golf clubs out at Wailua. Nancy joined the Kaua'i Women's Golf Club, and I joined the Aole Makana Club. Golf, then, became a large part of our lives. We played for years, and I still play the game today.

Another sport that we got into was sailing. The Kauai Yacht Club got in a few sunfish sailboats, and several of the members bought boats. Then, we started having races. It took a little while for some of us to get the hang of sailing, but we all got so that we could hold our own. For a while, we had annual races with the Outrigger Canoe Club from Honolulu. I don't think that I ever scored a point for our team, but we beat them three out of four times. Our children all kept asking us to let them take the boats by themselves. Before I would let any of them out by themselves, I would take them out one at a time and turn the boat over and make them right it several times. This was so they would not panic if it happened when they were out in the boat alone. When you want something bad enough, you can learn in a hurry, and hurry they did. We had several years of fun with the boats, but then golf got in the way. One by one, the boats were sold, and everyone started to play golf instead.

David went off to Hawai'i Prep in the fall of 1964 and graduated in 1967. He, then, went to Colorado State University in Fort Collins, Colorado. While there, he became a member of the swimming and water polo teams. They traveled over much of the West participating in games and meets. He graduated from Colorado State in 1972. He said that it was hard for a jock to finish in four years. So, after graduating, he took a tour of the country in his car. He visited his great-grandmother Reynolds in Flint, Michigan, while on his travels. He also drove up into Canada and into Maine to visit his Aunt and Uncle the Hamilton Mitchells, but he bypassed New York City because of traffic. After returning home, David tried doing lawn and garden maintenance in the Princeville area but that didn't work out. He, then, went to work for his grandmother at Hā'ena and Limahuli, since Mother was just starting to develop a garden there.

Kathy was the next to go to boarding school. She went to Seabury Hall at Makawao, Maui, and an Episcopal boarding school for girls that had just started. She was one of the first students. After graduating in 1969, she was accepted at the University of Northern Colorado in Greeley, just a few miles from David. Nancy, David, and I went to help get her settled. We had a couple of days in San Francisco and then took the train to Denver going up the Feather river Canyon in California. We got into Denver late, and our rental car was not ready. So we took a taxi to the hotel and got settled in. We got our car the next morning, and David made sure to take us to the Coors Brewery. After two days in Denver, we started north for Greeley

Just as we turned off the interstate heading toward Greeley, suddenly Kathy exclaimed, "What is that smell?"

I opened the window and took a good sniff and reported, "Sugar beets and cow shit. You better get used to it." Greeley was the home to a substantial sugar beet refinery, and the Moffat Meat Company had a large slaughterhouse and feedlot here. They used the sugar beet pulp for roughage in the fattening process. We got Kathy moved in and, then, went to a bank to open an account for her. For all of our children, I had the head of the First Hawaiian bank in Līhue write a letter of introduction to the manager of the bank where they were going to school. It sure made a difference in how the student was treated. I think it was the manager of the bank where we took Joan in Des Moines to open an account who said, after he had read the letter and seen Clyde French's signature, "I know him. I went to banking school with him a couple of years ago."

After taking care of Kathy, we went to Fort Collins with David. He got us into a Best Western Motel on the outskirts of town. The next day, David took us on a tour of the town and the school campus. That night, David asked us to come to his house where he was living and cook dinner for him and his roommates. We found a Safeway supermarket that had all the makings for chicken hekka. I had asked David about how many there would be for dinner and he said about a dozen. I knew how young men's appetites were, so I got plenty of food. That was a smart move because we fed about twenty people that night.

The next morning, Nancy and I headed south sightseeing. We drove up to Estes Park and went to the summit. We were advised at lunch to start back because it looked like snow and the gates would be locked. If we didn't get out before this happened, we would be stuck for the night. Driving up the canyon, we were amazed at the landscape. How the first pioneers ever found their way through the mountains was truly amazing. Now we know why they are called the Rockies.

The next day, we checked out of the motel after making reservations to return in two days. We drove around Denver to Silver City to see a quaint old town and a gold mine. Then it was down south to Colorado Springs with a visit to the Air Force Academy and to the top of Pike's Peak. We spent the night in Colorado Springs and had dinner at The Red Barn. I had a steak, and Nancy had mountain oysters. At eight-thirty, a good country music band started playing, so we worked off some of the dinner by dancing to the country style music. The following day, we headed south again to the Royal Gorge and drove across the bridge spanning the gorge. I had gone through the gorge on my way to Texas during World War II. Our train had stopped just under the bridge, and we were able to get out and look up. I have always wanted to go back and look down. Here I was able to see the river from the top of the gorge. We, then, went west to Durango and north through Leadville to Vail where we had lunch. Finally, we headed back to Fort Collins. As I remember, it was about a five-hundred mile drive that day. That night, we picked up Kathy and David who joined us for dinner. It was David's birthday dinner a few days early. The next day, we drove south to Denver and our flight home.

I played a lot of golf in those days and also a lot of cribbage. I played with Bill Schwallie, Frank Sullivan, and Glen Lovejoy, the manager of the Kauai Yacht Club. We settled all of our debts on Christmas Eve every year. One year, very close to Christmas, I had a streak of good luck and had Frank Sullivan down several dollars when he made the comment that I had "jerked all the presents right out from under [his] Christmas Tree." A couple of days later, Nancy and I went over to Kalāheo to pick out a tree for ourselves. I told Nancy that I was going to get a tree for Frank and deliver it to him on the way home. This we did, and the look on Frank's face was worth every cent that the tree cost me. Frank was very careful about what he said after that.

Another fellow who became one of the assistant pros was Gordon Rabideau, a retired policeman from around Detroit, Michigan. Every Friday afternoon, Frank hosted a scramble game at the Surf. The players were divided into two teams; three team if there were more that twenty-one players. The stakes were one dollar automatic with the winners paying for the drinks. There usually wasn't enough money in the pot, so we always had to dig into our pockets. If someone happened to make a hole in one, he had to treat everybody who played. We never had a hole in one during the Friday scramble, but I had it happen to me four times in our Wednesday games.

The first time we were playing in two five-somes, so the bill was a goodly sum. That time, as we were sitting around the table, Frank moaned, "There are eleven of us here and only two have not had holes in one yet. And one of them, my dad, does not play golf. The other one is me." There wasn't much sympathy for poor, old Frank. Sympathy was not an emotion that ever surfaced in any of these matches.

At the Kauai Surf, I played Wednesdays with Wayne Ellis and Bill Schwallie, with Jud Atchison as my partner. It was with this group that I made four holes in one. It was an expensive proposition because these men were pretty good drinkers, as long as it was on my money. On Saturdays, I would play with Clyde French, Jack Sheehan, and Warren Robinson. Jack Sheehan always wanted to bet me a dollar automatic, and there were days when I would separate him from thirty to forty dollars. He was one of the nicest losers you would ever want to play with, but he was an obnoxious winner. Slowly, this group started to break up as people moved away and new players took their places. Finally the Kauai Surf was sold to Chris Hemmeter, and the golf course was reconfigured with Jack Nicholas as the architect.

The Saturday gang now moved to Kiahuna in Kōloa and picked up a couple of new players—Dave Hughson and Bill Balfour. This group lasted for four years when, then, both Balfour and Hughson were transferred to Oʻahu. After they left, we were down to Warren and myself, but were able to get Jack Canute and Bob Prosser to play with us at Wailua. We played at Wailua for several years, and I got another hole in one on the fourteenth hole there. This one wasn't so expensive, as it was early in the morning and none of us had more than one beer.

I started playing with a group in the late sixties who played on Thursdays, and, with some changes, they are still playing. I was the token haole, as all the snowbirds who used to play with us in the winter are either dead or don't come to Hawaiʻi anymore. The last of this gang are Mervyn Masumura, Walter Yamamoto, Val Hataishii and Tad Takiguchi. One time, my mother asked me to take her to church on a particular Sunday morning. So Nancy and I did, and Mother was happy. That afternoon, in a Yacht Club golf tournament, I got another hole in one on the fifth hole. When I next saw Mother, I told her she was an expensive luxury that I couldn't afford. No more going to church with her on the day of a tournament. I now have had six holes in one in my golf career.

In 1961, Sam Cooke and I went up to the Big Island for the International Billfish Tournament. We fished with Sam's brother Charles IV for five days with only one strike and no hookups. After the tournament was over, Wayne Ellis asked me if I would like to help him bring his boat back to Kauaʻi, and I accepted. We had a fun time coming home. I saw a lot of the Hawaiian Islands from the sea—views that I had never seen before. Clint Childs, who was working for Lihue Plantation at the time, was on board for this trip. After we left Lahaina, on the way to Molokaʻi, he pointed out where the new Amfac development of Kāʻanapali would be. From Lahaina to Kalaupapa we caught a twenty-pound mahimahi. I cleaned and filleted the fish, and we had half grilled for dinner, and the other half Clint poached for breakfast the next morning. We spent the night anchored off Kalaupapa and motored to Honolulu the next day. We got into Honolulu early enough to get fueled up so that we could get an early start the next morning. When we were about ten miles from Nāwiliwili, we got a good strike. Everyone was tired, and nobody wanted to reel in the fish. So Wayne told me to do the job. He slowed down slightly, but I still had one hell of a time reeling that ono in. It weighed about fifty pounds and was a nice fish.

Later in the year, I went out with Wayne over to Niʻihau with Sam Cooke and Brother Wilcox. On the way over to Hanalei, where we were supposed to pick up Jud Atchison, we got a big strike. Sam Cooke took the reel, and, in an hour, he had a one-hundred-fifty pound 'ahi up to the boat. We got into Hanalei around dark and spent the night anchored. Early the next morning, Jud showed up but made all kinds of excuses for not going with us. So, we left for Ni'ihau without him. Along the way, we caught a couple of ono and spent the night anchored off Ni'ihau. The next day, we caught nine more ono for a total of eleven. Over the next two years, we went to Ni'ihau on Memorial Day and Labor Day weekends. The usual crew was Wayne Ellis, Sam Wilcox, Clint Childs, Bob Morton, Bob Herkes, and myself. Bob Herkes was the cook, and I took care of icing the fish. One weekend, we caught thirty-seven ono, and I had my hands full trying to save the ice for the fish instead of for cocktails. On the Memorial Day weekend of 1963, while trolling over the flats of Ka'ula at about eleven o'clock in the morning, we got a strike. It was my turn to catch a fish, so I went right to work reeling the fish in and soon had the fish up to the boat. As soon as I saw that it was a rainbow runner, I told everybody that it was a new world's record. I held the record for thirteen years until a fisherman from California broke it. Later, I saw several rainbow runners that were fifteen to twenty pounds heavier than mine. Mine was only 31.5 pounds. The rainbow runner had just recently been recognized as a game fish, so I had an open field. On another one of our trips, we anchored off Ni'ihau. I always threw the anchor and made sure it was set right and then went to re-ice the fish that we had caught that day. Bob Herkes, as our cook, had gone below and showered. When he came up on deck, he was dressed in a tuxedo shirt and coat with raggedy shorts and a towel over his arm and said, "What will it be gentlemen." Everyone was so stunned that no one could say anything for a minute or two. Dinner that night was shrimp cocktail, Caesar salad, Chateaubriand and cherries jubilee for dessert.

We always entered the Hawai'i Big Game Fish Club's annual tournament in Kona, and we won more that our share of the awards. This was back in the days when the Honolulu boats hadn't really discovered Ka'ula Rock, and we had the place to ourselves.

One night, we anchored up at the Lehua end of Ni'ihau in a place we had never anchored before. At two in the morning, I got up to check the anchor line. But Wayne was already there doing the same thing. I told him that I couldn't sleep, and he said he couldn't also. We stayed up on the bow for about forty minutes more and then went back into the cabin and had a good sleep. The next morning, we heard men on a couple of Honolulu boats talking on the radio and asking each other what they had done about the tsunami alert at two. Wayne and I looked at each other and smiled. We knew why we couldn't sleep. The next time we went to Ni'ihau, our wives made us promise to call the Coast Guard and let them know where we were. The first night we tried and tried to raise the Coast Guard, but we couldn't raise a soul. Just before going to bed, I tried one more time and got an answer. This was in the days of the AM ship-to-shore radios, which were mostly a line of sight instruments. I talked to the answering party and found that they were on Lake Ponchatrain in Louisiana. They were as surprised as we were. I had a nice talk with them and signed off and went to bed. After 1964, Wayne sold the boat and the fishing trips were over.

This is our total catch for the trip in April of 1963 with the crew. Clint Childs, Hobey, Wayne Ellis, and Tom Replogle.

Weighing and measuring the world record rainbow runner that I caught on this trip. With me are Clint Childs and Yoshi Ogata.

Joan Goodale Evans.

Richard Goodale at Hawaii Prep in the 1970s.

Katherine Goodale Richardson.

David Goodale with son Matthew.

Nancy with our first grandchild, Matthew Goodale.

Juliet Rice Wichman, my mother, taken when she was in her seventies.

CHAPTER TEN

The Seventies and the Ni'ihau Rescue

The seventies started with a bang. In June, we were off to Maui for Joan's graduation from Seabury Hall and learned that she would be going to college at Drake University in Des Moines. We would be going there with her on our way back from Africa to help her get settled in School. In late July, we were off to San Francisco with Mother, our four children, and Wendy Wichman. We flew from Honolulu to San Francisco and spent the night at an airport hotel. The next afternoon, we flew over the Pole to London. In London, we stayed at the Grosvenor House for about three days. Mother hired a car and driver who took us sightseeing—Westminster Abbey, St. Paul's Cathedral, the Tower of London, and the Crown Jewels. We also went to several of the best stores like Harrods, Fortnum and Mason, and Thomas Cook for china where we saw displays of place settings they had made for the coronations and birthdays of the British royalty.

David, Rick, and I went with Mother to Kew Gardens one afternoon. Mother said, "I want to see the Tropical House." This we did, and then she said, "Let's go back to the hotel." The boys and I wanted to see more, but Mother was the boss. She was so afraid that we would get lost that we were not allowed to go out of the hotel without her.

At last, the day of our flight to Africa arrived, and, after much waiting at the hotel, we departed for Heathrow Airport and a late afternoon flight to Entebbe, Uganda, and an unexpected snag in the plans. Our guide, Butch Visage, was not at the airport to meet us as expected because the driver of the truck with our camping equipment tried to pass another car in a rainstorm and was in a bad accident in which he was killed. Ten dozen eggs were smashed on the road, all of our tenting equipment was lost, and the cook was badly injured. The manager of our hotel finally met us and took us to our rooms. The native people there were having a dance at the hotel. So, trying to get to sleep with the song "Little Arrows" playing over and over until after one in the morning was an impossibility. The next day, Butch arrived and spent the rest of the day booking us into lodges and other accommodations. He did a wonderful job at such short notice.

We had a very memorable time on this trip and saw many animals and birds. One of the sights to boggle the mind was Murchison Falls where the Nile River was compressed into a narrow waterfall. Here were millions of gallons of water flowing in a mass of confusion with crocodiles waiting in the still water below the falls. After Uganda, we motored to Kenya and to Lake Naivasha where we stayed in tents but took all of our meals in the lodge's dining room. One day, we motored to Lake Nakuru and saw over a million lesser flamingos on the lake. It was a sight to behold. Then, it was off to the Masai Mara and over 250,000 wildebeests, giraffes, lions, and buffalo. Next, it was off to the Serengeti in Tanzania where we saw our first cheetahs. At the Seronera Wildlife Lodge, a tented camp, we caught Wendy and Richard bellied up to the bar getting rum-and-cokes. Rick was fourteen and Wendy thirteen. I guess the Bar tender figured, if they are big enough to look over the top of the bar, they are old enough to drink. Next, it was Ngorongoro Crater and more lions and other animals. We continued on to Lake Manyara, Arusha, and up the slopes of Mount Kilimanjaro for a night, and then on to Amboseli National Park in Kenya. Here were more lions, cheetahs, and elephants. Then, back to Nairobi and on to London and Gatwick Airport. Here our driver missed us, and we had to get into two taxis and get to the hotel by ourselves. When we got to the hotel, the Grosvenor House, we found that they had given our room to another family named Rice. Mother always used Rice as her middle name, and the hotel people were confused but got us taken care of quickly. We had a wonderful time on the safari. While in London, we did a little more sightseeing and more shopping before heading for home. Nancy, Joan, and I left the group and flew to Des Moines to see Joan settled in college.

A funny thing happened after we left that morning. Rick got up early, walked to Carnaby Street in Soho. He bought some very mod clothes, had them fitted, and returned to the hotel before anyone knew he was not in his room. So much for Mother's fear about us getting lost. There was a large map of London in Mother's apartment where Rick traced his route to and from Carnaby Street. David was not happy for being upstaged by his baby brother. This trip opened the floodgates of travel for Nancy and me.

In Late November, I got word that Garden Island Motors had won an incentive contest from Goodyear Tire and Rubber Company and the prize was trip for two to Portugal and Spain. I asked Bill Tanji, our parts manager, to go, but he declined. So Nancy and I went. We got there in the middle of April, and all the flowers were in bloom. We had flown from Kaua'i to New York City where we spent a couple of days seeing the city and several plays. On the night of our departure from New York to Portugal, we found that our flight was a chartered one, and there would only be other winning dealers and Goodyear personnel. Each couple had a row of three seats together, so we were not crowded at all. Both countries were interesting. In Portugal, we were on the coast at Lisbon and, in Spain, in Madrid in the middle of the country. I was amazed at how short the people seemed in both countries. In Madrid, we had one hour at the Prado Museum of Art. We had a wonderful informative lecture on Spanish art and the Spanish masters. There were three different groups in the room when we got there, each one speaking a different language. It was hard to concentrate. One hour only whetted our appetites, then it was off for more sightseeing. On the way back to our hotel, riding on a bus, we came over a hill and there were my cousin George Kimball and his wife walking on the side of the road. There was no way that we would have been able to find them even if we had tried. On the day of our departure for home, we were told that our flight would be delayed because of weather and stacking at Kennedy. A couple from Des Moines and ourselves took a taxi to the Louvre Museum and Palais Royale, which we had not been able to visit on our first day because Emperor Haili Selassie of Ethiopia was at the Museum and it was closed to the public for that day. We got there as the doors opened, got an English-speaking guide, toured the whole museum, and got back to the hotel for lunch. No one even knew that we had been missing.

In September of 1972, Mother took Nancy and I to Africa again for a month. This time it was only Kenya. We saw new places and some new animals. On the coast we visited an old deserted city called Gedi. It was very interesting. In a little museum, we saw a rusted safety pin and part of a pair of scissors. They were very old, and it was interesting to see how similar they were to the modern product. We spent several nights at two resorts on the Indian Ocean. Nancy and I got to go out on the reef at low tide. I always take a stick with me when I go out on the reef, and this time I found a big, black, sea urchin in a hole. With the stick, I got it out of its hole and started to break all the spines off. Before I was finished, two black men appeared and watched me. When I had denuded the urchin of all its spines, I broke it open and started to eat the eggs like we do in Hawai'i. I asked the men if they ate these, and they shook their head and said no. I guess they must have thought we whites were funny people.

Upon returning home I found out that we had won another sales incentive, this time from Ford Motor Company's parts department. This trip was to the Canary Islands off the coast of northwestern Africa. These islands belong to Spain. Again Bill Tanji refused to go, but a couple of years later when we won a trip to Las Vegas. As I stated earlier, with the Vegas trip, he accepted right away. We flew to Oakland, California, and spent the night at a hotel at the airport. The next morning we flew to Bangor, Maine, and then to Las Palmas on the Gran Canaria Island. This trip was on a 707 again, and it was completely filled. The month was November, and there were not many flowers in bloom at this time of the year. The Canaries are rather dry because they lie in the lee of the Sahara Desert and the clouds have nowhere to pick up water. Las Palmas has a desalination plant that produces about five-million gallons of potable water each day. We did some touring, and one day Nancy and I played golf. We had a seven and an eight year old as our caddies, and they were cute, friendly kids. One thing that impressed us both was how finicky the average American is about food. They always wanted to know what they were eating, and, if it wasn't meat and potatoes, they wouldn't touch it. On our return, we stopped on the Island of Santa Maria in the Azores. These Islands belong to the Portuguese and are rather windswept and desolate. We were forced to land there because of fog on the East Coast. We finally took off and landed in Bangor again at two in the morning. We had to walk about one-hundred yards from the plane in two degree weather to a big barn where we went through immigration and customs. We spent another hour or so while the plane was refueled. This gave all the finicky Americans a chance to get some real American food— hot dogs and hamburgers. The Ford people told us that we were the second to last group of about eight thousand for the year. The tours had started in September. Ford was a big spender in those days.

Our next excursion was in the fall of 1973. Al Kocher, his wife H. M., Nancy, and I had talked about a trip to Europe for several years. We had agreed that, when our children were all in school, we would do Europe. We did England, France, the Rhine River on a riverboat, Austria, Italy, and Switzerland. The details of this trip are in a travel section as an addendum.

There were other trips during the seventies that Nancy and I took. These were mostly to Hayden Lake, Idaho, where I played in a local Ford dealer's golf tournament. Nancy would do four days of bridge with some of the wives while I played golf. Many of the Idaho people had built homes at Princeville on Kaua'i, and we had played a lot of golf with them. I haven't been back to Hayden Lake since then.

After David's graduation from college he returned home and started the yard maintenance business. That lasted about a year or so until he was stiffed by customers a couple of times and gave up the business. He worked for Mother for a while as the gardener at Limahuli. Then, in 1975, he decided that he would like to go into the charter fishing business on Kaua'i. He and I found a nice thirty-eight-foot haole sampan for sale in Honolulu and bought it. It was in dry-dock, so we had a marine surveyor look it over. We did all the repair work that the surveyor recommended and got the boat back into the water. We had it blessed and came back to Kaua'i with it. We were back in Nāwiliwili in September of 1975, and David went right to work building up a charter business. The business started slowly, and, when there were no charters for a couple of days, he would go commercial fishing. The first time we went to Ni'ihau and Ka'ula Rock, an island about nineteen miles south of Ni'ihau, we had very good luck. When we had gotten to Ka'ula, we found a school of medium sized 'ahi and some ono. In a few hours, we had no more room or ice for any more fish. We came back to Ni'ihau, had dinner, and went to sleep until about midnight. At midnight, we up anchored and started back for Nāwiliwili where we sold most of the fish. David made several more trips to Ka'ula with about the same results.

At that point, his charter business started to pick up, so the trips to Ni'ihau became further and further apart. In November, one of Thomas Hashimoto's daughters was getting married. So David, Heidi Hydrick, Wendell Fu, and Paul Lawrence went over to Ni'ihau to catch some fish for the wedding. However, he did not return. He was supposed to be home by Friday, and, by Saturday morning, there was still no word from him. He had a citizens band radio and a VHS band radio on board, so we weren't too worried at first. But, by midmorning Saturday, we called the Coast Guard. They had heard nothing, and, because there had been a hoax SOS call a couple of weeks before, they were averse to sending the C-130 search-and-rescue plane out to look for the boat. The next morning, I called the Navy out at PRMF at Barking Sands, and they had a helicopter out in a very short time. There happened to be a man here on Kaua'i, married to a distant relative of ours, who was the Port Captain at Kodiak, Alaska. When he heard of our concern, he called and asked about the search plane. When I told him what the Coast Guard had said, he called them and asked about the plane. When he couldn't get a positive answer, he told them he was calling the admiral in Seattle to do something about it. Anyway, the plane was dispatched and a helicopter, too.

Jack Harter, Joan, and I flew all the way out to Ka'ula Rock in Jack's helicopter and back on Sunday morning but never saw a thing. That afternoon, we started out again and finally got word that the four of them had been found on Ni'ihau. One of the men with David, Wendell Fu, had gone over the mountain and reached the village. The people living in that village on Ni'ihau were leery about calling out on a Sunday but did call Bruce Robinson on Kaua'i about what had happened. Bruce told them to go get the rest of the crew out immediately. He then called the base to let them know where the rest of the crew was. The Navy sent a helicopter and they lifted the three remaining people out of a rugged little valley and brought them back to Kaua'i. In the meantime, the Coast Guard helicopter picked Wendell up and brought him back to Kaua'i. All the kids were pretty dehydrated but okay otherwise. Paul Lawrence, who was the most dehydrated, was kept in the hospital for another day before being released. Then came the inquisition. All the forms that the Coast Guard wanted filled out—how it happened, why it happened, and so forth—and all this the week before Thanksgiving. We had our whole family back together safe and sound. It was truly a time to be thankful.

We found out later that the boat had had a lot of electrical problems in the past. Some of the problems had been fixed, and other had not. A carpenter at the Hawaiian Tuna Packers Shipyard told us that the whole stern half of the boat had had new screws placed in the hull, but the owner didn't want to spend the money on the bow half. David had had a marine surveyor look over the boat, but he never caught the problem. Coming back from Ni'ihau that Friday night, the boat just opened up as it went over a wave and started to sink before David could get an SOS off. The Coast Guard only picked up half of the boat's call sign before it was under water. The four young people got life preservers on before the boat went down and vowed to stay together. They started swimming toward Kaua'i at first, but, after about half an hour, they still smelled diesel fumes they decided to swim the other way.

They swam for nineteen hours before they got to Ni'ihau. The waves were pretty big, and there they were separated. Wendell and Paul went in first and got up into a valley where Wendell could, then, climb out and get to the village. Only Wendell could make the trek because Paul was still suffering from an earlier accident that had left him pretty much paralyzed from the chest down for a long time. On the swim, Paul had a recurrence of the paralysis and had to be towed by Wendell most of the way. Wendell got him ashore and went to look for David and Heidi. David and Heidi tried several times to get ashore, but the waves kept pushing them back. David was getting pretty discouraged, but Heidi made him keep trying. Finally, they made it to shore. The next morning, David and Heidi saw Wendell on the cliff above them and signaled for him to try and get to the village. Wendell started out, but night fell before he reached the village. He went to sleep under a kiawe tree, and, in the middle of the night, he awoke in full moonlight and saw what he thought were the faces of angels looking at him. He was quite scared, but the faces were only the faces of some curious sheep.

Early the next year, David and I went to Honolulu to look at a new boat. This one was one that Sherry Dowsett had made for himself to fish out of Kāne'ohe. It was fifty-five feet long and about twelve feet wide. It was powered by two V6.71 diesel engines and could produce about six hundred horsepower. It was a long, thin pencil of a boat, but could it catch fish. It was named the *Goof Off*. The first thing we did was to have the boat blessed and the name changed to "*Kamanu*." David named it the *Kamanu* after the fish also known as the rainbow runner or Hawaiian salmon. He made this decision because I had held the world's record for this fish for thirteen years. We brought the boat back to Kaua'i as soon as some minor dry-dock work and all the legal paperwork were done. Once back on Kaua'i, David started out in the charter business with a vengeance.

We planned a trip to Ni'ihau and Ka'ula with David, Heidi, Wendell Fu, Rick Goodale, Frank Sullivan and myself on board. We left Nāwiliwili at ten p.m. and headed for Ka'ula Rock. By six in the morning, we were off Ka'ula, the lines were put out, and we started fishing. By mid-morning, we had caught some small fish when we got a big strike and David made me take the pole. After about forty minutes, we had a large marlin up to the boat. We did not want to land the fish, and it was pretty lively. So we took pictures of it in the water and let it go. The fish was estimated to be about four-hundred pounds. This was my first marlin, and one is enough. A little while later, we got another big strike and Wendell Fu took the pole. After about an hour, a large 'ahi was brought to gaff, and, when we returned to Kaua'i and had the fish weighed, it tipped the scales at two-hundred-thirty-seven pounds. After more trolling, we returned to Ni'ihau for the night. While coming in toward Ni'ihau, David wanted to find a good place to do some bottom fishing that night and asked Rick to put on a face mask and go over the side and look for a good rocky bottom. As Rick was getting into the water, we were going over a reef and we could see the bottom. Just as he got into the water and put his face down so he could see, we had gone over the edge of the reef and he saw nothing but blue water and no bottom. He got back into the boat so fast it made us laugh, but he was quite upset with his brother. We finally anchored at an anchorage known as Kamalino.

That evening, after we had cleaned up and I was waiting for the rice to cook, we started the cocktail hour. The evening was a gorgeous one with a beautiful sunset. There were little clouds in the west that showed like black spots in the sky against the different shades of red within the sunset. All was quiet after a long day of the roar of the engines, and one could hear the small waves as they swirled around the rocks on the shoreline. Everything was so nice and peaceful when Frank Sullivan took a sip of his martini and said, "Say fellows, wouldn't you rather be on a freeway in Los Angeles about now." If he weren't so big, we might have thrown him overboard. Anyway, everyone got a good laugh. By then, the rice was done, and I went below to cook the rest of the meal. On all of our fishing trips, I would cook one-pot meals that went well with rice. The next day, we had breakfast, up-anchored, and left for home. We went around the west end of Ni'ihau, caught a couple of small fish, and got into Nāwiliwili at about four in the afternoon. David sold the big 'ahi, but there were enough fish so everyone got enough to take home.

This was the first boating trip for David, Heidi, and Wendell since the trip when their boat sank. Heidi had some bad moments the first night while watching the white water of the wake, but all had a good time anyway. It was a good healing experience for them. Once that first trip was out of the way, there were many more good trips on the Kamanu. It was a lucky boat as far as fishing was concerned.

From the middle of 1976 until 1981, David pursued the vocation of a charter boat skipper and commercial fisherman. Whenever there were no charters for a few days, he would take off for Ni'ihau and Ka□ula Rock. Most of the time, I would go with him and whoever his deck hand was. Every Fourth of July and Labor Day weekend, David would take a group of Līhue businessmen over to Lehua Island where they camped and fished for three days. We would go to Ka'ula or fish around Ni'ihau. On the third day, we would pick the fellows up and bring them back to Port Allen on Kaua'i and then return to Nāwiliwili. There were some really memorable moments during those years.

One time, David and I took Frank Sullivan and Gordon Rabideau on a trip to Ni'ihau and Ka'ula to break in Frank's new rod and reel. Frank had a friend named Les Eichorn who owned the Sevenstrand Fishing Tackle Company. Les had given Frank a brand new graphite rod with a reel and about five hundred yards of fifty-pound test line. Frank was just itching to try this new tackle out, so David arranged the trip. We left Nāwiliwili at one in the afternoon heading to spend the night at Ni'ihau. When we got almost directly south of Port Allen, we spotted a flock of birds working a school of small fish and decided to check them out. On our first pass through the birds, we got a solid strike on Frank's pole. We knew that it was probably a big 'ahi but not how big it really was. Frank got into the fighting chair and started to fight the fish. We kept encouraging Frank, and, after an hour, David poured a bucket of water over him to cool him off while the three of us had a beer. We told him that there would be no beer for him until he got the fish landed. After another hour and fifteen minutes, the fish surfaced.

When we saw how big it was we thought of a world record. We would not do anything to disqualify the fish if it was indeed a record.

After another half an hour, we were able to grab the double line and bring the fish next to the boat so that we could gaff it. After we got the fish aboard and iced, we realized that it was too late to get to Niʻihau before it was too dark to see where we could anchor safely. So we headed into Port Allen. David called his wife Heidi and asked her to bring his truck to Port Allen so he could get the fish to market. When she arrived, we loaded the fish into the truck, and David and Frank left to sell the fish. I got dinner started, and Gordon, Heidi, and I had a drink. When David and Frank returned, we learned that the fish weighed two-hundred-forty-five pounds and was just eleven pounds under the world record. That record was broken by twenty-five pounds three weeks later in Kona. Marilyn and Michael Sullivan and Nancy came over to Port Allen to see the fish, but David and Frank had already gone to sell the ʻahi.

The next morning, we left for Niʻihau, but Kaʻula was out of the question for this trip. On our way over to Niʻihau, we saw several jets fly over us and some had the Rising Sun insignia under their wings. Gordon freaked out. We found out later that, in World War II, his ship had been attacked by the Japanese. So he was not comfortable seeing Japanese planes again. We found after our return that the Japanese Navy and our Navy were having joint exercises in our waters. Near Niʻihau, we got another two-hundred-five-pound ʻahi and some smaller fish. We spent the night at Niʻihau and returned to Nāwiliwili the next morning.

Les Eichorn was most pleased with Frank's feat but said we should have taken pictures of the fish. The next time Les came to Kauaʻi, he brought three new lures with him. One looked like a mahimahi, one like an aku, and the other like an ʻahi. There were comments about what fish would bite one of those lures, but Les said, "Just let's try them." Later that week, after one of David's half-day charters, we took Les and his friend Frank Conti out for an afternoon of fishing. We trolled out toward Oʻahu for about an hour and then found some birds working so we chased them.

Just as we came up to the birds, we got a nice big strike on the mahimahi lure, and we made Les fight the fish. While Les was busy with the fish, I said to Frank Conti, "The next one is yours."

Frank said, " No way. I'll cut the line." He didn't have to worry, as we didn't get any more strikes.

Les was tickled when we weighed the fish and it weighed one-hundred-fifty-six pounds. This time, we were sure to take pictures with Les and his fish. Later, we saw a brochure with Les and his fish and the mahimahi like lure. Then there came a duffel bag full of lures for David to try. The only request was to take pictures of the fish and the lure whenever you caught a fish on one of those lures.

Once, on a long weekend, Bill Akana went along on his boat with us to Ni'ihau while Curly Carswell was coming around from Hanalei in his boat to join us. We had anchored for the night in the lee of Ni'ihau with Bill tied up to our stern. We waited a while for Curly and finally raised him on the radio. He was still a long way off, so we went ahead and had our drinks and dinner and didn't wait for Curly. As we were getting ready to call it a day, here comes Curly wanting something to eat. As he approached us, he got too close to our anchor rope and got tangled. If you know Curly, this didn't bother him at all and we finally got him all squared away and fed. Another time with Bill Akana, we were at the furthest western edge of the Ka'ula shoal when we noticed that the birds were all leaving the island. This was a sign that there were planes in the vicinity, and the birds knew that soon the bombs would be falling. David radioed Bill, who was on the other side of the island, to warn him there was going to be a bombing run and to get out of the way. Bill made some snappy comment and didn't leave. Luckily, the planes always made a low pass over the island before coming in to bomb. Two planes came over the island right over Bill's head and scared the heck out of him. As he was getting out of the way, the planes came over and dropped their bombs. One bomb missed the island and hit the water about a half-mile away. Later, David called Bill and got his son, Scott. Scott said that his father was so shaken up that they were going back to Ni'ihau and home. That was the last we saw of them for that trip. I don't think Bill ever went back to Ka'ula again.

One time with four of us aboard, we found a school of 'ahi, which looked to be about one-hundred-twenty-five pounds apiece. We followed the birds, and, each time we caught up to the school, we could see the fish in the waves behind the boat. They were right on the surface and plainly visible. Each time we would get a strike and land one of the big fish. This happened seven times, and, then, the fish disappeared. It was getting late in the afternoon, so we headed back to Ni'ihau for the night. David said we could go back the next day and try to catch some more. I told him we only had room or ice for two more fish of that size. So it would not be profitable to go back, and we should go home the next day.

The next morning, we left Ni'ihau right after breakfast and headed east past South Point of Ni'ihau. We were headed right into the morning sun and couldn't see what was in the water ahead of us when we got a mahimahi strike. While bringing the mahimahi in, we saw several more in the water behind the hooked one. We quickly rigged up another rod with fresh aku for bait. We threw this other line into the water and promptly had another fish on the line. We kept this up until we had seven twenty-five pound mahimahi in the boat. After about the fifth fish, a seven- or eight-foot shark appeared and started to chase the hooked fish. Every time the shark was just about to bite the fish, the mahimahi would jump into the air and change directions. The shark would have a much slower time in getting turned around, so we were able to pull the fish out of the water and into the boat before the shark could get the fish. Since there were more mahimahi in the water, we kept putting another bait into the water. We would quickly pull the hooked one into the boat and start fighting the new one. This happened with three fish, and, when we finally landed the last one, the shark in frustration rammed into the stern of the boat. He must have dazed himself, for he just kind of rolled in the water, shook his head, and slowly swam away. It was only then that we saw the large cargo net that had attracted the mahimahi. Thank god we didn't run over the net because no one would want to go into the water with an angry shark around. When all the excitement was over, I reminded David that we didn't need to go back for two more 'ahi.

The Kamanu, being a wooden-hulled boat and being used for charter, had to be dry-docked every six months. There was no place on Kaua'i where we could pull it out of the water, so we had to go to Honolulu for the semi-annual dry-dock. David tells the story of their being off Wai'anae, O'ahu, on their way to Kewalo Basin when he saw a periscope cutting through the water. Several minutes later, along comes a helicopter, and David gets a life jacket and starts to wave it at the helicopter. The pilot flies over to the boat, and David motions to the pilot in the direction the sub was going. The helicopter flew in the right direction and soon returned and flew low over the boat and waved a thank you to him. He had completed his mission and was heading home.

In 1980, David started working for Garden Island Motors and had to give up active fishing. But, he had a couple of fellows who could run the boat for him. These fellows were not too reliable, for they would never tell David when they needed new hooks or swivels and the like. The maintenance of the boat started to slip. David finally agreed to sell the boat to a Chinese man in Honolulu who had tried to buy the boat every time David came to dry-dock. We got more for the boat than what we paid for it. It was a sad time for all of us, but it was time to move on. I have since heard that the Kamanu or Coreen C II, as it was renamed, sank at its mooring and was left on the bottom for about six months and now will be scrapped. What a waste of a wonderful boat.

David and I went out fishing one more time with Tom Haeddeas and John Hankinson on the *Kuuhuapala*. Our destination was Nihoa Rock about one-hundred-fifty miles from Kaua'i. We left Nāwiliwili in the late afternoon and were at the twenty-five fathom shoal, which is out half way to Nihoa from Kaua'i at daylight. We fished that spot for a while and caught a small marlin and other small fish then decided to head for Nihoa. The seas were quite calm, and there was a slight breeze. But the visibility was not very good because of volcanic smog or "vog." We never found Nihoa, although, that night, we saw a light in the distance about where Nihoa should have been. The next morning, we could hardly see a mile ahead of us, so we started for home. Tom had had a new alternator installed on one of the engines and had not had the time to have it shielded. So, every time he engaged the alternator, the compass would swing forty-five degrees. We had to turn the alternator on periodically, but the automatic pilot was not affected. So, once we were headed in the right direction, it was okay. As long as there was enough electricity to run the AM radio, we could tell that we were getting closer to Kaua'i by the strength of the signal. At about five in the afternoon, David and I were at the helm when David said, "Dad, what island is that over to our starboard?" pointing to the south. We finally decided that it was Ka'ula Rock, so we headed for it. Just when we crossed over the edge of the twenty-five-fathom mark, we got a triple strike and landed three nice mahimahi. We later heard from Tom that the mahimahi more than paid for the trip. The next morning, we could barely make out Ni'ihau nineteen miles away, and we started home. After we passed Ni'ihau, we went blind for the better part of an hour before we could see Kaua'i. We made it home safely, but I don't want that kind of a trip again.

In the middle seventies, we had two weddings to put on. The first was between Kathy and Richie Richardson, which was a big formal affair; and then David and Heidi Hydrik's over at Hanalei at Mahamoku. This one we prepared for about four hundred, but, once it got dark, the bushes started quivering. I think that we fed over five hundred. In 1979, Heidi had a little boy, which made us grandparents. That was enough action for one decade.

CHAPTER ELEVEN

The Eighties & Travel

The eighties was a period of work at Garden Island Motors interspersed with several trips to foreign places. We celebrated three marriages and the births of a bunch of grandchildren. And the worst hurricane I had ever seen visited Kaua'i.

In November of 1982, Kaua'i was hit by Hurricane Iwa packing winds up to one-hundred-twenty miles per hour. We had adequate warning, but almost everyone was quite complacent about the whole idea, and quite a few people were caught unprepared. We did not save very much water, but the water was restored within twenty-four hours. The telephone and electricity, however, would take a whole month to get back on line. We were fat cats once the water was turned on again because we had a gas stove and a gas hot water heater. We didn't have any ice, but we could cook and have hot showers. Our house had only minor damage, as did our Hā'ena house. We lost a medium sized orange tree at Hā'ena and one breadfruit tree in Līhue. Our orange tree in Līhue lost its whole crop of immature fruit, though, and all the leaves were gone. New growth started to appear within ten days like hair on a dog's back. Our condo at Princeville, one of the Hanalei Villas units, lost its roof in the wind. We were told that the roofs acted like large Frisbees as they sailed about in the wind. The four big roof support beams were only nailed to the building actually with two nails in each of the four corners. After doing the repair work to the building, we soon sold the condo and got out of that mess. The building fared better in Iniki, as it only lost a couple of windows broken. Telephone and electric poles were down all over the place. Many of them were practically hollowed out by termites. The Douglas fir poles will only accept treatment to the depth of one and one-half inches deep, and the centers are completely untreated. From the outside, the poles look like they're in good condition, but, when the high winds came, they went over like match sticks.

Nancy and I went for a ride with Jack Harter in his helicopter about two weeks after the storm. We had another young couple who I think were on their honeymoon along on the trip also. She wasn't too keen about going up with no wings. What impressed us most was the damage to the bamboo thickets. They had been torn into an unrecognizable mess. At Brennecke's Beach, we could see all the sand about two-hundred yards out from shore. It has never come back, and the county keeps bringing in more sand and out it goes again. As usual, Kaua'i as a community pulled together, cleaned up the island, and repaired most of the damage very quickly.

Joan and Randy Evans were married on September 26, 1981 at All Saint Church in Kapa'a, and the reception was held at the Coco Palms Hotel. Their first child, Anthony, was born on April 6, 1983 in Honolulu. Kathy and Ritchie's son, Wayne Richardson IV, was born in Honolulu on October 21, 1981. That made grandchild number three. We were getting started with kids to spoil and send back to their parents to shape up.

Rick Goodale and Karen Fisher, of Detroit, Michigan, were married at Limahuli in Hā'ena on October 19, 1985, and their reception was held at Mother's house at Hā'ena. Nancy and I vacated our house at Hā'ena so Karen's family could stay together. Nancy and I got a room at the Hanalei Colony Resort for a couple of nights. Little did Karen and Rick know that their room was directly over ours, and did we ever tease them the next day. They planned to spend their first night at the resort and go on to Kōke'e for their honeymoon the next morning. Wrong! That night, it started raining, and, by the next morning, the bridge at Hanalei was closed until late in the morning because of the high water. After their honeymoon, they went back to Huntsville, Alabama, to pack up all their belongings and move back to Kaua'i. Rick had finished his stint in the Army and had been offered a position with the Kauai Medical Group at their clinic at Princeville.

Juliet Evans was born on February 9, 1985 in Honolulu. Kathy and Richie's daughter Katherine Emalia was born on December 23, 1985, and, on February 27, 1989, Rick and Karen's little boy Ian was born here on Kaua'i. Now we had six grandchildren to spoil.

The next one to get married was David, who married Patrice Pendarvis on November 26, 1988. They got married around the Bamboo Bridge in the Lawai Gardens. The reception was held at Lawai Kai for a short duration. Then, everything was packed up, and almost everyone moved across the island to Princeville where the party again started up at the Princeville Golf Clubhouse. When this part of the party closed down I don't know because Nancy and I had left long before the end.

Ron Harker, the manager of Garden Island Motors, retired at the end of 1982, and I took over as manager. After about two and a half years, I had decided that I was not cut out for the job. So I asked Kathy's husband if he would like to come and run the company. Kathy and Richie came with their two children Wayne IV and Katie. They lived with us for a short while then bought a house on Kanani Street from Nancy. Nancy had bought the lot from David and had built a house, which she rented. Luckily, the renters moved out about the time the Richardson's arrived on Kaua'i. Now we had three of our four children living here on Kaua'i.

In 1984, I was elected to the board of trustees of the National Tropical Botanical Garden (NTBG) where I have served for over twenty-five years. I am still going strong and enjoy the work and the opportunity to travel around the country for meetings. Every year, the board goes to a different city in the continental U.S., so Nancy and I have gotten to visit about a dozen major cities on the mainland. When we visit a U.S. city, there are always side trips either before or after the meeting. During the meetings, there are always visits to gardens in the area. These trips have given us great opportunities to get to know our country. In 1986, after one of our fall meetings on Kaua'i, a dozen board members and their spouses flew to Cairns, Australia, with one of our trustees, Eleanor Bleakie, as our leader. From Cairns, we flew to Sydney, Canberra, and Melbourne visiting private gardens and other botanic gardens. From Melbourne, we flew across the Tasman Sea to New Zealand. Here we saw Christchurch, Rotorua, and Auckland before flying home to Hawai'i.

The next year, 1985, I was elected to the board of directors of Island School. At that time, I had one grandchild, Matthew, attending the school. The school was located in the old Kealia Store building. Island School is a college preparatory school with grades Pre-K to twelfth and is accredited by the Hawai'i Association of Independent Schools. It is a school that gives children on Kaua'i a chance for a better education. In 1989, the school purchased ten acres of land from Lihue Plantation immediately behind the Kaua'i Community College in Puhi. Here we built an elementary school. It opened in 1991. I am a firm believer in affording an opportunity for our children to have a strong college preparatory education here on Kaua'i. There is only one boarding school in the state, and that is on the island of Hawai'i. It is hard for a family to arrange to find someone who will take a teenager for four years.

In the late 1980s, I started clearing an area of our lot at Hā'ena where we intended to build a new house. It took me a couple of years of weekends to get this done. Nancy and I asked Ron Agor, an architect who had finished drawing the plans for the new church at St. Michael and All Angels in Līhue, to do our plans. This was the easy part. It took almost two years to get the plans approved by the State Department of Land and Natural Resources, as this property is in a conservation zone. Once the plans were completed, we went to our contractor. Then it was the county's turn for the building permits. The biggest holdup was the State Department of Health. Finally, in late July 1992, everything was a go and the work was started. The columns for the foundation were in place but not grouted with concrete when the Hurricane Iniki hit on September 11, 1992. When we were finally able to get to Hā'ena, we found that six of the columns had been blown over in the wind. Now everything was stopped until November when the contractor started to work again. We finally moved into the new house on August 3, 1993.

In 1988, Jan Rudinoff, rector of St. Michael and All Angels, got together with me and a few other church members and started the ball rolling to build a new church. Steve Shackleton, an architect, said he would love to design the building and was given the okay to go ahead. Before Steve had finished the complete plans, he was offered a chance to attend the Frank Lloyd Wright Institute in Arizona. He left the unfinished plans with his partner Ron Agor to finish. When Ron was ready with the plans, Jan called a meeting of the congregation to review the plans and approve them so we could go ahead and start raising the money. It took Ron, Jan, and me over two hours one Sunday morning after church to convince the congregation that it could be done. Curtis Law was hired to be the contractor, I was the finance and fund drive chairman, and off we went. We were able to build and pay for the church building with a little money left over, so we decided to go ahead with the administration building. We had to take out an eight-hundred-thousand dollar mortgage, and, on Shrove Tuesday 2004, the mortgage was fully paid up. The church was finished before Iniki in 1992. The administration building was just about competed, and we were able to let the American Red Cross use it as a Disaster Center. The church building itself suffered only ten broken windows and nothing else of any consequence.

In 1980, Nancy and I met up with the Kochers and flew to Anchorage, Alaska. We toured Anchorage and its environs, then flew to Kotzebue for a quick visit, and then on to Nome for the night. This trip was in early August, so the night never really came. The next day, we flew back to Anchorage for the night and left for Fairbanks the next morning. Halfway to Fairbanks, we stopped and got off the train and, then, spent the night in Denali. The next morning, we had an hour's ride to the vantage point for viewing Mount McKinley. Along the way up and back, we saw Dall sheep, moose, caribou, and grizzly bears. On our return to the railroad, we got on the train again and continued to Fairbanks. After a day in Fairbanks, we flew to Barrow, the most northern town in the United States. Here we spent the night, then back to Fairbanks for a day of rest, and then by bus to Whitehorse in Canada's Yukon Territory. We had one night in Whitehorse and then on to the narrow gauge railroad to Skagway back in Alaska. A night in Skagway and then we boarded one of the Princess-line ships for Vancouver and back to Kaua'i.

In the summer of 1984, Nancy and I met with our friends Tom Gillespie and his wife Mary Ann in Seattle and drove to Banff, Canada, for some golf. We then went on to Lake Louise for the Fourth of July, and it was bitterly cold. After two days, we continued north to Jasper and stayed at the lodge there. Here we played golf three times and moved on by driving west to the Harrison Hot Springs, where the Gillespies left us. After dinner on the first night of our stay, there was dancing to an orchestra that played our kind of music from the forties and fifties. We had a wonderful time just the two of us dancing like we were teenagers again. There was a nine-hole golf course at Harrison Hot Springs where Nancy and I played twice. We rented a car and drove into Vancouver for a few days while we took in the sights of Expo '84. After a short stay in Vancouver, we motored down to the Sea-Tac Airport and stayed the night at an airport motel. While looking around before dinner, we spotted a farmer's market just across the street from the hotel. We decided to check it out and, to our pleasant surprise, we found some Rainier cherries. These were the kind that Mother had asked us to look for. So, we bought a couple of bags and brought them home for her. They really made a hit with her.

The Gillespies and the Jack Henrys talked us into going with them on a British Airways Golfing Tour to Scotland in the summer of 1986. We played the Royal Troon, Turnberry (both courses), Gleneagles (two courses), Carnoustie and St. Andrews (the old course). It was a thrill to have the opportunity to play those courses, as this is the birthplace of the game of golf. We, then, took the train down to London for a few days where we saw the play *Singin' in the Rain* with Gene Kelley as the star. Then, it was the long flight back to Kaua'i.

In the fall of 1987, Nancy and I with the Gillespies joined the People to People Organization and went to the Orient to play golf with people of different countries. We started in Tokyo, Japan, where we played with the Japanese at the Kasumigaseki Golf Club. Our itinerary now took us to Beijing, China, to play with the Chinese on a course financed by the Japanese. The Chinese we played with were just starting to learn the game, so they couldn't play too well. But they were further handicapped by stern-looking cadre who were watching their every move. While we were in Beijing, we had to march in a column of four to see the embalmed body of Chairman

Mao Tse Tung. The Great Wall of China was a thrill for me because, as a child, I had grown up with the National Geographic Magazine. Seeing such masterpieces was a dream come true. We also saw the Forbidden City and the Ming Tombs and had some very tasty dinners. The Northern Chinese cooking is a little different than what we were used to here at home where, in the old days, all the Chinese cooking was Southern Cantonese. After Beijing, it was south to Singapore for play on two interesting courses. Here we played twice by ourselves. It was so hot and muggy that you would be sweating just standing in the shade. This was where, after five holes, I took off my second set of gloves and have not worn a golf glove since. We did not play with any locals here in Singapore. We then flew to Hong Kong for a couple days of sightseeing and shopping, and, then, it was off the Macau by hovercraft. The next two days we traveled across the border into China to the village of Chung Shan to play on a course designed and built by Arnold Palmer for the Macauans. Here, on our last day, we played with young Chinese and they whipped our butts. Sometimes it was hard to understand the languages, but, at most places, they could understand a little English. On the third day, we left Macau and headed for Guangzhou (Canton) for a couple of days of sightseeing. Then, it was back to Hong Kong and more golf once again with locals. This time, everyone spoke English. The next evening, it was our flight back to Hawai'i and the most horrible experience at the hands of the custom inspectors. This was just after our ex-governor's wife had been caught with undeclared jewelry. It took Nancy and I, with nothing to declare, over forty-five minutes to get past the inspector.

As a young woman, Mother had been to China and Japan and wanted us to give her a full report on what we saw. When we left on this trip, Mother was not too well. I swear that she stayed alive for the report, which I dutifully made. We got home for her eighty-sixth birthday, and she died two weeks later. She wanted no full-blown funeral service, but we had a memorial service for her at the cemetery and took her ashes out to Hā'ena to be scattered. Jack Harter flew his helicopter out to Hā'ena to take Bruce and myself along with Thomas Hashimoto up to scatter her ashes. Jack would not take any payment for this because Mother had helped Jack buy his first helicopter to get him started in his own business.

Mother left me all her books on Hawaiiana. I would go down to her house in the evenings to catalogue the collection. Several people asked me if I was afraid she would come and humbug me. I would tell them that there were still some questions I would like answers to and wished that she would come a talk to me, but she never came.

It the late eighties, Kathy organized the Rice-Wilcox 'Ohana with a few close friends, and we started going to Camp Sloggett in Kōke'e for Thanksgiving. These were large affairs. The lowest attendance was about thirty-eight people, and the largest was the Thanksgiving after Hurricane Iniki when the attendance was eighty-four. Every one brings something, and it is a BYOB party. Every year, there are at least three turkeys, and John Plews brings a ham. There are also usually three kinds of stuffing, mashed potatoes, peas and carrots, and three or four kinds of pies. Everyone gets plenty to eat, and there is always enough turkey for sandwiches throughout the next couple of days. Weather permitting, there is always at least one hike every day, sometimes more if the hikes are short ones. It has gotten so that certain people will bring the same thing every year, so deciding the menu is pretty easy.

CHAPTER TWELVE

The Nineties & Iniki

The 1990s started well for Nancy and me. We were going to Brazil and South Africa on another People to People golf tour. We played twice in Rio de Janeiro and six times in South Africa. We arrived in Johannesburg and did some sightseeing and played golf twice. Johannesburg was no fun because it was too dangerous to go out on the streets for fear of getting mugged. We went by the native enclave of Soweto, and the bus drivers wouldn't take us in there even in the daylight. One of the men in our group was mugged on an escalator in the shopping mall below our hotel. Durban and Cape Town were much safer.

We also spent a night and morning at Mala Mala, a private game reserve that abuts Kruger National Park. At Mala Mala, we got into open cars with a white guide and a black tracker who didn't do any tracking but rode on a seat just above us and looked for animals while the white guide drove through the forest. We saw quite a few different animals during the afternoon. Just before dark, we spotted two wild dogs and followed them until dark. At dark, we stopped and had cocktails. After cocktails, we started to look for the dogs but came upon two lionesses out hunting. We followed them through the trees for about an hour but never saw them go after anything. The next morning, we went out again and found a Martial eagle, which had caught an impala calf and was about to start eating it. We were going to watch the eagle, but we got a radio call that one of the other cars had found a leopard in a tree with a kill. We hurried over and parked almost under the leopard. One of the women wailed, "What if it pees on us?" All I could think about was, if the leopard had wanted to, he could have slid off the branch, bitten any of us in the head, and that would be the last of us. After getting our fill of a sleeping leopard, we returned to camp and breakfast. After breakfast, we packed up and left Mala Mala for the enclave called Swaziland. Here we played golf with some of the locals and spent the night. The next day, we left for Durban in a bus with no air-conditioning because no one could get any new parts due to a boycott over racial discrimination.

On the way from Swaziland to Durban, we stopped for lunch at a wayside inn. At the entrance, was a topless Zulu girl, in full native regalia, who was the inn's greeter. Most of the men wanted their picture taken with her. But I guess that people in this part of the world don't get a chance to bathe too often, so she smelled pretty bad. Their first ardor sure waned in a jiffy. The food at the inn was good, but the beer was better.

While in Durban, South Africa, we were the guests of the Jockey Club for a day at the races. We arrived at the track at eleven-thirty in the morning, had cocktails before lunch, and watched a couple of races. The races here, as with the British, world start and run counterclockwise and not clockwise as in America. We were then ushered into the dining room for lunch. We had good food and more wine than was necessary and then back to the races. At four o'clock, it was time for tea, although one could have anything else you wanted besides tea for a beverage. Then, it was back to the races until the last race was over at about five-thirty. We headed back to the dining room for some goodbye drinks, and then we staggered to the bus and were back at the hotel by eight o'clock. We were staying at a hotel owned and operated by people from India, so the featured meal was curry. Both Nancy and I loved curry, so that is what we selected. We both asked for the medium curry, and it was hot but not killing hot. One condiment looked like the mango seed that we so like in Hawai'i, so I took two big pieces. Then, when I bit into the first piece, I thought that I had bitten into a red-hot iron. It was mango seed, all right, but with a blowtorch attached. Once I got through with the first piece, the second piece was a lot easier to handle. After this snack, my taste buds were dead.

On our last night in Cape Town, six of us went to a seafood restaurant for dinner. The special of the house that night was a local fish similar to a sea trout and it came fried. One of the women in the group, who had grown up in New Orleans, and I had the special. When it came, it was a whole fish about fifteen inches long and shaped like a trout. The fish was delicious, and both of us ate it all so that there were only bones left. The waiter patted me on the shoulder and said, "You sure know how to eat fish." It was one of the best tasting fish I ever have had. On the way back to the U.S., we stopped in Rio again for the day. The lunch was a typical Portuguese meal. There were black beans and rice and pigs feet cooked in a dark liquid, along with ears and tails. There were other foods that I didn't try because I was having too much fun with the "trotters," as the pigs' feet are called in Rio. There was one woman from the mainland sitting with Nancy and me who couldn't stand to see me chew on the feet, so she finally left the table.

On July 1, 1991, the entire master lease on the Ke'eaumoku property expired, and we were able to execute a seventy-five-year lease with Haseko

Company, a Japanese development firm. After five years, the Japanese economic bubble burst, and they bought their way out of the lease. Then, my bothers Charles and Bruce and I had to scramble to get an income stream rolling again. We had already connected with a land management group in California and bought a small shopping center in Edmonds, Washington, and a warehouse in Union City, California. We tried selling or leasing the remaining property ourselves. We had a lot of bites and a few that paid earnest money down but never followed through with a sale. A deal to lease fell through over a disagreement between Walmart and Sam's Club. But, a year later, suddenly Walmart came back and made an offer to buy. We took the deal, and they paid us for the property. They have now built a huge Walmart and Sam's Club complex on the property. My brother Charles found a management company from Boston who agreed to help us invest in property on the East Coast. We were able to beat the real estate boom and buy another shopping center in Florida and a warehouse in Pennsylvania.

I had been elected to the board of trustees of the, then, Pacific Tropical Botanical Garden (now the National Tropical Botanical Gardens) in 1984. In July of 1992, our director, William Theobald, suffered a crippling stroke and could not continue leading the garden. This is when I started going to the garden at least once a week to try and keep things going on an even keel until we could find a new director.

In August of 1992, Nancy and I went on a trip through the Aleutian Islands on an eighty-five-passenger ship from Dutch Harbor to the Island of Attu. Then, we traveled across the Pacific to Kamchatka, Russia, down the Kuril Island chain to Kushiro, on to Hokkaido Island of Japan, then to Tokyo, and home to Hawai'i. My only disappointment was not being able to visit the island of Shemya where I was stationed while I was in the Army. The reason given was that there was still a spy plane in operation there.

On the island of Iturup, which is halfway down the Kuril chain, the boat stopped for a day and we went ashore. In the bay, there were salmon traps in operation as the salmon run was on. On the way to shore, we could see salmon under the zodiacs and almost touch them. Once ashore, we were led to a schoolhouse for a demonstration of Russian folk dances. These were done by young children and were quite amusing. After the dances were over, we were escorted to a large bus and transported into the hills to view a salmon hatchery. The fish were not quite ripe, we were told, and were being held back for another week by a weir preventing them from going beyond the hatchery. The woman who was the head of the hatchery told us that, when the Russians took over from the Japanese, there was only about a ten-million fish return each year. But, with the Russians, the return was now over one-hundred-million fish per year. She also told us that the fish we saw being taken out of the traps were being canned for human consumption. She then said the fish that were harvested for their eggs and milt were canned for pet food so nothing was wasted. We toured a little bit more of the island, and most of us went back to the ship. The friendly Russians plied one of the women who stayed ashore with straight vodka, and she almost had to be carried back to the ship.

That evening, a party of nineteen Russians came aboard for cocktails and dinner. One of the nineteen was a young soldier who was sent along to see that none of our guests would defect. He was the only one who didn't want to go ashore at the end of the evening. There was a twelve-year-old Russian girl who sat at the piano and banged out classical rock without any sheet music to help her. I remember thinking that this meeting with the Russians was a good example of why we should be friends. It is not the common people who make the trouble but the commissars. These people were distinctly happy to see us and get to know that we are not the kind of people their leaders were making us out to be.

After arriving home from our Aleutian trip on Wednesday September ninth, we woke up to the sound of a warning siren at five-thirty on Friday morning the eleventh of September. We were in for a storm, and what a storm it was! It was named Hurricane Iniki. The winds kept increasing velocity all morning, and Nancy and I tried to batten down as best we could. At about one o'clock, the telephone rang. It was Matthew Goodale calling from Sun Valley, Idaho, looking for his father. By then, David's telephone was out of service, and ours was about to go. Matt said that he was watching the progress of the storm on TV, and it looked like the eye was nearly on Kaua'i. He wanted to know if the wind was blowing hard, and Nancy told him it was getting pretty bad. He said that he would try and reach his dad in the morning. The next day, there was no telephone service on Kaua'i at all. We lost most of our pitch and gravel roofing, and a piece of plywood from someone else's garage hit the front of our house. It smashed several windows and part of the wall. Luckily, I had saved a large cooler of clean drinking water along with a wheelbarrow and a couple trashcans of water for bathing and flushing toilets. Water service was not restored for another five days.

Kathy appeared on her bicycle with word that they were okay. We didn't hear from the boys for another day. On the following Tuesday, I went over to the garden at Lawai to check on things there. It was a mess! This was the first day that the full staff had come to work. We set up three different committees to go out into the garden, assess the damage, and see what could be saved. For the next few days, we worked the staff at the garden and then sent them home at noon to take care of their own homes. I returned to Līhue to help Richie pick up some generators at the airport, which a friend Peter Cannon had sent to Kaua'i. Here lo and behold comes Douglas Kinney, the chairman of the NTBG. He was here to see first hand how the garden had fared and to give encouragement and assurance that the staff still had their jobs. I asked him how long he would be staying on Kaua'i, and he replied that he would try to go back to Honolulu that night. I told him that he was welcome to spend the night with us if he couldn't fly out that night. Sure enough, at six that evening he showed up at our door. We had a meal of chopped leg of lamb with rice and the last of the frozen peas sautéed in soy sauce and Worcestershire. This was the last meal that we had from our freezer.

On Thursday, Nancy, Kathy, and I went to Hā'ena to check on the damage there. We met up with David at Hā'ena. The house was in shambles with no hope of repair. We tried to salvage whatever we could and brought it back to Līhue. The contractor had just started our new house next door. When we got there, we saw that (along with the six un-grouted concrete tile columns that had toppled over) the batter boards had completely disappeared. There were very few leaves on the trees, so it looked like winter on the mainland before the snows came.

We got our place in Līhue pretty well cleaned up in two weeks, but the repairs of the building took a lot longer. I was lucky to get our roof repapered by Monday after the storm. Hā'ena was a different matter. We waited a month and then asked for an insurance adjuster to look at the damage. When she came, she never quibbled, and we got a very equitable settlement for both houses. At Hā'ena she just paced off the length and the width of the house and said that she would call us in two weeks. While we were on our Aleutian trip, Nancy had a painter come in and paint the outside of the Līhue house. On Thursday, the day before the storm, Nancy paid the painter for repainting the exterior of the house. The paint was still tacky when the storm hit. About three days after the storm, the painter came to checked the paint job. The house was covered with bits of leaves all stuck to the new paint. He told us not to touch the sides of the house until the insurance adjuster had seen the mess. After we received our check for the damages, we washed down the walls. All the mess came right off, and we had what looked like a freshly painted house.

It would be several months before any semblance of normal life as it was returned to Kaua'i. However, the people were great. They pulled together helping their neighbors wherever they could. The spirit of the people was amazing.

Kathy and Richie had a soup kitchen for up to forty people for dinner for about two months. Some people got electricity sooner than others, so they would bring ice to the have-nots. Everyone shared what food they had in their freezers until the supply ran out. By then, the stores were open, and, again, you went shopping almost every day because there was no electricity at home. Kathy and Richie had just started to remodel their kitchen when the hurricane hit, but Richie was able to buy a two-burner gas stove and a ten-gallon tank of propane early the next morning after the storm.

After we got our settlement from the insurance company for the loss of the Hā'ena house, Kathy said that she would like to see what she could do about getting it replaced or a new one built. She asked Larry Smith, a carpenter from the mainland who had done some repair work for Dick Sloggett, Kathy's uncle, if he were interested. He agreed, and together they found a plan that fitted our price range. We approved of Kathy's estimate, and the materials were ordered. The house was completed in good time and under the amount we had received from the insurance company. With that, our children and grandchildren had a place of their own to stay in. We have deeded half of the house and lot to our four children and the other half to the seven grandchildren. Later, our estate advisor told us to give away some of the lot and the new big house to the grandchildren so we wouldn't have to pay so much in estate taxes. And now the grandchildren own seventy-four percent of the house and lot.

At the end of September, the board of trustees of the garden held their fall meeting in San Francisco. It was a welcome getaway from the recovery on Kaua'i. At this meeting, we set in motion the search process for a new director of the garden to replace Dr. Theobald. After eight months, we hired Dr. William Klein, who was currently the Director of the Morris Arboretum in Pennsylvania. For the next four years under Dr. Klein, we finished the recovery work and started on a major planning process to upgrade the direction of the garden for a new nursery and maintenance buildings. Things were going smoothly. Then, in early 1997, Dr. Klein, while in Florida for meetings at the Kampong National Tropical Botanical Garden, had a major heart attack while jogging and died. Then, we were back to square one. Luckily, we had the resumes from the previous search and were able to convince Dr. Paul Alan Cox from Utah to accept the Directorship. Dr. Cox's specialty was ethnobotany, and it fits nicely into our plans for the future. We already had the world's largest collection of breadfruit, over two hundred cultivars from throughout the Pacific. This collection is now located at our branch garden at Kahanu on Maui. Our focus at the garden is to become the best in the world at saving Native Hawaiian and South Pacific plants. All through this I have continued to check the operation almost every Tuesday morning and have progressed from trustee to senior vice-chairman on the board and also the chairman of the finance committee.

The year 1985 was when I became the director of the Island School. In 1997, the school opened a high school starting with the ninth grade and adding a grade every year until there was a full high school concentrating on college prep.

The school first started in the old Kealia Plantation Store building and, in 1990, was given ten acres of land in back of the Kaua'i Community College in Puhi by the Lihue Plantation Company. With a donated building and funds from the community and foundations, the new school opened in the fall of 1991. Hurricane Iniki did considerable damage to the buildings, but the school re-opened by the first of 1993. We were able to get three portable classrooms to get us going again. These temporary buildings are now permanent, after some major renovations. In 1998, the school purchased twenty more acres of land from the Lihue Plantation Company for building of athletic fields, classrooms, a gymnasium, and other ancillary buildings. I am now the chairman of the development committee.

After Grove Farm developed the first increment of its new, residential Puakea complex, we bought a lot in 1995. This section was called Puak☐ or sugarcane flower. We hired architect Bill Bess to design a house for us. While in the planning stage, we also talked to Rob Brower, who had built our house at Hā'ena, about building this one for us. He agreed and, one day, while meeting with the architect, Rob invited us to go to a friend's home, not far from Kīlauea town, to look at a new wood from New Zealand called Rimu. We liked what we saw and opted for it for all our built-in cabinets, baseboards, moldings, and doors. When we knew the amount of wood needed, we had the wood ordered. As luck would have it, there was a couple we knew who were packing up to return to Kaua'i from New Zealand. Their household goods would need only half the container, so we piggy-backed with them. We then contracted with Gunnar Wickman to do the cabinets for us. So we had the fancy woodwork taken care of, and Gunnar did a superb job on the cabinets. The house we had designed was a concrete-slab, low-profile, stucco building. While still in the framing stage, we decided to have insulation put in the ceilings. The house turned out to be very comfortable in the summer but quite chilly in the winter. We moved in on December 6, 1996 and have never looked back. Like the house on Hinahina Street, this was the third house in this subdivision. The lanai faces the west, and we have wonderful views of beautiful sunsets and the mountains of Wai'ale'ale and the Ha'upu Range. We had the lot professionally landscaped, and we have a yard service for our maintenance. We are next to the tee on the eighth hole of the Puakea Golf Course, and, on the opposite side of the fairway, there is the old Līhue Landfill. This landfill will remain untouchable until the year 2040 and no development can happen before that. We are very comfortable here.

In 1997, the trustees meeting of the NTBG was held at the Kampong in Miami, Florida. After the meeting was finished, a party of twenty of us left for Costa Rica with Larry Schokman. We spent four days combing the highlands forests and one of the lowland parks. On the last day, we ended up at a spa where the stream was fed with hot water from a volcano. It was fun swimming there because the water was so hot you could only stay for a few minutes and then had to move a few feet where the water was so cold that in a few minutes you went back the hot water. The people of Costa Rica were very friendly to the Americans.

In 1999, Nancy and I flew to Midway Island for my seventy-sixth birthday. We spent four days there looking at birds and the foliage of the island. The Laysan albatross had not returned to nest yet, so we were able to see all the lesser birds that inhabit the island. There are several noxious weeds growing there, and nothing seems to be done to control them. One in particular is a member of the sunflower family, and it is taking up all the available space for the albatrosses to take off. One of the more noticeable birds was the Bonin petrel. They would return to their burrows at dusk, and you could see them digging out their burrows in the dark. Two other birds that we saw were imports and were considered pests. One was the yellow canary, which was brought to the island by the wife of one of the Navy commandants and was left on the island when his tour of duty was finished. They have multiplied considerably and have stabilized their numbers to about one-hundred birds. The other bird is our common mynah. There are still few enough of them that someone with a good shotgun could get rid of them in a hurry. I'm afraid that the U.S. Fish and Wildlife people would not like this strategy.

Nancy and I continued traveling through the decade throughout the continental United States for the annual NTBG trustees meeting. Other trips included a trip down the Mississippi on the Delta Queen to New Orleans and another from Honolulu to Hong Kong, Bali, Komodo, Java, and finally Singapore with the Kochers. In June of 1998, Nancy and I took our four children and their four spouses and our seven grandchildren on a one-week cruise around the Hawaiian Islands to celebrate our fiftieth wedding anniversary on the *SS Independence*.

One funny little incident about this trip was the question by Matthew to his grandmother when he saw some of the crew starting to grill hamburgers and hot dogs. He asked, "Grandma, how much do you think they charge for the hamburgers?"

Nancy replied, "All the food on this trip is paid for, and you can eat as much as you want. But you can't get any liquor."

Matt's reply was, "Boy! This is my kind of trip!" Then off he went with Wayne to get hamburgers.

The two ex-charter boat captains and I were always on deck to help the captain and pilot with the arrivals and departures from port. One thing that was nice was that, at each port, each family could go their own way and do what they wanted. This trip was a success because the children still talk about it.

David Goodale was the Manager of Garden Island Motors at this time, but he wasn't interested in running the company anymore. On February 28, 1998, we sold Garden Island Motors to Midpac Auto Center, whose principals were Walsh Hadley and Pat Fitzgerald from Hilo. This sale brought an end to sixty–eight years of my family's ownership in the company. It was a great relief because the automobile business was no fun anymore—too much government and Ford Motor Company interference. When I got home that evening, I had a good stiff drink and the best night's sleep in years.

I still do a little light yard work at Hā'ena on weekends. I'm not as active as I used to be, but I try to keep busy. I still play golf two times a week. In 2000, I was able to shoot my age at Wailua with a seventy-six gross for eighteen holes. I even have a hole in one. Really only the first one counts; after that, the rest are only frosting on the cake. But, the truth is that I really have six holes in one. The only major accomplishment in golf I haven't achieved is a two on a par five. This one is now out of reach for me because there is no way that I can hit the ball that far any more.

The decade of the nineties and the century closed for us on the upbeat, having sold the auto business and having overcome some daunting medical problems. Nancy and I looked forward to the new century ahead and more wonderful times.

CHAPTER THIRTEEN

Development on Kaua'i 1950–2005

This chapter is about the development and changes that have occurred on Kaua'i since the fifties. During this period, this island was hit by two major hurricanes, along with two minor ones, and a tsunami, with costs running into millions of dollars worth of damage to buildings and vegetation. The vegetative damage was most noticeable in the forests where the indigenous and endemic plants are located.

The first major development was the building of the Kauai Surf Hotel at Kalapaki. After Hawai'i was granted statehood in 1959, there seemed to be a lot more interest in big resort development in Hawai'i, and Kaua'i was no exception. In 1960, the Interisland Resorts group headed by Dudley Child approached my grandfather Charles Rice about Kalapaki. Kalapaki had been on the market since the tsunami of 1946, and there had been no takers. Kalapaki had been given to my grandfather as a wedding present from his parents. When the Kimball family of Honolulu heard that the Childs were interested, they wanted to get in on the action. My grandfather told the parties that the only fair way was to have competitive bidding. So he gave them two months to submit their bids. When the envelopes with the bids were in my grandfather's hands, he opened the Childs' bid first. Their bid was eight-hundred-thirteen-thousand dollars, and the Kimballs tried to take their envelope back and substitute another envelope. My grandfather would not accept the new envelope. The Kimball's original bid was six-hundred-sixty-thousand dollars, and their other bid was going to be one-million dollars. Land preparation started immediately, the construction followed as soon as the land was leveled, and the first ten-story tower was built with the hotel opening in 1961. About ten years later, another ten-story tower was built. After the second tower was built, four two-story buildings from the Kauai Inn in Līhue were moved down around the lily pond. The Kauai Inn then closed for good. These four buildings were later moved to Niumalu in the late eighties when Chris Hemmeter remodeled the Kalapaki property. These four buildings are now being operated as the Kauai Inn in Niumalu.

In the beginning of Kauai Surf's life, the resort built a nine-hole golf course and later had nine more holes added. When Hemmeter came into the picture, he got Jack Nicklaus to design two golf courses where the old one was. Not one of the old holes was kept intact. After Hurricane Iniki, Hemmeter left, and the Marriott took over the operation and built another ten-story wing. This wing is now made up of hotel rooms, and the two towers have been turned into timeshares.

Statehood in 1959 brought all kinds of changes to Kaua'i in the sixties. Development took off like a scalded cat! Central Līhue was completely remade. The old Tip Top Cafe and Lihue Store complex gave way to the round building and Foodland Supermarket. Later, the county purchased the building and land from Harry Weinberg and Big Save Market replaced Foodland.

Down on Rice Street, the old Crawford home became Central Pacific Bank, and, across the street on the site of Hale Nani, the old William Hyde Rice home became a small business complex. Next, the site of the old William Hyde Rice, Ltd. office became Rice Shopping Center. The first anchor was Big Save Market, and then it was turned into a bowling alley when Big Save vacated to move up the street to where Foodland had been. Proceeding further down the south side of Rice Street, Yoneji Store was remodeled into an office complex. Just beyond Kalena Park, the UPW Union built an office building for themselves next to the fire station. All the old Kauai Inn buildings were razed, and a completely new apartment complex now known as the Kalapaki Villas was built on the land. Then, what used to be cane field became a subdivision for low-income housing.

On the opposite side of Rice Street, the Lihue Plantation Company developed a light industrial park, which was quickly sold out. Garden Island Motors was the one of the first companies to move in. This occurred in the fall of 1965. This land was only sold as leasehold at first, but soon Lihue started to sell the fee to lessees. Garden Island was not able to afford to capitalize on the opportunity to purchase their holdings because their mortgage was so great, so the land was sold to Harry Weinberg. Heading west from the industrial park, a large area was set aside for commercial development. Pay 'n' Save took almost all of this space, built there, and occupied it for a few years. It, then, became Longs Drug, then Payless, and now Ace hardware.

Years ago, the State Highways Department had built a nice, two-lane highway, with room for two more lanes from Kūhiō Highway in Līhue to the airport. This road is now called Airport Road. The state next connected Rice Street to the Airport Road and named it Kapule Highway. This highway was just east of the original industrial park. Lihue Plantation then developed another industrial park on the other side of the highway, and this park was bought up instantly.

At the northern end of the first industrial park, a football/soccer stadium was built. The federal government then built a Veterans Memorial Hall. Next to the hall and parking lot, the state erected a huge new judicial building, and, just west of the judicial building, a new police station. We have an awful lot of government for a small island. And, now, because of the tight security needed to counter the threat of terrorism, both buildings are equipped with very tight security systems. Now the general public cannot just walk in as in the past but must undergo a close check.

Back in central Līhue on Kūhiō Highway, opposite the movie theater, more development was taking place. Where there were camp houses the area was cleared and filled with small businesses all the way to Airport Road. On the northeast corner of Kūhiō Highway and Airport Road, there was a bowling alley, which was later turned into Hilo Hatties, a tropical clothing store for tourists. Between Hilo Hatties and the Wilcox Memorial Hospital, Walmart built a huge store and parking lot. Wilcox Hospital has undergone several expansions over the years. A three-story clinic was built next to the hospital as the Kauai Medical Clinic. East of the hospital, Sun Village, a retirement complex, was built for which residents have to be at least fifty-five years old.

On the southwest side of Līhue, Grove Farm Company built a major shopping center and commercial village. Businesses in this complex include Kmart, Macy's, Sears, Home Depot, and most recently Costco. A residential subdivision called Puakō was opened 1995, and, by 2005, almost all the lots have been built on. An eighteen-hole golf course named Puakea has been built between the shopping center and the Puakō subdivision. To the north and west of the Puakō subdivision, Grove Farm has another residential subdivision that called the Pīkake subdivision. The entrance to this subdivision is a continuation of where Pīkake meets Nūhou. It wraps itself around the front nine of the golf course and numbers about two-hundred-fifty lots. Work started in 2004.

At Puhi, Grove Farm donated two hundred acres of land to the University of Hawai'i for a community college. This college serves both first and second year students in being able to complete their first and second year requirements while being able to stay at home in doing so. The school offers night school courses to the adult population, and it also offers a selection of commercial and trade courses including a culinary arts school. Island School is located behind the college.

In 1962, Wailua Golf Course opened its second nine holes, becoming one of the premier public golf courses in the country. On the south side of the golf course, a condominium and a hotel were built. The hotel has changed owners several times and is now called the Radisson. Moving north from the golf course there are the Kaha Lani Condominiums, Lydgate Park, and the Kauai Resorts hotel. Next comes the Wailua River and the Coco Palms hotel. The Coco Palms has been closed since Iniki, and there's been a disagreement with the owners and the insurance company that has not been satisfactorily settled. Now the state highway department is talking about widening the highway and will need some of the frontage land from the hotel.

The old polo field and racetrack (later a pasture) at Waipouli is now the Coconut MarketPlace. This is a series of small shops and at least three small hotels, none of the four-star type. On the outskirts of Kapaʻa proper, and on the west side of the highway, are two small shopping centers, one anchored by Foodland and the other by Safeway supermarkets. Across the street from these shopping centers, is a time-share complex of several four-story buildings. There have been a few major changes in downtown Kapaʻa, but most of the old buildings have had facelifts and remodels. The exceptions being a shopping center anchored by Big Save Markets and the razing of the old pineapple cannery with a condominium and timeshare complex called Pono Kai Resort built in its place.

Heading north again on Kūhiō Highway just before Anahola, the Hawaiian Homes have opened up an area where now stands a village of homes built for people of Hawaiian ancestry. Beyond Anahola where there used to be pineapple fields, there is now a cluster of Hawaiian Home farm lots that have been built on and some farming is taking place.

The north shore of Kauaʻi has changed. The former Princeville Ranch is no more and is now a huge residential development. Along with that, Hanalei is no longer a sleepy little country town. Hanalei began to move in the fifties when the surfers discovered the fine winter surf. Then came the hippies and their counter-culture lifestyles of the sixties. Hanalei town now has about a dozen eating places and many more other retail establishments. Prior to the 1957 tsunami, there were two small general stores. Land prices have gone through the roof making it difficult for the old timers to be able to afford the land taxes. Hanalei School has gone from a school where most of the children had brown or black hair to a school where a good percentage are blonds. Almost all the old families are gone from the beachfront properties, and their places have been taken over by the wealthy newcomers. The same is true of Hāʻena to the north.

The Poʻipū area is considered the Gold Coast of Kauaʻi. This is the major resort area of Kaua'i. The Kimball family of Honolulu started the Waiohai Beach Club in the late fifties as a single story cottage resort on the site of the old Eric Knudsen home. After about ten years of operation, the cottages were all torn down and a new four-star hotel was built in its place. The new Waiohai went through both hurricanes—Iwa in 1982 and Iniki in 1992. During Iniki, the building suffered extensive damages from both the wind and water. After several years of bickering with their insurance company, the case was settled and the property taken over by the Marriott chain and rebuilt as a timeshare complex. The Poipu Beach Hotel, which was adjacent to the Waiohai, also suffered major damage and rebuilt. Closer to the Kōloa Landing, the Sheraton Hotel built a low-rise building along the shoreline. It suffered wind and water damage but was back in operation within two years of Iniki. Inland of the Sheraton and mauka of Po'ipū Road, a resort shopping center was built along with an eighteen-hole golf course called Kiahuna. I must mention that, in the sixties, the county planners designated Po'ipū as a major resort area and a new road was constructed parallel to the shoreline about a thousand feet inland. This now serves as the main road through Po'ipū. Going east from the Waiohai is the Po'ipū Beach Park. This park has been enlarged over the years so that now it is over three times the original size. Several private homes were condemned and the land purchased for this enlarging. So, today there is no private property from the Waiohai to Brennecke's Beach on the ocean.

From there to around the Crater Hill, there are several condos that have been built and are in full operation. Going east again you come to the Hyatt Hotel. The Hotel suffered minor damage from the Iniki but was never closed and was the only major hotel open for business. East of the hotel is the Poipu Bay Golf Course. In the nineties, a bypass road was built so traffic from the Hyatt did not have to go through Kōloa town.

Heading west from Kōloa, there has not been much major development over the years except at the end of the road at Mānā where there is the Pacific Missile Base. The U.S. Navy operates this base with civilian contractors. At last count, there were over six-hundred Navy and civilian employees at the base. The base is one of the largest employers on the island. Waimea and Hanapēpē have resisted change, and the only major changes are the restoration of old building in both towns. Waimea has a small technology center and a bungalow type hotel operated by the Faye family.

Up on the Mountain at Koke'e several NASA installations were built for the tracking of the first astronauts in our space program. These are now standing idle. At Kalalau Lookout there is an Air National Guard radar station, which is still in use. It monitors all airplanes and missiles that might be coming into our air space. Also at Koke'e there is a wonderful little natural history museum and a visitor center and restaurant.

In the Kukui'ula section if Kōloa district, McBryde and Alexander and Baldwin created another one-thousand-lot subdivision with a golf course intertwined among the homes. This luxury resort area is aimed at the wealthy.

On the west side at Pākala, Gay and Robinson has plans for an ecotourism resort on the lands below the main highway just east of Waimea. As of 2011, the plans for this development are on hold.

Near Hanamā'ulu, where the old belt road meets Kūhiō Highway, another big development is in the wings. This one will also have a golf course. The triangle of the land from the stop light at Kūhiō Highway to the school in Hanamā'ulu down to the highway and back to the stoplight is planned for an affordable priced housing subdivision. Grove Farm has built a surface treatment plant to process ground water for this development.

The State Harbors Division has plans for further docking space at Nāwiliwili primarily due to the increase in cruise ship dockings that have numbered about three hundred in recent years.

The State Highways Department is planning to widen Kamuali'i Highway into a four-lane road from the Tree Tunnel to Līhue. This widening is needed but will not be completed for a few more years. Kūhiō Highway from the Hanamā'ulu stoplight to Kapa'a town needs to be a four-lane road also but when we don't know.

CHAPTER FOURTEEN

The Twenty-First Century

While my book *All About Hobey* was still stuck at the editor's desk, I had time to write this last chapter.

In 2000, Nancy and I took a steamship tour of the Baltic Sea and the countries that border it. At Heathrow in London, we met up with the Kochers and flew to Stockholm, Sweden. We found our ship and boarded without our baggage. At about one o'clock in the morning, we were awakened and told that our bags would be coming up to our deck very soon and that we were to get the bags out of the hall as soon as possible. This we did and went right back to sleep until time for breakfast. The next morning, we started touring with a trip around Stockholm, and, that evening, we sailed for Helsinki, Finland. Here we saw people walking around in shorts while we were bundled up in sweaters. The highlight here was the chapel that had been cut out of solid rock and was huge. Next on the list was Saint Petersburg in Russia where we had an early dinner and were transported by bus to an officers club and a ballet performance of Swan Lake by young dancers. You just couldn't find a flaw in the whole performance. The next morning, we went to the Hermitage and saw room after room of procommunist finery. In one room, we were told that by this time in our tour we had probably seen over twenty tons of gold. That afternoon, we went to a chapel where all the tsars and their families are buried, even the bones of Anastasia's family whose remains had only recently been found. Estonia was our next port of call. Nancy stayed aboard, but I went on the tour. Nothing much to see but beautiful countryside. The cemeteries were all in forests among the trees.

We were soon back in Copenhagen for a more detailed tour of the city and countryside. We then left for Oslo, Norway, and more museums full of old Viking relics. Al and I had to replenish our vodka supplies, but what a rigmarole. We had to go to a bank and get traveler checks cashed. Then we went back to the store and got whatever we wanted and were able to pay the crone. Our ship was moored about three places away from the Norwegian ship the *Windjammer*, a Norwegian Navy training ship. She at one time had gone to New York on a training mission and a musical was made about her and her crew. Next, we headed south to Amsterdam in the Netherlands where we visited the Delft and the Porcelain pottery works. Here we saw a copy of Ruben's "Night Watch" done with Delft blue tiles. The work twelve feet by eight feet, all set in eight-inch square tiles. We were then off to Brussels and Bruges in Belgium. Here we saw diamonds being cut and polished for sale. Bruges is an old, charming city, and we hated to leave. Le Harve, France, was next, and most people wanted to go to Omaha Beach in Normandy. Nancy and I and a few others stayed at a small town before we got to Normandy, and we browsed and naturally bought some trinkets to bring home. That evening, we had our farewell dinner, and, the next morning, it was off the ship and into a car for London Town. In London, we joined up with the Richard Goodales and Patrice and Dylan Goodale. They did the tourist things, while we did shopping on our first day. The second day, we all went out on the Tube to Kew Gardens and spent the day looking at plants. That evening, we all went to *The Lion King*. It was a wonderful show. The group then started for home. We were the last to leave London and flew to Santa Barbara. We got in at quarter-to-five and were met at the airport by a friend of Joan's who took us to Tony's school for his graduation. We got there just as the class was marching in. After the ceremony, the principal of the school wanted to meet us because Tony had used us for an excuse to get two extra tickets for the ceremonies. He was quite impressed that we had made it on time. After that, we had a couple of days in Santa Barbara, then it was back the Kaua'i.

In the fall, we went to Seattle for the NTBG's trustees meeting, and Nancy and I took a supplemental trip to Vancouver Island and the City of Victoria. While there, we spent the better part of a day touring the Butchart Gardens. All the fall flowers were in full bloom, and what a splash of color that was. You could wonder what it was like in the spring. The next day, we took the ferry back to Vancouver town and back home the following day.

The first trip of the year in 2001 was to Barbados where we had three days of sightseeing before boarding the cruise ship *The World*. *The World* has a condominium configuration and, while we were aboard, it was sold condo-by-condo to individuals. We landed at the island of Tobago and then over to the island of Trinidad for another three days. Then, we sailed to the Orinoco River and upriver to Puerto Ordaz where we boarded small airplanes for the flight to the Angel Falls. These falls drop three thousand feet and are considered the tallest falls in the world. After returning to the ship, we motored downriver into the Atlantic Ocean to the Île du Diable (Devil's Island), the most infamous prison isle in the new world. We, then, had had a couple of days at sea before we reached the mouth of the Amazon

River. Here we were delayed because a couple of our group had not finished with their yellow fever shots. When everything was in order, we headed upriver for three days before we came to the town of Santarém and had a day's rest. We went ashore and visited a farm where they showed us how they tapped the trees for rubber and processed the cassava to make flour for the baking of bread, plus there was a whole table of fruit. Only three of the fruits were new to me.

After returning to the ship, we steamed another day and stopped at a small village where we were told to watch the water at the stern of the ship when we started up again. As soon as the water started to roil, the pink dolphins showed themselves. They were a real pink. The next morning, we were at Manaus and the end of our trip. We spent the next two days touring and shopping before returning to the United States.

Later in the fall, our NTBG trustees meeting was held in Dallas, Texas, and, after the meeting, Nancy and I joined a group on a post meeting tour. We first visited Lady Bird Johnson's preserve, then west to Admiral Chester Nimitz's birthplace, and then to Betsy Matthews's ranch. Here we had dinner and then back into the bus for the ride into San Antonio. This trip was quite something as we encountered sixty-mile-an-hour winds all the way to San Antonio. The next morning, we first visited the Alamo and the San Antonio Botanical Gardens. That evening, we took a boat ride on some of the canals of San Antonio with a dinner and then off to bed. The next morning, we left San Antonio for Dallas and on to Santa Barbara and a visit with Joan. Then it was back home to Kaua'i.

The year 2002 was one during which we didn't take any major trips. The only one was to Charleston, South Carolina, for the NTBG trustees meeting in the fall. We did the Old Charleston tour on foot and then into the countryside. One night, we were treated to boiled oysters. But most of our group was interested in the other sights, so I took advantage of the oysters. After about two-dozen of these nice, fat oysters, I didn't need any dinner. At the farm, I got to the gift shop way before any of the rest did and got two beautiful stuffed birds for Christmas tree ornaments. By the time the others woke up to the fact that there was a gift shop, the shop was closed and I had a couple of family members mad at me. On the way home to Hawai'i, we stopped in Santa Barbara and visited with Joan and her family again.

In 2003, the trustees meeting would be held in San Francisco. So we took one of Jim Elders's pre-meeting tours of Napa Valley. Before we could go on any tour, though, Nancy had trouble walking. So I stayed with her and went to a hospital in Napa. The doctor gave her a prescription, but this was the start of Nancy's troubles. After taking the medicine, Nancy seemed to get better. But, by the time we got into San Francisco, she fell trying to get up at one of the meetings. One of our trustees, Harlan Amsteth of UCLA, called UCSF and talked to a friend of his who was a neurologist. We were told to go to UCSF immediately. We got there at about seven in the evening and were taken right in because they had been waiting for us. When the doctor came to check on Nancy, I got out of the vestibule and stood in the hall. Now I had one of those small world experiences. An older, female patient asked me if I was the guy from Hawai'i. I told her yes and she asked me what island. I told her Kaua'i. She said that her son lived there, and that he owned a restaurant at a golf course. I asked her if the place's name was "Joe's on the Green" and she said yes. I told her that I had had meals there and the food was good and that I would tell Joe that I had talked to her. She told me that Joe was one of ten children. When we got back to Kaua'i, I had lunch at Joe's on the Green and told him of the chance meeting. He, then, went to his office and called her because she had never told him that she had been in the hospital. Nancy had tests all night and finally got to sleep at about four in the morning. Some of the tests had to be done in Atlanta, Georgia, though, so we didn't get the results for three weeks. The final report came in about three weeks later. The doctor said, "We know that you have something, but we don't know what it is."

Nancy did, however, stay well enough to travel. In 2004, our big trip was to take a French ship and tour the Great Lakes. We flew to Toronto and checked into the hotel and then went shopping. I needed a new pair of slacks and, much to our surprise, the Canadians were happy to see us. The service was just like in the older days. A tailor fit the slacks, and we were told come back after lunch and the slacks would be ready. And so they were. The next day, we boarded the *Le Levant* for our trip and started out. We went through what little there was to see of Ontario and then into Lake Erie and the locks. They were interesting, but, to our jaundiced eyes after Europe and the Panama Canal, we had seen bigger and better. The next morning, we had gone to the northwestern end of Erie and were docked at Windsor where we were welcomed to Canada by the town crier dressed in the traditional clothes of yesterday. It was fun. This particular morning, we went across the bridge into the U.S. again. We went to the Ford Motor Museum where we spent the day. We looked at all the old cars, had lunch at the cafeteria, and then took a train that circles the whole museum property. It was then the gift shop's turn. We bought a couple of jigsaw puzzles and a whole lot of small presents for Christmas. Then, it was back to the bridge and going through Canadian immigration, which was a lot quicker that the good old U.S.A. The next day, we motored through Lake Huron and into Thunder Bay where we spent the night. The following day, we spent the morning touring an old mission site that the Native Americans from the area had burned but that was never replaced. In the afternoon, we motored to Mackinac Island where we spent the night. Mackinac has a regulation that only emergency and delivery trucks are allowed. The alternative transportation is by horse-drawn wagons and carriages. We took the "Around-the-Island Tour" on a wagon and had a great time. We left Mackinac in the late afternoon and woke up going into Green Bay. What a production this was—rush-hour traffic and all the drawbridges going up and down for us. We found out later that Green Bay had wanted the tour boats to come to town, but we were the first, and they loved it. One of our people walked into town for a newspaper and couldn't get back to the boat until he had been, both, interview by the publisher of the newspaper and part of an interview for T.V. We left that evening for Chicago and the end of our tour of the Great Lakes. Our checkout from the ship was a comic relief, as we had been in the U.S.A. and Canada but the ship was French. So all our onboard bills were in Euros.

After landing in Chicago, we were taken to the O'Hare Airport for a flight to Albuquerque, New Mexico. After arriving in Albuquerque, we took the bus to Santa Fe and our hotel where we would attend the NTBG trustees meeting. Santa Fe was a town we really enjoyed. It was friendly, and the walks were not too long as to be tiring. After the meetings were over, we took the bus back to Albuquerque the plane to Denver, Los Angeles, and direct to Kaua'i.

Our big trip in 2005 would be the Rhine and Danube riverboat trip. Nancy and I, along with the Kochers, had done the Rhine to Heidelberg way back in 1973. This time, we split the flying with a layover in Washington, D.C. We landed in Amsterdam much more rested and ready to go, but the weather did not cooperate. It rained that afternoon, and we were supposed to take an open-boat tour of the canals. That afternoon, instead, we were allowed early boarding. So we got to settle into out rooms that were to be home for ten days or more. The next morning, we were bused to Arnhem and had a chance to see some more van Gogh paintings. When we got there, the van Gogh room was full if viewers, so they sent us out into the yard where there were several sculptures of all kinds. While were we looking at the items, I spotted a name on the t-shirt of one of our group that read, "Hay Creek Ranch." I knew that this woman was from Madras, Oregon, so I introduced myself to her and asked if this Hay Creek Ranch was twelve-miles east of Madras. She asked, "How do you know this?" I replied that my stepfather had owned the place in the thirties and forties and that I had ridden over most of the ranch on horseback. She said, "Do we want to talk to you!" This was the start of a great friendship. The next night at dinner we were five women and myself at the table, and, thanks that Nancy was one of them. All the men wanted to know how come I got all the pretty girls to sit with me. It's no fair. The next day, after the van Gogh viewing, we motored up the Rhine River to Mainz and down the through the Mainz Canal to the Danube and to Budapest. On the way, Nancy found a riverside soup kitchen, and we went and had wonderful oyster chowder for lunch.

In Budapest, we were bused to a ranch south of the city about an hour away and came to a ranch where they raised and gave the early training to the young prospective Lipizzaner colts. The Hungarians put on a show riding their own horses. These were big beautiful bays that were wonderfully trained. After the show, the leader brought out an empty wine bottle and set it up on a fence post in front to the crowd. He explained that there would be a contest to try to knock the bottle off the post with the whip. You would win a bottle of wine if you could do the trick in three tries. Nobody seemed daring, but Nancy and some of the others started to yell at me to try. I went up and the darn whip was so unbalanced it took me two tries. But I did get my bottle of wine. Monte Richards from Kahua Ranch on the Big Island made his on his third try, and Molly Clark from Hay Creek Ranch just didn't know how to swing the whip.

After Budapest, some of us who had signed up for the post trip left by bus for Krakau and Prague. We started with Krakau, and we visited the salt mine first. We went down four-hundred feet and saw the huge chapel that the salt miners had carved out at that depth. I am not really claustrophobic, but I was glad to get back to sunlight. The next day, we bussed our way into Prague for a couple days of shopping and sightseeing. We were able to go out into the city by ourselves, as the hotel we were staying at was right on the main street. The time spent on this side trip was just enough to bring us back to Washington for the NTBG trustees meeting. After the meeting was over, we flew right back to Kaua'i. We had had enough traveling for one year

In 2006, the meetings we were back to Portland. Kathy, Nancy, and I came up early for a side trip of our own to Hay Creek Ranch. On the Rhine trip last year, the women we had met who now owned Hay Creek Ranch. Niki Clark, had told us that, if we ever were in the vicinity, we should to come and stay with them for a couple of nights and look over the ranch. The previous owners had stripped the place of all historically interesting data, so the Clarks wanted to know what there must have been. We had two nights with them and had a great time—them listening to my stories and me reliving four summers of working on the ranch. Gordon Clark,

Niki's husband, had gotten a lot of press in California where he had a foam surfboard forming company and was not handling some of the toxic waste in the approved manner. He was a good friend of Jimmy Pflueger. After having my brain picked dry of information by the Clarks, Nancy, Kathy, and I drove back to Portland for the NTBG trustees meeting. After the meeting, we drove first to Tillamook to buy some cheese to take home with us and to buy some Christmas presents, thanks to UPS. Later that afternoon, we got in touch with Jim Bethel, and he gave us directions to their new house overlooking the Pacific Ocean. We spent the night with Ann and Jim Bethel and had a wonderful time reminiscing about their two-year stay on Kaua'i. The next morning, we motored south along the coast until we got to Coos Bay where we stayed the night and then went inland and headed north to the Portland Airport the next day. We caught the Hawaiian direct flight to Honolulu and the shuttle to Kaua'i and home.

Our big trip in 2007 was to St. Louis, Missouri, for the NTBG trustees meetings. The first day, Nancy and I walked to the Missouri Zoo by ourselves and saw quite a bit more than our big group that came after we had gotten started. One day, was spent touring the Missouri Botanical Garden. Nancy and I had been to these gardens before, so we saw a great many changes. The trustees meetings had slowly been tamed to the point of ennui. There were no points of discussion that got people moved, and the meetings were down to two hours from four to five hours as in the past. After the meetings, we went to Santa Barbara and spent couple days with Joan and her family before flying back to Kaua'i.

January fifth of 2008 was Richie Richardson's mother Caroll's ninetieth birthday, and we (Hobey, Nancy, Kathy, and Richie) left Kaua'i with a cooler full of laulaus and octopus lū'au for the start of a Hawaiian meal. Kathy was able to get lomi salmon, Honolulu poi and a can of coconut milk for the lū'au in San Mateo. With these items, we had the makings for a real Hawaiian meal. We were met in San Mateo by Wayne and Katie for the weekend. After the birthday dinner, Ritchie got us the makings for a Crab Louis for a farewell dinner. Each Louis was made with one whole crab. Now it was back to Kaua'i to await the next trip to Chapel Hill.

On June twenty-fifth, Nancy and I celebrated sixty years of a wonderful, happy marriage with a dinner at Dondero's at the Hyatt. Kathy, Ritchie, and Katie were there to help us, and help us they did. They had gotten the staff to figure out a six- or seven-course dinner with a different wine for each course. The chief chef came and explained each course, as did the sommelier with the wine. That's why I don't remember how many courses we had for dinner.

This year, our big doings meant a trip back to Chapel Hill for the NTBG trustees meetings and a short side trip to see our Pennsylvania property. This was our second trip to Chapel Hill in thirteen years. Nancy really enjoyed it this time around. We saw a farm where they raised Belted Galloway cattle. These animals are mostly black with the exception of a wide white stripe around their middles. Nancy and Kathy went down to the stables as the cattle came in for their late afternoon feeding and got to pet some of the calves.

As a last gasp, we were taken by bus for one last shopping stop at the replenishments store. Here Nancy was able to buy some dinner plates to fill in her trousseau from sixty years ago. The plates were Wedgewood's "Edme" pattern from their Queen's Ware line from our everyday set of china.

After shopping, we went to the airport, flew to Newark, and stayed at the airport Marriott. The next day, we were driven south to Pennsylvania and were shown our property—a large warehouse with three tenants. After lunch, we were driven back to the airport and flew to Santa Barbara for a couple of days with the Evans family. Joan and Randy drove us around and showed us some of the damage done by the fire the summer before. Then, we bused back to the L.A. airport and home to Līhue on Friday.

The next evening, we went with Kathy and Ritchie to the Robinson's for dinner. While talking to one of her friends, Nancy fell over backwards and hit her head on the concrete floor. She never came to. We air-evacuated her to Queen's Hospital in Honolulu where Nancy died. We brought her ashes home to Kaua'i, and she is buried at the Līhue Cemetery.

Nancy's funeral was one of the largest ever at the cemetery. At the get-together to celebrate her life, the caterer had to get more food two more times because the crowd was so large. Nancy was a quiet type of person, and you never knew how many people she touched in some way here on Kaua'i. But, at the service and party, all this became obvious.

Christmas was quiet this year. I went to church after dinner at Kathy's house. She had the usual forty or more for a sit down dinner. After church, I went home and went to bed. I must have been pretty tired, for I didn't hear a thing all night. The next morning when I went out to the kitchen, I noticed that all the presents under the tree were gone. There was a large note in the kitchen saying that the Grinch had taken the presents and that I was to go to the Richardson's for breakfast or I would never see the presents again.

Breakfast was great, and I got to open my presents with company. Christmas night dinner was at my house, and we had the traditional oyster stew and turkey broth for those who didn't like the oysters.

The year 2009 was rather uneventful with the exception of the marriage of Matt and Meagan in May. Matt was the first of our grandchildren to get married. Matt is working for the garden as their "it" man. It is sure is nice to have a son who is a doctor and a grandson who is a computer expert, although Matt is not keen on the Mac products. Well, you can't have it all.

The big news for the year and decade is that, after over one-hundred years, sugar is no more on the island of Kaua'i. Gay and Robinson harvested and processed the last sugar in 2010. Now most of the old sugar lands have been turned over to the seed corn growing. Much of Grove Farm Company's flat land has likewise been converted to seed corn production. This is matter of pure economics—seed corn production returns almost ten times that of cattle ranching.

Our NTBG trustees fall meeting was held in Chicago this year. Kathy and I decided to break up the long flight, so we stopped at San Francisco Airport and stayed with Carroll Richardson for a couple of days. Joan joined us at the airport, and we flew to Minneapolis and joined up with Chipper and Hauoli and Charlie and Jeanne Wichman. Warren Wichman joined the group later. We all were met by our real estate agents and driven to Minnetonka where we were shown around the office building we had bought there. We had lunch and then flew to Chicago for a week of meetings and tours. One whole day was spent at the Chicago Botanic Garden. We were an envious group when we heard how much money they got from the City of Chicago.

After Nancy died, we found that she had kept all the letters that we written to each other while we were at school. As you know, Nancy went to Pine Manor Junior College in Wellesley, Massachusetts, while I was going to Menlo Junior College in Menlo Park, California. The letters cover from September 1947 to March 1948. I made copies of the letters, and my grandson Wayne Richardson IV used a couple of pictures of Nancy and me together taken in 1947 for the cover. I had the whole works bound and used for Christmas presents for the children and grandchildren. The telephone rate across country at that time was a dollar per minute. That's why the letters.

This is the end of my story...or is it? I have taken on being a trustee of the Kauai Museum, and, at the last annual meeting, I was elected chairman of the board. I just haven't learned how to say "no!" The grandchildren are more or less out on their own but no great grandchildren yet. I kid about this saying, "I am eighty-six years old but no great grandchildren. I need at least one for my obituary." Tony Evans has graduated and has passed his certification exam to be a radiology technician; Katie Richardson will soon be a pastry chef; Wayne Richardson a photographer and designer; Julie

Evans is a bakery chef; Ian Goodale an auto technician; Dylan Goodale is a professional surfer; and Matt Goodale is our computer guru and the only one who is married.

I keep myself busy with the Kauai Museum, Lihue Cemetery, the National Tropical Botanical Garden, and now my position as director emeritus of the Island School board.

For hobbies, I collect stamps and do jigsaw puzzles and crossword puzzles to keep my idle moments filled.